America's
"War on Terrorism"

Michel Chossudovsky

America's "War on Terrorism"

Second Edition

Global Research

America's "War on Terrorism", by Michel Chossudovsky — Second Edition.

© Michel Chossudovsky, 2005. All rights reserved – Global Research, Center for Research on Globalization (CRG).

No part of this book may be used or reproduced in any manner whatsoever without written permission of the publisher.

Global Research is a division of the Centre for Research on Globalization (CRG), 101 Cardinal-Léger Blvd, P.O. Box 51004, Pincourt, Québec, J7V 9T3, Canada.

For more information, contact the publisher at the above address or by email at our website at www.globalresearch.ca.

SECOND EDITION

Cover Photo © Pavel Filatov/Alamy
Cover Graphics by Nicolas Calvé, © Global Research 2005

Printed and bound in Canada.
Printed on acid free paper.

ISBN 0-9737147-1-9 (paperback)

Library and Archives Canada Cataloguing in Publication

Chossudovsky, Michel

America's "War on Terrorism" / Michel Chossudovsky. – 2nd ed.

Previously published under the title:
War and Globalisation: The Truth behind September 11.

Includes index.

ISBN 0-9737147-1-9

1. September 11 Terrorist Attacks, 2001. 2. War on Terrorism, 2001-   . 3. United States—Politics and government—1993-   . 4. United States—Military policy. United States—Foreign relations—1989-   . I. Title.

HV6431.C46 2005   973.931   C2005-904499-3

To the Memory of André Gunder Frank

Also by Michel Chossudovsky

The Globalization of Poverty and the New World Order

TABLE OF CONTENTS

PREFACE TO THE SECOND EDITION

At eleven o'clock, on the morning of September 11, the Bush adminstration had already announced that Al Qaeda was responsible for the attacks on the World Trade Center (WTC) and the Pentagon. This assertion was made prior to the conduct of an indepth police investigation.

That same evening at 9:30 pm, a "War Cabinet" was formed integrated by a select number of top intelligence and military advisors. And at 11:00 pm, at the end of that historic meeting at the White House, the "War on Terrorism" was officially launched.

The decision was announced to wage war against the Taliban and Al Qaeda in retribution for the 9/11 attacks. The following morning on September 12th, the news headlines indelibly pointed to "state sponsorship" of the 9/11 attacks. In chorus, the US media was calling for a military intervention against Afghanistan.

Barely four weeks later, on the 7th of October, Afghanistan was bombed and invaded by US troops. Americans were led to believe that the decison to go to war had been taken on the spur of the moment, on the evening of September 11, in response to the attacks and their tragic consequences.

Little did the public realize that a large scale theater war is never planned and executed in a matter of weeks. The decision to launch a war and send troops to Afghanistan had been taken well in advance of 9/11. The "terrorist, massive, casualty-producing event" as it was later described by CentCom Commander General Tommy Franks, served to galvanize public opinion in support of a war agenda which was already in its final planning stage.

The tragic events of 9/11 provided the required justification to wage a war on "humanitarian grounds", with the full support of World public opinion and the endorsement of the "international community".

Several prominent "progressive" intellectuals made a case for "retaliation against terrorism", on moral and ethical grounds. The "just cause" military doctrine (*jus ad bellum*) was accepted and upheld at face value as a legitimate response to 9/11, without examining the fact that Washington had not only supported the "Islamic terror network", it was also instrumental in the installation of the Taliban government in 1996.

In the wake of 9/11, the antiwar movement was completely isolated. The trade unions and civil society organizations had swallowed the media lies and government propaganda. They had accepted a war of retribution against Afghanistan, an impoverished country of 30 million people.

I started writing on the evening of September 11, late into the night, going through piles of research notes, which I had previously collected on the history of Al Qaeda. My first text entitled "Who is Osama bin Laden?", which was completed and first published on September the 12th. (See Chapter II.)

From the very outset, I questioned the official story, which described nineteen Al Qaeda sponsored hijackers involved in a highly sophisticated and organized operation. My first objective was to reveal the true nature of this illusive "enemy of America", who was "threatening the Homeland".

The myth of the "outside enemy" and the threat of "Islamic terrorists" was the cornerstone of the Bush adminstration's military doctrine, used as a pretext to invade Afghanistan and Iraq, not to mention the repeal of civil liberties and constitutional government in America.

Without an "outside enemy", there could be no "war on terrorism". The entire national security agenda would collapse "like a deck of cards". The war criminals in high office would have no leg to stand on.

It was consequently crucial for the development of a coherent antiwar and civil rights movement, to reveal the nature of Al Qaeda and its evolving relationship to successive US administrations.

Amply documented but rarely mentioned by the mainstream media, Al Qaeda was a creation of the CIA going back to the Soviet-Afghan war. This was a known fact, corroborated by numerous sources including official documents of the US Congress. The intelligence community had time and again acknowledged that they had indeed supported Osama bin Laden, but that in the wake of the Cold War: "he turned against us".

After 9/11, the campaign of media disinformation served not only to drown the truth but also to kill much of the historical evidence on how this illusive "outside enemy" had been fabricated and transformed into "Enemy Number One".

The Balkans Connection

My research on the Balkans conducted since the mid-1990s enabled me to document numerous ties and connections between Al Qaeda and the US Administration. The US military, the CIA and NATO had supported Al Qaeda in the Balkans. Washington's objective was to trigger ethnic conflict and destablize the Yugoslav federation, first in Bosnia, then in Kosovo.

In 1997, the Republican Party Committee (RPC) of the US Senate released a detailed report which accused President Clinton of collaborating with the "Islamic Militant Network" in Bosnia and working hand in glove with an organization linked to Osama bin Laden. (See Chapter III.) The report, however, was not widely publicized. Instead, the Republicans chose to discredit Clinton for his liason with White House intern Monica Lewinsky.

The Clinton Adminstration had also been providing covert support to the Kosovo Liberation Army (KLA), a paramilitary group supported by Al Qaeda, which was involved in numerous terrorist attacks. The Defense Intelligence Agency (DIA) and Britain's Secret Intelligence Service, more commonly known as MI6, together with former members of Britain's 22nd Special Air Services Regiment (SAS) were providing training to the KLA, despite its extensive links to organized crime and the drug trade. Meanwhile, known and documented, several Al Qaeda operatives had integrated the ranks of the KLA. (See Chapter III).

In the months leading up to 9/11, I was actively involved in research on the terror attacks in Macedonia, waged by the self-proclaimed National Liberation Army (NLA) of Macedonia, a paramilitary army integrated by KLA commanders. Al Qaeda Mujahideen had integrated the NLA. Meanwhile, senior US military officers from a private mercenary company on contract to the Pentagon were advising the terrorists.

Barely a couple of months prior to 9/11, US military advisers were seen mingling with Al Qaeda operatives within the same paramilitary army. In late June 2001, seventeen US "instructors" were identified among the withdrawing rebels. To avoid the diplomatic humiliation and media embarrassment of senior US military personnel captured together with "Islamic terrorists" by the Macedonian Armed Forces, the US and NATO pressured the Macedonian government to allow the NLA terrorists and their US military advisers to be evacuated.

The evidence, including statements by the Macedonian Prime Minister and press reports out of Macedonia, pointed unequivocally to continued US covert support to the "Islamic brigades" in the former Yugoslavia. This was not happening in the bygone era of the Cold War, but in June 2001, barely a couple of months prior to 9/11. These developments, which I was following on a daily basis, immediately cast doubt in my mind on the official 9/11 narrative which presented Al Qaeda as the mastermind behind the attacks on the World Trade Center and the Pentagon. (Chapter IV.)

The Mysterious Pakistani General

On the 12th of September, a mysterious Lieutenant General, head of Pakistan's Military Intelligence (ISI), who according to the US press reports "happened to be in Washington at the time of the attacks", was called into the office of Deputy Secretary of State Richard Armitrage.

The "War on Terrorism" had been officially launched late in the night of September 11, and Dick Armitage was asking General Mahmoud Ahmad to help America "in going after the terrorists". Pakistani President Pervez Musharraf was on the phone with Secretary of State Colin Powell and the following morning, on the 13th of September, a comprehensive agreement, was reached between the two governments.

While the press reports confirmed that Pakistan would support the Bush adminstration in the "war on terror", what they failed to mention was the fact that Pakistan's military intelligence (ISI) headed by General Ahmad had a longstanding relationship to the Islamic terror network. Documented by numerous sources, the ISI was known to have supported a number of Islamic organizations including Al Qaeda and the Taliban. (See Chapter IV.)

My first reaction in reading news headlines on the 13th of September was to ask: if the Bush adminstration were really committed to weeding out the terrorists, why would it call upon Pakistan's ISI, which is known to have supported and financed these terrorist organizations?

Two weeks later, an FBI report, which was briefly mentioned on ABC News, pointed to a "Pakistani connection" in the financing of the alleged 9/11 terrorists. The ABC report referred to a Pakistani "moneyman" and "mastermind" behind the 9/11 hikackers.

Subsequent reports indeed suggested that the head of Pakistan's military intelligence, General Mahmoud Ahmad, who had met Colin Powell on the 13th of September 2001, had allegedly ordered the transfer of 100,000 dollars to the 9/11 ringleader Mohammed Atta. What these reports suggested was that the head of Pakistan's military intelligence was not only in close contact with senior officials of the US Government, he was also in liason with the alleged hijackers.

My writings on the Balkans and Pakistani connections, published in early October 2001 were later incorporated into the first edition of this book. In subsequent research, I turned my attention to the broader US strategic and economic agenda in Central Asia and the Middle East.

There is an intricate relationship between War and Globalization. The "War on Terror" has been used as a pretext to conquer new economic frontiers and ultimately establish corporate control over Iraq's extensive oil reserves.

The Disinformation Campaign

In the months leading up to the invasion of Iraq in March 2003, the disinformation campaign went into full gear.

Known and documented prior to the invasion, Britain and the US made extensive use of fake intelligence to justify the invasion and occupation of Iraq. Al Qaeda was presented as an ally of the Baghad regime. "Osama bin Laden" and "Weapons of Mass Destruction" statements circulated profusely in the news chain. (Chapter XI.)

Meanwhile, a new terrorist mastermind had emerged: Abu Musab Al-Zarqawi. In Colin Powell's historic address to the United Nations Security Council, detailed "documentation" on a sinister relationship between Saddam Hussein and Abu Musab Al-Zarqawi was presented, focussing on his ability to produce deadly chemical, biological and radiological weapons, with the full support and endorsement of the secular Baathist regime.

A Code Orange terror alert followed within two days of Powell's speech at the United Nations Security Council, where he had been politely rebuffed by UN Weapons Inspector Dr. Hans Blix.

Realty was thus turned upside down. The US was no longer viewed as preparing to wage war on Iraq. Iraq was preparing to attack America with the support of "Islamic terrorists". Terrorist mastermind Al-Zarqawi was identified as the number one suspect. Official statements pointed to the dangers of a dirty radioactive bomb attack in the US.

The main thrust of the disinformation campaign continued in the wake of the March 2003 US-led invasion of Iraq. It consisted in presenting the Iraqi resistance movement as "terrorists". The image of "terrorists opposed to democracy" fighting US "peacekeepers" appeared on television screens and news tabloids across the globe.

Meanwhile, the Code Orange terror alerts were being used by the Bush administration to create an atmosphere of fear and intimidation across America. (See Chapter XX.) The terror alerts also served to distract public opinion from the countless atrocities committed by US forces in the Afghan and Iraqi war theaters, not to mention the routine torture of so-called "enemy combatants".

Following the invasion of Afghanistan, the torture of prisoners of war and the setting up of concentration camps became an integral part of the Bush adminstration's post 9/11 agenda.

The entire legal framework had been turned upside down. According to the US Department of Justice, torture was now permitted under certain circumstances. Torture directed against "terrorists" was upheld as a justifiable means to preserving human rights and democracy. (See chapters XIV and XV.) In an utterly twisted logic, the Commander in Chief can now quite legitimately authorize the use of torture, because the victims of torture in this case are so-called "terrorists", who are said to routinely apply the same methods against Americans.

The orders to torture prisoners of war at the Guantanamo concentration camp and in Iraq in the wake of the 2003 invasion emanated from the highest levels of the US Government. Prison guards, interrogators in the US military and the CIA were responding to precise guidelines.

An inquisitorial system had been installed. In the US and Britain the "war on the terrorism" is upheld as being in the public interest. Anybody who questions its practices—which now include arbitrary arrest and detention, torture of men, women and children, political assassinations and concentration camps—is liable to be arrested under the antiterrorist legislation.

The London 7/7 Bomb Attack

A new threshold in the "war on terrorism" was reached in July 2005, with the bomb attacks on London's underground, which resulted tragically in 56 deaths and several hundred wounded.

On both sides of the Atlantic, the London 7//7 attacks were used to usher in far-reaching police state measures. The US House of Representatives renewed the USA PATRIOT Act "to make permanent the government's unprecedented powers to investigate suspected terrorists". Republicans claimed that the London attacks showed "how urgent and important it was to renew the law."

Barely a week prior to the London attacks, Washington had announced the formation of a "domestic spy service" under the auspices of the FBI. The new department—meaning essentially a Big Brother "Secret State Police"—was given a mandate to "spy on people in America suspected of terrorism or having critical intelligence information, even if they are not suspected of committing a crime." Significantly, this new FBI service is not accountable to the Department of Justice. It is controlled by the Directorate of National Intelligence headed by John Negroponte, who has the authority of ordering the arrest of "terror suspects".

Meanwhile, in the wake of the 7/7 London attacks, Britain's Home Office, was calling for a system of ID cards, as an "answer to terrorism". Each and every British citizen and resident will be obliged to register personal information, which will go into a giant national database, along with their personal biometrics: "iris pattern of the eye", fingerprints and "digitally recognizable facial features". Similar procedures were being carried out in the European Union.

War Criminals in High Office

The anti-terrorist legislation and the establishment of a Police State largely serve the interests of those who have committed extensive war crimes and who would otherwise have been indicted under national and international law.

In the wake of the London 7/7 attacks, war criminals continue to legitimately occupy positions of authority, which enable them to redefine the contours of the judicial system and the process of law enforcement. This process has provided them with a mandate to decide "who are the criminals", when in fact they are the criminals. (Chapter XVI).

From New York and Washington on September 11 to Madrid in March 2004 and to London in July 2005, the terror attacks have been used as a pretext to suspend the writ of habeas corpus. People can be arbitrarily arrested under the antiterrorist legislation and detained for an indefinite period. More generally, throughout the Western World, citizens are being tagged and labeled, their emails, telephone conversations and faxes are monitored and archived. Thousands of closed circuit TV cameras, deployed in urban areas, are overseeing their movements. Detailed personal data is entered into giant Big Brother data banks. Once this cataloging has been completed, people will be locked into watertight compartments.

The witch-hunt is not only directed against presumed "terrorists" through ethnic profiling, the various human rights, affirmative action and antiwar cohorts are also the object of the antiterrorist legislation.

The National Security Doctrine

In 2005, the Pentagon released a major document entitled *The National Defense Strategy of the United States of America* (NDS), which broadly sketches Washington's agenda for global military domination. While the NDS follows in the footsteps of the Administration's "preemptive" war doctrine as outlined in the Project for a New American Century (PNAC), it goes much further in setting the contours of Washington's global military agenda. (See Chapter XIX.)

Whereas the preemptive war doctrine envisages military action as a means of "self defense" against countries categorized as "hostile" to the US, the 2005 NDS goes one step further. It envisages the possibility of military intervention against "unstable countries" or "failed nations", which do not visibly constitute a threat to the security of the US.

Meanwhile, the Pentagon had unleashed a major propaganda and public relations campaign with a view to upholding the use of nuclear weapons for the "Defense of the American Homeland" against terrorists and rogue enemies. The fact that the nuclear bomb is categorized by the Pentagon as "safe for civilians" to be used in major counter-terrorist activities borders on the absurd.

In 2005, US Strategic Command (STRATCOM) drew up "a contingency plan to be used in response to another 9/11-type terrorist attack". The plan includes air raids on Iran using both conventional as well as tactical nuclear weapons.

America's "War on Terrorism"

The first ten chapters, with some changes and updates, correspond to the first edition of the book published in 2002 under the title *War and Globalization: The Truth behind September 11.* The present expanded edition contains twelve new chapters, which are the result of research undertaken both prior as well as in the wake of the invasion of Iraq. (Parts III and IV.) The sequencing of the material in Parts III and IV corresponds to the historical evolution of the post 9/11 US military and national security agendas. My main objective has been to refute the official narrative and reveal—using detailed evidence and documentation—the true nature of America's "war on terrorism".

Part I includes four chapters on September 11, focusing on the history of Al Qaeda and its ties to the US intelligence apparatus. These chapters document how successive administrations have supported and sustained terrorist organizations with a view to destabilizing national societies and creating political instability.

Part II entitled *War and Globalization* centers on the strategic and economic interests underlying the "war on terrorism".

Part III contains a detailed analysis of War Propaganda and the Disinformation Campaign, both prior and in the wake of the invasion of Iraq.

Part IV entitled *The New World Order* includes a review of the Bush administration's preemptive war doctrine (Chapter XIX), a detailed analysis of the post-Taliban narcotics trade protected by US intelligence, and a review of the 9/11 Commission Report focusing specifically on "What Happened on the Planes on the Morning of 9/11".

Chapter XX focuses on the system of terror alerts and their implications. Chapter XXI follows with an examination of the emergency procedures that could be used to usher in Martial Law leading to the suspension of Constitutional government. In this regard, the US Congress has already adopted procedures, which allow the Military to intervene directly in civilian police and judicial functions. In the case of a national emergency—e.g., in response to an alleged terror attack—there are clearly defined provisions, which could lead to the formation of a military government in America.

Finally, Chapter XXII focuses on the broad implications of the 7/7 London Bombs Attacks, which were followed by the adoption of sweeping Police State measures in Britain, the European Union and North America.

Writing this book has not been an easy undertaking. The material is highly sensitive. The results of this analysis, which digs beneath the gilded surface of US foreign policy, are both troublesome and disturbing. The conclusions are difficult to accept because they point to the criminalization of the upper echelons of the State. They also confirm the complicity of the corporate media in upholding the legitimacy of the Administration's war agenda and camouflaging US sponsored war crimes.

The World is at an important historical crossroads. The US has embarked on a military adventure which threatens the future of humanity. As we go to press, the Bush Administration has hinted in no uncertain terms that Iran is the next target of the "war on terrorism".

Military action against Iran would directly involve Israel's participation, which in turn is likely to trigger a broader war throughout the Middle East, not to mention an implosion in the Palestinian occupied territories.

I have attempted to the best of my abilities to provide evidence and detailed documentation of an extremely complex political process.

The livelihood of millions of people throughout the World is at stake. It is my sincere hope that the truth will prevail and that the understanding provided in this detailed study will serve the cause of World peace. This objective, however, can only be reached by revealing the falsehoods behind America's "War on Terrorism" and questioning the legitimacy of the main political and military actors responsible for extensive war crimes.

I am indebted to many people, who in the course of my work have supported my endeavors and have provided useful research insights. The readers of the Global Research website at www.globalresearch.ca have been a source of continuous inspiration and encouragement.

I am indebted to Nicolas Calvé for the creative front cover graphics, which vividly portray the New World Order, as well as his support in the typesetting and production of this book. I owe a debt of gratitude to my daughter Natacha, who assisted me in the editing of the final manuscript. I also wish to thank Dr. Leuren Moret and Professor Glen Rangwala whose carefully researched texts are included as appendices.

Michel Chossudovsky
Terrasse-Vaudreuil, Québec, August 2005

PART I
September 11

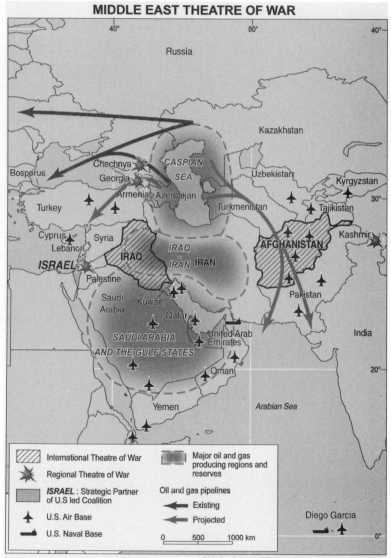

MIDDLE EAST THEATRE OF WAR

Realisation : Cartography Laboratory, Department of Geography, Laval University.

Chapter I
Background: Behind September 11

The world is at the crossroads of the most serious crisis in modern history. In the wake of the tragic events of September 11, in the largest display of military might since the Second World War, the United States has embarked upon a military adventure which threatens the future of humanity.

Barely a few hours following the terrorist attacks on the World Trade Center and the Pentagon, Osama bin Laden and his Al Qaeda network were identified by the Bush administration—without supporting evidence—as "the prime suspects". Secretary of State Colin Powell called the attacks "an act of war", and President George W. Bush confirmed in an evening-televised address to the Nation that he would "*make no distinction between the terrorists who committed these acts and those [foreign governments] who harbor them*".

Former CIA Director James Woolsey pointed his finger at "state sponsorship", implying the complicity of one or more foreign governments. In the words of former National Security Adviser Lawrence Eagleburger, "I think we will show when we get attacked like this, we are terrible in our strength and in our retribution."[1]

Meanwhile, parroting official statements, the Western media had approved the launching of "punitive actions" directed against civilian targets in Central Asia and the Middle East. According to William Safire writing in the *New York Times*: "When we reasonably determine our attackers' bases and camps, we must pulverize them—minimizing but accepting the risk of collateral damage— and act overtly or covertly to destabilize terror's national hosts."[2] The Bush administration, using the US media as its mouthpiece, was preparing the Western World for the merciless killing of thousands of innocent civilians in Afghanistan and beyond.

Osama bin Laden: Pretext for Waging War

At the outset, the "war on terrorism" had conveniently been used by the Bush administration not only to justify the extensive bombing of civilian targets in Afghanistan, but also to repeal constitutional rights and the Rule of Law at home, in the context of the "domestic war" on terrorism.

It turns out that the prime suspect in the New York and Washington terrorists attacks, Saudi-born Osama bin Laden, is a creation of US foreign policy. He was recruited during the Soviet-Afghan war "ironically under the auspices of the CIA, to fight Soviet invaders". Our analysis in Chapters II, III and IV amply confirms that Osama bin Laden's Al Qaeda network is what the CIA calls an "intelligence asset".

During the Cold War, but also in its aftermath, the CIA—using Pakistan's military intelligence apparatus as a "go-between"—played a key role in training the Mujahideen. In turn, the CIA-sponsored guerrilla training was integrated with the teachings of Islam. Both the Clinton and Bush administrations have consistently supported the "Militant Islamic Base", including Osama bin Laden's Al Qaeda, as part of their foreign policy agenda. The links between Osama bin Laden and the Clinton administration in Bosnia and Kosovo are well documented by congressional records. (See Chapter IV.)

A few months after the attacks, Defense Secretary Donald Rumsfeld, stated that it will be difficult to find Osama and extradite him: "It's like searching for a needle in a stack of hay." But the

US could have ordered, with no problem, his arrest and extradition on several occasions prior to the September 11 attacks. Two months before the September 11 attacks bin Laden, America's "Most Wanted Fugitive", was in the American Hospital in Dubai (United Arab Emirates) receiving treatment for a chronic kidney infection. If the US authorities had wanted to arrest Osama bin Laden prior to September 11, they could have done it then. But then they would *not* have had a pretext for waging a major military operation in Central Asia.

The US Support of the Taliban

While the Western media (which echoes the Bush administration) portrays the Taliban and Osama bin Laden's Al Qaeda as the "incarnation of evil", they fail to mention that the Taliban's coming to power in Afghanistan 1996 was the result of US military aid, channeled to Taliban and Al Qaeda forces through Pakistan's ISI. *Jane Defense Weekly* confirms that "half of Taliban manpower and equipment originate[d] in Pakistan under the ISI".[3]

Backed by Pakistan's ISI, the imposition of the hardline Taliban Islamic State largely served American geopolitical interests in the region. The hidden agenda behind US support to the Taliban was oil, because no sooner had the Taliban taken Kabul in 1996 and formed a government, than a delegation was whisked off to Houston, Texas for meetings with officials of Unocal Corporation regarding the construction of the strategic trans-Afghan pipeline. (See map page 2.)

Largest Display of Military Might Since World War II

Presented to public opinion as a "campaign against international terrorism", the deployment of America's war machine purports to enlarge America's sphere of influence not only in Central Asia and the Middle East, but also into the Indian sub-continent and the Far East. Ultimately, the US is intent upon establishing a permanent military presence in Afghanistan, which occupies a strategic position bordering on the former Soviet Union, China and Iran. Afghanistan is also at the hub of five nuclear powers: Russia, China,

India, Pakistan and Kazakhstan. In this regard, the Bush administration has taken the opportunity of using the "war against terrorism" to establish US military bases in several former Soviet republics including Uzbekistan, Kazakhstan, Tajikistan and the Kirgyz Republic. (See Chapter VI.)

Authoritarian State

Under the Bush administration, the military and intelligence apparatus has clearly taken over the reins of foreign policy in close consultation with Wall Street. With key decisions taken behind closed doors at the CIA and the Pentagon, "civilian political institutions" including the US Congress increasingly become a façade. While the illusion of a "functioning democracy" prevails in the eyes of public opinion, the US President has become a mere public relations figurehead, with visibly little understanding of key foreign policy issues:

> [O]n too many issues, especially those dealing with the wider world of global affairs, Bush often sounds as if he's reading from cue cards. When he ventures into international issues, his unfamiliarity is palpable and not even his unshakable self-confidence keeps him from avoiding mistakes.[4]

When a journalist asked Governor Bush during the 2000 election campaign what he thought about the Taliban:

> [H]e just shrugged his shoulders, bemused. It took a bit of prompting from the journalist ("discrimination against women in Afghanistan") for Bush to rouse himself: "Taliban in Afghanistan! Absolutely. Reprisals. I thought you were talking about some rock group." That's how well-informed about the outside world the prospective US President is, [e]ven about very important present-day developments that are on everyone's lips—that is, everyone with the slightest pretensions to culture; developments that he, if elected, will have to deal with.[5]

George W. Bush's statement on the Taliban was made to a *Glamor* correspondent. While commented on by a number of newspapers outside the US, it has barely been acknowledged by the American media.[6]

Who decides in Washington? In the context of a major military operation which has a bearing on our collective future and global security—not to mention Washington's "first strike" use of nuclear weapons—this question is of the utmost significance. In other words, apart from reading carefully prepared speeches, does the President wield any real political power or is he an instrument of the military intelligence establishment?

Military Planners Call the Shots

Under the New World Order, military planners in the State Department, the Pentagon and the CIA call the shots on foreign policy. They are not only in liaison with NATO, they also maintain contacts with officials in the IMF, the World Bank and the World Trade Organisation (WTO). In turn, the Washington-based international financial bureaucracy, responsible for imposing deadly "economic medicine" in the Third World and in most of the countries of the former Soviet block, maintains a close working relationship with the Wall Street financial establishment.

The powers behind this system are those of the global banks and financial institutions, the military-industrial complex, the oil and energy giants, the biotech and pharmaceutical conglomerates and the powerful media and communications giants, which fabricate the news and overtly influence the course of world events by blatantly distorting the facts.

"Criminalization" of the US State Apparatus

Under the Reagan administration, senior officials in the State Department had used the proceeds of illicit narcotics trade to finance the supply of weapons to the Nicaraguan Contras. In a bitter twist, the same State Department officials implicated in the "Iran-Contragate" scandal now occupy key positions in the Bush administration's inner cabinet.

These same "Iran-Contragate officials" call the shots in the day-to-day planning of the "war on terrorism". Richard Armitage "worked closely with Oliver North and was involved in the Iran-Contra arms smuggling scandal".[7] (See Chapter XII.)

Bush has been choosing people from the most dubious part of the Republican stable of the 1980s, those engaged in the Iran-Contra affair. His first such appointment, that of Richard Armitage as Deputy Secretary of State, went through the Senate quietly back in March by a voice vote. Armitage served as Assistant Secretary of Defense for International Security Affairs in the Reagan years, but a 1989 appointment in the elder Bush administration was withdrawn before hearings because of controversy over Iran-Contra and other scandals.

Bush followed up the Armitage appointment by appointing Reagan's Assistant Secretary of State, Elliot Abrams, as the National Security Council's senior director for democracy, human rights and international operations, a post which does not require Senate approval. Abrams pleaded guilty to two misdemeanor counts of lying to Congress during the Iran Contra hearings and was subsequently pardoned by George H. W. Bush.[8]

Richard Armitage was also one of the main architects behind US covert support to the Mujahideen and the "Militant Islamic Base", both during the Afghan-Soviet war as well as in its aftermath. Financed by the Golden Crescent drug trade, this pattern has not been fundamentally altered. (See Chapters II and XVI.) It still constitutes an integral part of US foreign policy. Moreover, amply documented, the multi-billion dollar drug trade has been been a major source of illicit funding by the CIA.[9]

Destroying the Rule of Law

Since September 11, state resources have been redirected towards financing the military-industrial complex, while social programs have been slashed. Government budgets have been restructured and tax revenues have been channeled towards beefing up the police and the domestic security apparatus. A "new legitimacy" has emerged, which undermines the fabric of the judicial system and destroys "the Rule of Law". Ironically, in several Western countries including the US, Great Britain and Canada, "existing democracies" are being repealed by democratically elected governments.

While "national security" has been reinforced, the new legislation is not meant to "protect citizens against terrorism". Rather, it largely upholds and protects the "free market" system. Its purpose is to disarm the civil rights and anti-war coalitions as well as to curb the development of a meaningful anti-globalization protest movement. (See Text Box 1.2) With the civilian economy in a free-fall, "Homeland Security" and the military-industrial complex constitute America's new economic growth centres.

Text Box 1.2

The Anti-Globalization Protest Movement and Canada's proposed Bill C-42

Proposed shortly after the September 11 attacks, Bill C-42 would have allowed the government to arbitrarily define military zones anytime and anywhere it wished. Had Quebec City been declared a military zone during the Free Trade Area of the America's (FTAA) Summit in the Spring of 2001, anyone caught inside the perimeter, including Quebec City residents, could have been declared a terrorist, arrested on the spot and detained indefinitely without recourse. (Bill C-42 was rescinded by the Canadian Parliament in April 2002.)

The New "Anti-Terrorist" Legislation

In the US, the "PATRIOT Act" criminalizes peaceful anti-globalization protests.[10] Demonstrating against the IMF or the WTO, for instance, is considered "a crime of domestic terror". Under the Act, "domestic terrorism" includes any activity which could lead to "influencing the policy of a government by intimidation or coercion".[11]

The US "anti-terrorist legislation", rubber-stamped by the US Congress, was decided upon by the military-police-intelligence establishment. In fact, several features of this legislation had been designed prior to the September 11 terrorist attacks in response to the growing anti-globalization protest movement.

In November 2001, President George W. Bush signed an executive order establishing "military commissions or tribunals to try suspected terrorists".[12]

> Under this order, [at the discretion of the President,] non-citizens, whether from the United States or elsewhere, accused of aiding international terrorism ... can be tried before one of these commissions. These are not court-martials, which provide for more protections. ... Attorney General Ashcroft has explicitly stated that terrorists do not deserve constitutional protections. These are "courts" of conviction and not of justice.[13]

Immediately following the September 11 attacks, hundreds of people in the US were arrested on a variety of trumped up charges. High school students were dismissed for holding "anti-war" views, university professors were fired or reprimanded for opposing the war.

> A Florida University professor has become the first post-September 11 academic casualty of the war against terrorism. Dr. Sami Al-Arian, a tenured professor of computer sciences at the University of South Florida (USF) ... had been investigated by the FBI and had never been arrested or charged with a crime. ... Professor Al-Arian received death threats and was quickly suspended, with pay, by university President Judy Genshaft.
>
> [In November 2001] ... the American Council of Trustees and Alumni (ACTA) issued a report titled "Defending Civilization: How Our Universities Are Failing America, and What Can Be Done About It." The report reproduced statements from some 117 college and university faculty who dared to speak out against or raise questions about the President's war on terrorism. "Defending Civilization" called these academics, the "weak link in America's response to the attack" of September 11.[14]

Extending More Powers to the FBI and the CIA

According to the new legislation, the powers of the FBI and the CIA have been extended to include routine wiretapping and surveillance of non-governmental organizations and trade unions, as well as journalists and intellectuals:

Under the new law, the same secret court will have the power to authorize wiretaps and secret searches of homes, in criminal cases—not just to gather foreign intelligence. The FBI will be able to wiretap individuals and organizations without meeting the stringent requirements of the Constitution. The law will authorize the secret court to permit roving wiretaps of any phones, computers or cell phones that might possibly be used by a suspect. Widespread reading of e-mail will be allowed, even before the recipient opens it. Thousands of conversations will be listened to, or read, that have nothing to do with the suspect or any crime.

The new legislation is filled with many other expansions of investigative and prosecutorial power, including wider use of undercover agents to infiltrate organizations, longer jail sentences and lifetime supervision for some who have served their sentences, more crimes that can receive the death penalty and longer statutes of limitations for prosecuting crimes.

The Act [also] creates a number of new crimes. One of the most threatening to dissent and those who oppose government policies is the crime of "domestic terrorism". It is loosely defined as acts that are dangerous to human life, violate criminal law and "appear to be intended to intimidate or coerce a civilian population" or "influence the policy of a government by intimidation or coercion". Under this definition, a protest demonstration that blocked a street and prevented an ambulance from getting by could be deemed domestic terrorism. Likewise, the demonstrations in Seattle against the WTO could fit within the definition. This was an unnecessary addition to the criminal code; there are already plenty of laws making such civil disobedience criminal without labelling such a time-honoured protest as terrorism and imposing severe prison sentences.

Overall, the new legislation represents one of the most sweeping assaults on liberties in the last 50 years. It is unlikely to make us more secure; it is certain to make us less free.

The US Government has conceptualized the war against terrorism as a permanent war, a war without boundaries. Terrorism is frightening to all of us, but it's equally chilling to think that in the name of anti-terrorism, our government is willing to suspend constitutional freedoms permanently as well.[15]

The Canadian legislation broadly replicates the clauses of the US anti-terrorist laws. (See Text Box 1.3) In the course of two months following the September 11 attacks, "over 800 people in Canada have disappeared into Canada's detention system without being allowed to contact family or lawyers".[16] And this happened before the Canadian Anti-Terrorist Legislation was adopted by the Canadian Parliament:

> The "anti-terrorism" laws … do far more than eliminate civil liberties. They eliminate justice. They return to an inquisitorial system of arbitrary arrest and detention. Summarized police allegations replace evidence. The concept of evidence is gone. Accusation equals guilt. The concept of innocent until proven guilty is gone.[17]

TEXT BOX 1.3
Canada's Anti-Terrorist Legislation

"The two essential pillars of criminal law to establish guilt: *mens rea* (intention to do a crime) and *actus reus* (the fact of doing the crime), are gone. If the State decides a terrorist act was committed and you were in any way connected or associated with it, you are guilty whether or not you 'intended to do the criminal act'or whether or not you 'did the act'." 'The right to remain silent' is gone. The principle of confidentiality between lawyer and client is gone (akin to forcing a priest to reveal the contents of the confessional). The concept of a fair trial and the right to a full defense is gone.

"People or organizations accused of being 'terrorists'are put on a list. Anyone who associates with a 'listed'person or organization can, by association, be defined as a terrorist. Hence lawyers who defend people accused of being terrorists could find themselves being defined as terrorists.

"Property and bank accounts can be frozen and confiscated simply on the accusation of being a terrorist. Punishments are excessive and severe (life imprisonment in many cases). These are some of the horrors of [Canada's Anti-Terrorist Legislation under] Bill C-36."[18]

In the European Union, the "anti-terrorist legislation"—while contributing to derogating civil liberties and undermining the Rule of Law—is less drastic than that adopted in the US and Canada. In Germany, the Greens within the government coalition had pressured Interior Minister Otto Schily to "tone down" the original draft of the legislation presented to the Bundestag. The anti-terrorist legislation in Germany, nonetheless, grants extraordinary powers to the police. It also reinforces the laws pertaining to deportation. Of significance, the German government has allocated more than three billion marks to beefing up their domestic security and intelligence apparatus, largely at the expense of social programs.

Global Economic Crisis

The "war on terrorism" and the development of the authoritarian State are occurring at the outset of a huge global economic depression marked by the downfall of State institutions, mounting unemployment, the collapse in living standards in all major regions of the world, including Western Europe and North America, and the outbreak of famines over large areas.

At a global economic level, this depression could be far more devastating than that of the 1930s. Moreover, the war has not only unleashed a massive shift out of civilian economic activities into the military-industrial complex, it has also accelerated the demise of the welfare state in most Western countries.

Five days before the terrorist assaults on the World Trade Center and the Pentagon, President Bush stated almost prophetically:

> I have repeatedly said the only time to use Social Security money is in times of war, times of recession, or times of severe emergency. And I mean that. (September 6, 2001.)[19]

The tone of the President's rhetoric has set the stage for a dramatic expansion of America's war machine. The "recession" and "war" buzzwords are being used to mould US public opinion into accepting the pilfering of the Social Security fund to pay the producers of weapons of mass destruction—i.e., a massive redirection of the nation's resources towards the military industrial complex.

Since the terrorist attacks, "love of country", "allegiance" and "patriotism" pervade the media and day-to-day political discourse. The hidden agenda behind Bush's declaration of an "axis of evil" (Iraq, Iran, North Korea, Libya and Syria) is to create a new legitimacy, opening the door for a "revitalization of the nation's defenses", while also providing various justifications for direct military interventions by the US in different parts of the world. Meanwhile, the shift from civilian into military production pours wealth into the hands of defense contractors at the expense of civilian needs.

The boost provided by the Bush administration to the military-industrial complex will not in any way resolve the mounting tide of unemployment in America. (See Text Box 1.4) Instead, this new direction of the US economy will generate hundreds of billions of dollars of surplus profits, which will line the pockets of a handful of large corporations.

War and Globalization

War and globalization are intimately related processes. The global economic crisis, which preceded the events of September 11, has its roots in the New World Order "free market" reforms. Since the 1997 "Asian crisis", financial markets have plummeted, national economies have collapsed one after the other and entire countries (e.g., Argentina and Turkey) have been taken over by their international creditors, forcing millions of people into abysmal poverty.

"The post-September 11 crisis" in many regards announces both the demise of Western social democracy, as well as the end of an era. The legitimacy of the global "free market" system has been reinforced, opening the door to a renewed wave of deregulation and privatization, eventually conducive to the corporate take-over of all public services and State infrastructure (including healthcare, electricity, municipal water and sewerage, inter-city highways and public broadcasting, just to name a few).

Moreover, in the US, Canada and Great Britain, and also in most countries of the European Union, the legal fabric of society has been overhauled. Based on the repeal of the Rule of Law, the foun-

---

TEXT BOX 1.4

Job Creation in America's War Machine

"The Big Five defense contractors (Lockheed Martin, Northrop Grumman, General Dynamics, Boeing and Raytheon) have been shifting staff and resources from 'civilian'into 'military'production lines. Lockheed Martin (LMT)—America's largest defense contractor—has shifted resources out of its troubled commercial/civilian sectors, into the lucrative production of advanced weapon systems including the F-22 Raptor high-tech fighter-jet. Each of the F-22 Raptor fighters will cost $85 million. Three thousand direct jobs will be created at a modest cost of $20 million a job."[20]

Boeing, which is bidding for the $200 billion dollar contract with the Defense Department for the production of the Joint Striker Fighter (JSF), confirmed that while some 3,000 jobs would be created under this contract, as a result of the September 11 attacks it will fire as many as 30,000 workers. At Boeing, each job created in the JSF Program, will cost US taxpayers $66.7 million. No wonder the Administration wants to downsize Social Security programs.[21]

---

dations of an authoritarian state apparatus have emerged with little or no organized opposition from the mainstay of civil society. Without debate or discussion, the "war on terrorism" against "rogue states" is deemed necessary to"protect democracy" and "enhance domestic security".

A collective understanding of the root causes of America's war, based on history, has been replaced by the need to "combat evil", contain "rogue states" and "hunt down Osama". These buzzwords are part of a carefully designed propaganda campaign. The ideology of the "rogue state", developed by the Pentagon during the 1991 Gulf War, constitutes a new legitimacy, a justification for waging a "humanitarian war" against countries which do not conform to the New World Order and the tenets of the"free market" system.

Notes

1. PBS News Hour, 11 September 2001. http://www.pbs.org/newshour/bb/military/terroristattack/government.html.

2. *New York Times,* 12 September 2001.

3. *Christian Science Monitor,* 3 September 1998.

4. *Time Magazine,* 15 November 1999.

5. Alexander Yanov, "Dangerous Lady: Political Sketch of the Chief Foreign Policy Adviser to George Bush", *Moscow News,* 12 July 2000.

6. See also *The Irish Times,* 20 January 2001, *The Japanese Times,* 6 January 2002.

7. *The Guardian,* London, 15 September 2001.

8. Peter Roff and James Chapin, "Face-off: Bush's Foreign Policy Warriors", United Press International, 18 July 2001, Centre for Research on Globalization, http://globalresearch.ca/articles/ROF111A.html, 3 November 2001.

9. Alfred McCoy, "Drug Fallout: The CIA's Forty Year Complicity in the Narcotics Trade", *The Progressive,* 1 August 1997.

10. PATRIOT is an acronym based on George W. Bush's "Uniting and Strengthening America by Providing Appropriate Tools Required to Intercept and Obstruct Terrorism" Act. Soon followed by 'TIPS'—Terrorism Information and Prevention System.

11. Michael Ratner, "Moving Toward a Police State (Or Have We Arrived?)", *Global Outlook,* No. 1, 2002, p. 35. Also at Centre for Research on Globalization (CRG), http://www.globalresearch.ca/articles/RAT111A.html, 30 November 2001.

12. *Ibid.*

13. *Ibid.*

14. Bill Berkovitz, "Witch-hunt in South Florida, Pro-Palestinian professor is first casualty of post-9/11 conservative correctness", Centre for Research on Globalization (CRG), http://globalresearch.ca/articles/BER112A.html, dated 13 December 2001.

15. Ratner, *op. cit.*

16. See Constance Fogal, "Globalization and the Destruction of the Rule of Law", *Global Outlook,* No. 1, Spring 2002, p. 36.

17. *Ibid.,* page 37.

18. *Ibid.*

19. Remarks by President Bush in the presence of Mexican President Vicente Fox prior to their departure to Toledo, Ohio; US Newswire Inc., 6 September 2001.

20. See Michel Chossudovsky, "War is Good for Business", *Global Outlook,* No 1. Spring 2002.

21. *Ibid.*

Appendix to Chapter I
Where was Osama bin Laden on 9/11?

According to a Reuters report (quoting Richard Labevière's book *Corridors of Terror*), "negotiations" between Osama bin Laden and the CIA, took place two months prior to the September 11, 2001 attacks at the American Hospital in Dubai, United Arab Emirates, while bin Laden was recovering from a kidney dialysis treatment.[1]

Enemy Number One in hospital recovering from dialysis treatment "negotiating with the CIA"?

The meeting with the CIA head of station at the American Hospital in Dubai, UAE had indeed been confirmed by a report in the French daily newspaper *Le Figaro,* published in October 2001.[2]

As to "negotiations" between the CIA and Osama (a CIA "intelligence asset"), this statement seems to be contradictory.

Even though the CIA has refuted the claim, the report serves to highlight Osama as a bona fide "Enemy of America," rather than a creation of the CIA. In the words of former CIA agent Milt Bearden in an interview with Dan Rather on September 12, 2001, "If they didn't have an Osama bin Laden, they would invent one."

Intelligence negotiations never take place on a hospital bed. The CIA knew Osama was at the American Hospital in Dubai. Rather than negotiate, they could have arrested him. He was on the FBI most wanted list.

According to the Reuters report: "At the time, bin Laden had a multi-million dollar price on his head for his suspected role in the 1998 bombings of two US embassies in East Africa". So why did the hospital staff, who knew that Osama was at the American Hospital in Dubai, not claim the reward?

The *Figaro* report points to complicity between the CIA and Osama rather than "negotiation". Consistent with several other reports, it also points to the antagonism between the FBI and the CIA.

If the CIA had wanted to arrest Osama bin Laden prior to September 11, they could have done it then in Dubai. But they would not have had a pretext for waging a major military operation in the Middle East and Central Asia.

According to *Le Figaro*:

> Dubai ... was the backdrop of a secret meeting between Osama bin Laden and the local CIA agent in July [2001]. A partner of the administration of the American Hospital in Dubai claims that "public enemy number one" stayed at this hospital between the 4th and 14th of July. While he was hospitalized, bin Laden received visits from many members of his family as well as prominent Saudis and Emiratis. During the hospital stay, the local CIA agent, known to many in Dubai, was seen taking the main elevator of the hospital to go [up] to bin Laden's hospital room. A few days later, the CIA man bragged to a few friends about having visited bin Laden. Authorized sources say that on July 15th, the day after bin Laden returned to Quetta [Pakistan], the CIA agent was called back to headquarters. In the pursuit of its investigations, the FBI discovered "financing agreements" that the CIA had been developing with its "Arab friends" for years. The Dubai meeting is, so it would seem, within the logic of "a certain American policy."[3]

The *Figaro* report is confirmed by several other news reports including the London *Times*.[4] During his 11-day stay in the American hospital, Osama received specialized medical treatment from Canadian urologist Dr. Terry Calloway.[5]

Osama back in Hospital on September 10, 2001, one Day before the 9/11 Attacks

According to Dan Rather, CBS, bin Laden was back in Hospital, one day before the 9/11 attacks, on September 10, this time, courtesy of America's indefectible ally Pakistan. Pakistan's Military Intelligence (ISI) told CBS that bin Laden had received dialysis treatment in Rawalpindi, in a military hospital at Pak Army's headquarters:

> DAN RATHER, CBS ANCHOR: As the United States and its allies in the war on terrorism press the hunt for Osama bin Laden, CBS News has exclusive information tonight about where bin Laden was and what he was doing in the last hours before his followers struck the United States [on] September 11.
>
> This is the result of hard-nosed investigative reporting by a team of CBS news journalists, and by one of the best foreign correspondents in the business, CBS's Barry Petersen. Here is his report.
>
> BARRY PETERSEN, CBS CORRESPONDENT (voice-over): Everyone remembers what happened on September 11. Here's the story of what may have happened the night before. It is a tale as twisted as the hunt for Osama bin Laden.
>
> CBS News has been told that the night before the September 11 terrorist attack, Osama bin Laden was in Pakistan. He was getting medical treatment with the support of the very military that days later pledged its backing for the US war on terror in Afghanistan.
>
> Pakistan intelligence sources tell CBS News that bin Laden was spirited into this military hospital in Rawalpindi for kidney dialysis treatment. On that night, says this medical worker who wanted her identity protected, they moved out all the regular staff in the urology department and sent in a secret team to replace them. She says it was treatment for a very special person. The special team was obviously up to no good.
>
> "The military had him surrounded," says this hospital employee who also wanted his identity masked, "and I saw the mysterious patient helped out of a car. Since that time," he says, "I have seen many pictures of the man. He is the man we know as Osama bin Laden. I also heard two army officers talking to each other. They were saying that Osama bin Laden had to be watched carefully and looked after." Those who know bin Laden say he suffers from numer-

ous ailments, back and stomach problems. Ahmed Rashid, who has written extensively on the Taliban, says the military was often there to help before 9/11.

AHMED RASHID, TALIBAN EXPERT: There were reports that Pakistani intelligence had helped the Taliban buy dialysis machines. And the rumor was that these were wanted for Osama bin Laden.

PETERSEN (on camera): Doctors at the hospital told CBS News there was nothing special about that night, but they refused our request to see any records. Government officials tonight denied that bin Laden had any medical treatment on that night.

(voice-over): But it was Pakistan's President Musharraf who said in public what many suspected, that bin Laden suffers from kidney disease, saying he thinks bin Laden may be near death. His evidence, watching this most recent video, showing a pale and haggard bin Laden, his left hand never moving. Bush administration officials admit they don't know if bin Laden is sick or even dead.

DONALD RUMSFELD, DEFENSE SECRETARY: With respect to the issue of Osama bin Laden's health, I just am—don't have any knowledge.

PETERSEN: The United States has no way of knowing who in Pakistan's military or intelligence supported the Taliban or Osama bin Laden maybe up to the night before 9/11 by arranging dialysis to keep him alive. So the United States may not know if those same people might help him again perhaps to freedom.[6]

It should be noted that the hospital is directly under the jurisdiction of the Pakistani Armed Forces, which has close links to the Pentagon. US military advisers based in Rawalpindi work closely with the Pakistani Armed Forces. Again, no attempt was made to arrest America's best known fugitive, but then maybe bin Laden was serving another "better purpose". Rumsfeld claimed at the time that he had no knowledge regarding Osama's health.[7]

The CBS report is a crucial piece of information in the 9/11 jigsaw. It refutes the administration's claim that the whereabouts of bin Laden are unknown. It points to a Pakistani connection; it suggests a cover-up at the highest levels of the Bush administration.

Dan Rather and Barry Petersen failed to draw the implications of their January 2002 report. They failed to beg the key question:

where was Osama on 9/11? If they are to stand by their report, the conclusion is obvious: The administration is lying regarding the whereabouts of Osama.

If the CBS report is accurate and Osama had indeed been admitted to the Pakistani military hospital on the evening of September 10 (local time), courtesy of America's ally, he was in all likelihood still in hospital in Rawalpindi on the 11th of September, when the attacks occurred. Even if he had been released from the hospital the following morning on the 11th (local time), in all probability, his whereabouts were known to US officials on September 12, when Secretary of State Colin Powell initiated negotiations with Pakistan, with a view to arresting and extraditing bin Laden. (See Chapter IV.)

Notes

1. Reuters, 13 November 2003.

2. See Alexandra Richard, "La CIA aurait rencontré ben Laden en juillet", 2 November 2001, *Le Figaro*, English translation by Tiphaine Dickson, Centre for Research on Globalization, November 2001, http://www.globalresearch.ca/articles/RIC111B.html.

3. *Ibid.*

4. *The Times*, London, 1 November 2001.

5. See the Hospital's website at http://www.ahdubai.com/site/ps18_2.htm

6. Transcript of CBS report, 28 January 2002, http://www.cbsnews.com/stories/2002/01/28/eveningnews/main325887.shtml

7. *Ibid.*

Chapter II
Who Is Osama bin Laden?

Presented in stylized fashion by the Western media, "Osama bin Laden" constitutes the new bogeyman. He is both the "cause" and the "consequence" of war and social devastation. He is also held responsible for the civilian deaths in Afghanistan resulting from the US bombing campaign. In this regard, Secretary of Defense Donald Rumsfeld has stated that "he did not rule out the eventual use of nuclear weapons" as part of the US Government's campaign against Osama bin Laden's Al Qaeda.[1]

Background of the Soviet-Afghan War

Who is Osama? The prime suspect in the New York and Washington terrorists attacks, Saudi-born Osama bin Laden, was recruited during the Soviet-Afghan war, "ironically under the auspices of the CIA, to fight Soviet invaders".[2]

In 1979, the largest covert operation in the history of the CIA was launched in Afghanistan:

> With the active encouragement of the CIA and Pakistan's ISI, who wanted to turn the Afghan Jihad into a global war waged by all

Muslim states against the Soviet Union, some 35,000 Muslim radicals from 40 Islamic countries joined Afghanistan's fight between 1982 and 1992. Tens of thousands more came to study in Pakistani madrasahs. Eventually, more than 100,000 foreign Muslim radicals were directly influenced by the Afghan jihad.[3]

US Government support to the Mujahideen was presented to world public opinion as a "necessary response" to the 1979 Soviet invasion of Afghanistan in support of the pro-Communist government of Babrak Kamal. Recent evidence suggests, however, that the CIA's military-intelligence operation in Afghanistan had been launched *prior* rather than *in response to* the Soviet invasion. Washington's intent was to deliberately trigger a civil war, which lasted more than 20 years.

The CIA's role in support of the Mujahideen is confirmed in an 1998 interview with Zbigniew Brzezinski, who at the time was National Security Adviser to President Jimmy Carter:

> **Brzezinski:** According to the official version of history, CIA aid to the Mujahideen began during 1980, that is to say, after the Soviet army invaded Afghanistan, [on] 24 December 1979. But the reality, secretly guarded until now, is completely otherwise. Indeed, it was July 3, 1979, that President Carter signed the first directive for secret aid to the opponents of the pro-Soviet regime in Kabul. And that very day, I wrote a note to the President in which I explained to him that in my opinion, this aid was going to induce a Soviet military intervention.
>
> **Question:** *Despite this risk, you were an advocate of this covert action. But perhaps you yourself desired this Soviet entry into war and looked to provoke it?*
>
> **Brzezinski:** It isn't quite that. We didn't push the Russians to intervene, but we knowingly increased the probability that they would.
>
> **Question:** *When the Soviets justified their intervention by asserting that they intended to fight against a secret involvement of the United States in Afghanistan, people didn't believe them. However, there was a basis of truth. You don't regret anything today?*
>
> **Brzezinski:** Regret what? That secret operation was an excellent idea. It had the effect of drawing the Russians into the Afghan trap and you want me to regret it? The day that the Soviets officially

crossed the border, I wrote to President Carter. We now have the opportunity of giving to the USSR its Vietnam War. Indeed, for almost 10 years, Moscow had to carry on a war unsupportable by the government, a conflict that brought about the demoralization and finally the breakup of the Soviet empire.

Question: *And neither do you regret having supported the Islamic fundamentalists, having given arms and advice to future terrorists?*

Brzezinski: What is most important to the history of the world? The Taliban or the collapse of the Soviet empire? Some stirred-up Moslems or the liberation of Central Europe and the end of the Cold War?[4]

"The Islamic Jihad"

Consistent with Brzezinski's account, a "Militant Islamic Network" was created by the CIA. The "Islamic Jihad" (or holy war against the Soviets) became an integral part of the CIA's intelligence ploy. It was supported by the United States and Saudi Arabia, with a significant part of the funding generated from the Golden Crescent drug trade:

> In March 1985, President Reagan signed National Security Decision Directive 166 ... [which] authorize[d] stepped-up covert military aid to the Mujahideen, and it made clear that the secret Afghan war had a new goal: to defeat Soviet troops in Afghanistan through covert action and encourage a Soviet withdrawal. The new covert US assistance began with a dramatic increase in arms supplies—a steady rise to 65,000 tons annually by 1987 ... as well as a "ceaseless stream" of CIA and Pentagon specialists who traveled to the secret headquarters of Pakistan's ISI on the main road near Rawalpindi, Pakistan. There, the CIA specialists met with Pakistani intelligence officers to help plan operations for the Afghan rebels.[5]

The Central Intelligence Agency using Pakistan's ISI played a key role in training the Mujahideen. In turn, the CIA-sponsored guerrilla training was integrated with the teachings of Islam. The madrasas were set up by Wahabi fundamentalists financed out of Saudi Arabia: "[I]t was the government of the United States who supported Pakistani dictator General Zia-ul Haq in creating thousands of religious schools, from which the germs of the Taliban emerged."[6]

Predominant themes were that Islam was a complete socio-political ideology, that holy Islam was being violated by the atheistic Soviet troops, and that the Islamic people of Afghanistan should reassert their independence by overthrowing the leftist Afghan regime propped up by Moscow.[7]

Pakistan's ISI used as a 'Go-Between'

CIA covert support to the "Islamic Jihad" operated indirectly through the Pakistani ISI—i.e., the CIA did not channel its support directly to the Mujahideen. For these covert operations to be "successful", Washington was careful not to reveal the ultimate objective of the "Jihad", which consisted of not only destabilizing the pro-Soviet government in Afghanistan, but also destroying the Soviet Union.

In the words of the CIA's Milton Beardman, "We didn't train Arabs." Yet, according to Abdel Monam Saidali, of the Al-aram Centre for Strategic Studies in Cairo, bin Laden and the "Afghan Arabs" had been imparted "with very sophisticated types of training that was allowed to them by the CIA".[8]

The CIA's Beardman confirmed, in this regard, that Osama bin Laden was not aware of the role he was playing on behalf of Washington. According to bin Laden (as quoted by Beardman): "Neither I, nor my brothers, saw evidence of American help."[9]

Motivated by nationalism and religious fervor, the Islamic warriors were unaware that they were fighting the Soviet Army on behalf of Uncle Sam. While there were contacts at the upper levels of the intelligence hierarchy, Islamic rebel leaders in theater had no contacts with Washington or the CIA.

With CIA backing and the funneling of massive amounts of US military aid, the Pakistani ISI had developed into a "parallel structure wielding enormous power over all aspects of government".[10] The ISI had a staff composed of military and intelligence officers, bureaucrats, undercover agents and informers, estimated at 150,000.[11]

Meanwhile, CIA operations had also reinforced the Pakistani military regime led by General Zia-ul Haq:

Relations between the CIA and the ISI had grown increasingly warm following [General] Zia's ouster of Bhutto and the advent of the military regime. ... During most of the Afghan war, Pakistan was more aggressively anti-Soviet than even the United States. Soon after the Soviet military invaded Afghanistan in 1980, Zia [ul Haq] sent his ISI chief to destabilize the Soviet Central Asian states. The CIA only agreed to this plan in October 1984.

The CIA was more cautious than the Pakistanis. Both Pakistan and the United States took the line of deception on Afghanistan with a public posture of negotiating a settlement, while privately agreeing that military escalation was the best course.[12]

The Golden Crescent Drug Triangle

The history of the drug trade in Central Asia is intimately related to the CIA's covert operations. Prior to the Soviet-Afghan war, opium production in Afghanistan and Pakistan was directed to small regional markets. There was no local production of heroin.[13] Researcher Alfred McCoy's study confirms that within two years of the onslaught of the CIA operation in Afghanistan, "the Pakistan-Afghanistan borderlands became the world's top heroin producer, supplying 60 per cent of US demand. In Pakistan, the heroin-addict population went from near zero in 1979 ... to 1.2 million by 1985— a much steeper rise than in any other nation".[14]

CIA assets again controlled this heroin trade. As the Mujahideen guerrillas seized territory inside Afghanistan, they ordered peasants to plant opium as a revolutionary tax. Across the border in Pakistan, Afghan leaders and local syndicates under the protection of Pakistan Intelligence operated hundreds of heroin laboratories. During this decade of wide-open drug-dealing, the US Drug Enforcement Agency in Islamabad failed to instigate major seizures or arrests. ...

US officials had refused to investigate charges of heroin dealing by its Afghan allies "because US narcotics policy in Afghanistan has been subordinated to the war against Soviet influence there." In 1995, the former CIA director of the Afghan operation, Charles Cogan, admitted the CIA had indeed sacrificed the drug war to fight the Cold War. "Our main mission was to do as much damage as possible to the Soviets. We didn't really have the resources or the time to devote to an investigation of the drug trade .... I don't think that we need to apologize for this. Every situation has its fallout .... There was fallout in terms of drugs, yes. But the main objective was accomplished. The Soviets left Afghanistan."[15]

After the Cold War, the Central Asian region became not only strategic for its extensive oil reserves, but also produced, in Afghanistan alone, 75 per cent of the world's heroin, representing multi-billion dollar revenues to business syndicates, financial institutions, intelligence agencies and organized crime. With the disintegration of the Soviet Union, a new surge in opium production had unfolded.

The annual proceeds of the Golden Crescent drug trade (between 100 and 200 billion dollars) represented approximately one third of the worldwide annual turnover of narcotics, estimated by the United Nations to be of the order of $500 billion.[16] According to the US Drug Enforcement Agency (DEA), Afghanistan produced more than 70 per cent of the world's opium in 2000, and about 80 per cent of the opiate products in Europe.[17]

Powerful business syndicates in the West, and in the former Soviet Union, allied with organized crime, were competing for the strategic control over the heroin routes. According to UN estimates, the production of opium in Afghanistan in 1998-99—coinciding with the buildup of armed insurgencies in the former Soviet republics—reached a record high of 4,600 metric tons.[18] In other words, control over "the drug routes" is *strategic.*

The multi-billion dollar revenues of narcotics are deposited in the Western banking system. Most of the large international banks—together with their affiliates in the offshore banking havens—launder large amounts of narco-dollars. Therefore, the international trade in narcotics constitutes a multi-billion dollar business of the same order of magnitude as the international trade in oil. From this standpoint, geopolitical control over "the drug routes" is as strategic as oil pipelines. (On the post-Taliban narcotics economy, see Chapter XVI).

In the Wake of the Soviet Withdrawal

Despite the demise of the Soviet Union, Pakistan's extensive military-intelligence apparatus (the ISI) was not dismantled. In the wake of the Cold War, the CIA continued to support the Islamic Jihad out of Pakistan. New undercover initiatives were set in motion in Central Asia, the Caucasus and the Balkans. Pakistan's ISI essentially "served as a catalyst for the disintegration of the Soviet Union and the emergence of six new Muslim republics in Central Asia".[19]

Meanwhile, Islamic missionaries of the Wahabi sect from Saudi Arabia had established themselves in the Muslim republics, as well as within the Russian federation, encroaching upon the institutions of the secular State. Despite its anti-American ideology, Islamic fundamentalism was largely serving Washington's strategic interests in the former Soviet Union.

Following the withdrawal of Soviet troops in 1989, the civil war in Afghanistan continued unabated. The Taliban were being supported by the Pakistani Deobandis and their political party, the Jamiat-ul-Ulema-e-Islam (JUI). In 1993, the JUI entered Pakistan's government coalition of Prime Minister Benazir Bhutto. Ties between the JUI, the Army and the ISI were established. In 1996, with the downfall of the Hezb-I-Islami Hektmatyar government in Kabul, the Taliban not only instated a hardline Islamic government, they also "handed control of the training camps in Afghanistan over to JUI factions …".[20]

The JUI, with the support of the Saudi Wahabi movement, played a key role in recruiting volunteers to fight in the Balkans and the former Soviet Union.

Jane Defense Weekly confirms, that "half of Taliban manpower and equipment originate[d] in Pakistan under the ISI".[21] In fact, it would appear that following the Soviet withdrawal, both sides in the Afghan civil war continued to receive covert support through Pakistan's ISI.[22]

Backed by Pakistan's military intelligence, which in turn was controlled by the CIA, the Taliban Islamic State was largely serving American geopolitical interests. No doubt this explains why Washington had closed its eyes on the reign of terror imposed by the Taliban, including the blatant derogation of women's rights, the closing down of schools for girls, the dismissal of women employees from government offices and the enforcement of "the Sharia laws of punishment".[23]

The Golden Crescent drug trade was also being used to finance and equip the Bosnian Muslim Army (starting in the early 1990s) and later the Kosovo Liberation Army (KLA). In fact, at the time of the September 11 attacks, CIA-sponsored Mujahideen mercenaries were fighting within the ranks of KLA-NLA terrorists in their assaults into Macedonia. (See Chapter III.)

The War in Chechnya

In Chechnya, the renegade autonomous region of the Russian Federation, the main rebel leaders, Shamil Basayev and Al Khattab, were trained and indoctrinated in CIA-sponsored camps in Afghanistan and Pakistan. According to Yossef Bodansky, director of the US Congress'Task Force on Terrorism and Unconventional Warfare, the war in Chechnya had been planned during a secret summit of HizbAllah International held in 1996 in Mogadishu, Somalia.[24] The summit was attended by none other than Osama bin Laden, as well as high-ranking Iranian and Pakistani intelligence officers. In this regard, the involvement of Pakistan's ISI in Chechnya "goes far beyond supplying the Chechens with weapons and expertise: The ISI and its radical Islamic proxies are actually calling the shots in this war." [25]

Russia's main pipeline route transits through Chechnya and Dagestan. Despite Washington's condemnation of Islamic terrorism, the indirect beneficiaries of the wars in Chechnya are the British and American oil conglomerates which are vying for control over oil resources and pipeline corridors out of the Caspian Sea basin. (See map page 2.)

The two main Chechen rebel armies (led by Commanders Shamil Basayev and Emir Khattab), estimated at 35,000 strong, were supported by Pakistan's ISI, which also played a key role in organizing and training the rebel army:

[In 1994] the Pakistani Inter Services Intelligence arranged for Basayev and his trusted lieutenants to undergo intensive Islamic indoctrination and training in guerrilla warfare in the Khost province of Afghanistan at Amir Muawia camp, set up in the early 1980s by the CIA and ISI and run by famous Afghani warlord Gulbuddin Hekmatyar. In July 1994, upon graduating from Amir Muawia, Basayev was transferred to Markaz-i-Dawar camp in Pakistan to undergo training in advanced guerrilla tactics. In Pakistan, Basayev met the highest ranking Pakistani military and intelligence officers: Minister of Defense General Aftab Shahban Mirani, Minister of Interior General Naserullah Babar, and the head of the ISI branch in charge of supporting Islamic causes, General Javed Ashraf (all now retired). High-level connections soon proved very useful to Basayev.[26]

Following his training and indoctrination stint, Basayev was assigned to lead the assault against Russian federal troops in the first Chechen war in 1995. His organization had also developed extensive links to criminal syndicates in Moscow as well as ties to Albanian organized crime and the KLA. In 1997-1998, according to Russia's Federal Security Service (FSB), "Chechen warlords started buying up real estate in Kosovo ... through several real estate firms registered as a cover in Yugoslavia."[27]

Basayev's organization had also been involved in a number of rackets including narcotics, illegal tapping and sabotage of Russia's oil pipelines, kidnapping, prostitution, trade in counterfeit dollars and the smuggling of nuclear materials.[28] Alongside the extensive laundering of drug money, the proceeds of various illicit activities were funnelled towards the recruitment of mercenaries and the purchase of weapons.

During his training in Afghanistan, Shamil Basayev linked up with Saudi-born veteran Mujahideen Commander, Al Khattab, who had fought as a volunteer in Afghanistan. Barely a few months after Basayev's return to Grozny, Khattab was invited (in early 1995) to set up an army base in Chechnya for the training of Mujahideen fighters. According to the BBC, Khattab's posting to Chechnya had been "arranged through the Saudi-Arabian-based [International] Islamic Relief Organization, a militant religious organization, funded by mosques and rich individuals who channeled funds into Chechnya".[29]

Dismantling Secular Institutions in the former Soviet Union

The enforcement of Islamic law in the largely secular Muslim societies of the former Soviet Union has served America's strategic interests in the region. Previously, a strong secular tradition based on a rejection of Islamic law prevailed throughout the Central Asian republics and the Caucasus, including Chechnya and Dagestan (which are part of the Russian Federation).

The 1994-1996 Chechen war, instigated by the main rebel movements against Moscow, has served to undermine secular state institutions. A parallel system of local government, controlled by the Islamic militia, was implanted in many localities in Chechnya. In some of the small towns and villages, Islamic Sharia courts were established under a reign of political terror.

Financial aid from Saudi Arabia and the Gulf States to the rebel armies was conditional upon the installation of the Sharia courts, despite strong opposition of the civilian population. The Principal Judge and Ameer of the Sharia courts in Chechnya is Sheikh Abu Umar, who "came to Chechnya in 1995 and joined the ranks of the Mujahideen there under the leadership of Ibn-ul-Khattab …. He set about teaching Islam with the correct Aqeedah to the Chechen Mujahideen, many of whom held incorrect and distorted beliefs about Islam."[30]

Meanwhile, state institutions of the Russian Federation in Chechnya were crumbling under the brunt of the IMF-sponsored austerity measures imposed under the Presidency of Boris Yeltsin. In contrast, the Sharia courts, financed and equipped out of Saudi Arabia, were gradually displacing existing State institutions of the Russian Federation and the Chechnya autonomous region.

The Wahabi movement from Saudi Arabia was not only attempting to overrun civilian State institutions in Dagestan and Chechnya, it was also seeking to displace the traditional Sufi Muslim leaders. In fact, the resistance to the Islamic rebels in Dagestan was based on the alliance of the (secular) local governments with the Sufi sheiks:

> These [Wahabi] groups consist of a very tiny but well-financed and well-armed minority. They propose with these attacks the creation of terror in the hearts of the masses .... By creating anarchy and lawlessness, these groups can enforce their own harsh, intolerant brand of Islam .... Such groups do not represent the common view of Islam, held by the vast majority of Muslims and Islamic scholars, for whom Islam exemplifies the paragon of civilization and perfected morality. They represent what is nothing less than a movement to anarchy under an Islamic label .... Their intention is not so much to create an Islamic state, but to create a state of confusion in which they are able to thrive.[31]

Promoting Secessionist Movements in India

In parallel with its covert operations in the Balkans and the former Soviet Union, Pakistan's ISI has provided, since the 1980s, support to several secessionist Islamic insurgencies in India's Kashmir.

Although officially condemned by Washington, these covert ISI operations were undertaken with the tacit approval of the US Government. Coinciding with the 1989 Geneva Peace Agreement and the Soviet withdrawal from Afghanistan, the ISI was instrumental in the creation of the militant Jammu and Kashmir Hizbul Mujahideen (JKHM).[32]

The December 2001 terrorist attacks on the Indian Parliament—which contributed to pushing India and Pakistan to the brink of war—were conducted by two Pakistan-based rebel groups, Lashkar-e-Taiba (Army of the Pure) and Jaish-e-Muhammad (Army of Mohammed), both of which are covertly supported by Pakistan's ISI.[33]

The timely attack on the Indian Parliament, followed by the ethnic riots in Gujarat in early 2002, were the culmination of a process initiated in the 1980s, financed by drug money and abetted by Pakistan's military intelligence.[34]

Needless to say, these ISI-supported terrorist attacks serve the geopolitical interests of the US They not only contribute to weakening and fracturing the Indian Union, they also create conditions which favor the outbreak of a regional war between Pakistan and India.

The powerful Council on Foreign Relations (CFR), which plays a behind-the-scenes role in the formulation of US foreign policy, confirms that the Lashkar and Jaish rebel groups are supported by the ISI:

> Through its Inter-Service Intelligence Agency (ISI), Pakistan has provided funding, arms, training facilities, and aid in crossing borders to Lashkar and Jaish. This assistance—an attempt to replicate in Kashmir the international Islamist brigade's "holy war" against the Soviet Union in Afghanistan—helped introduce radical Islam into the long-standing conflict over the fate of Kashmir ....
>
> *Have these groups received funding from sources other than the Pakistani government?*
>
> Yes. Members of the Pakistani and Kashmiri communities in England send millions of dollars a year, and Wahabi sympathizers in the Persian Gulf also provide support.
>
> *Do Islamist terrorists in Kashmir have ties to Al Qaeda?*
>
> Yes. In 1998, the leader of Harakat, Farooq Kashmiri Khalil, signed Osama bin Laden's declaration calling for attacks on Americans, including civilians, and their allies. Bin Laden is also suspected of funding Jaish, according to US and Indian officials. And Maulana Massoud Azhar, who founded Jaish, traveled to Afghanistan several times to meet bin Laden.
>
> *Where were these Islamist militants trained?*
>
> Many were given ideological training in the same madrasas, or Muslim seminaries, that taught the Taliban and foreign fighters in Afghanistan. They received military training at camps in Afghanistan or in villages in Pakistan-controlled Kashmir. Extremist groups have recently opened several new madrasas in Azad Kashmir.[35]

What the CFR fails to mention are the links between the ISI and the CIA. Confirmed by the writings of Zbigniew Brzezinski (who also happens to be a member of the CFR), the "international Islamic brigade" was a creation of the CIA.

US-Sponsored Insurgencies in China

Also of significance in understanding America's "War on Terrorism" is the existence of ISI-supported Islamic insurgencies on China's Western border with Afghanistan and Pakistan. In fact, several of the Islamic movements in the Muslim republics of the former Soviet Union are integrated with the Turkestan and Uigur movements in China's Xinjiang-Uigur autonomous region.

These separatist groups—which include the East Turkestan Terrorist Force, the Islamic Reformist Party, the East Turkestan National Unity Alliance, the Uigur Liberation Organization and the Central Asian Uigur Jihad Party—have all received support and training from Osama bin Laden's Al Qaeda.[36] The declared objective of these Chinese-based Islamic insurgencies is the "establishment of an Islamic caliphate in the region".[37]

The caliphate would integrate Uzbekistan, Tajikistan, Kyrgyzstan (West Turkestan) and the Uigur autonomous region of China (East Turkestan) into a single political entity.

The "caliphate project" encroaches upon Chinese territorial sovereignty. Supported by various Wahabi "foundations" from the Gulf States, secessionism on China's Western frontier is, once again, consistent with US strategic interests in Central Asia. Meanwhile, a powerful US-based lobby is channelling support to separatist forces in Tibet.

By tacitly promoting the secession of the Xinjiang-Uigur region (using Pakistan's ISI as a "go-between"), Washington is attempting to trigger a broader process of political destabilization and fracturing of the People's Republic of China. In addition to these various covert operations, the US has established military bases in Afghanistan and in several of the former Soviet republics, directly on China's Western border.

The militarization of the South China Sea and of the Taiwan Straits is also an integral part of this strategy. (See Chapter VII.)

Washington's Hidden Agenda

US foreign policy is not geared towards curbing the tide of Islamic fundamentalism. In fact, it is quite the opposite. The significant development of "radical Islam", in the wake of September 11, in the Middle East and Central Asia is consistent with Washington's hidden agenda. The latter consists of sustaining rather than combatting international terrorism, with a view to destabilizing national societies and preventing the articulation of genuine social movements directed against the American Empire. Washington continues to support—through CIA covert operations—the development of Islamic fundamentalism, particularly in China and India.

Throughout the developing world, the growth of sectarian, fundamentalist and other such organizations tends to serve US interests. These various organizations and armed insurgents have been developed, particularly in countries where state institutions have collapsed under the brunt of the IMF-sponsored economic reforms.

The application of IMF economic medicine often breeds an atmosphere of ethnic and social strife, which in turn favors the development of fundamentalism and communal violence.

These fundamentalist organizations contribute by destroying and displacing secular institutions.

In the short term, fundamentalism creates social and ethnic divisions. It undermines the capacity of people to organize against the American Empire. These organizations or movements, such as the Taliban, often foment "opposition to Uncle Sam" in a way which does not constitute any real threat to America's broader geopolitical and economic interests. Meanwhile, Washington has supported their development as a means of disarming social movements, which it fears may threaten US economic and political hegemony.

Notes

1. Quoted in *The Houston Chronicle*, 20 October 2001. See also Michel Chossudovsky, "Tactical Nuclear Weapons" against Afghanistan? Centre for Research on Globalization (CRG), http://globalresearch.ca/articles/CHO112C.html, 5 December 2001.

2. Hugh Davies, "Informers point the finger at bin Laden; Washington on alert for suicide bombers." *The Daily Telegraph*, London, 24 August 1998, emphasis added.

3. Ahmed Rashid, "The Taliban: Exporting Extremism", *Foreign Affairs*, November-December 1999.

4. "The CIA's Intervention in Afghanistan, Interview with Zbigniew Brzezinski, President Jimmy Carter's National Security Adviser", *Le Nouvel Observateur*, Paris, 15-21 January 1998, published in English, Centre for Research on Globalization, *emphasis added in italics*, http://www.globalresearch.ca/articles/BRZ110A.html, 5 October 2001, italics added.

5. Steve Coll, *The Washington Post*, July 19, 1992.

6. Revolutionary Association of the Women of Afghanistan (RAWA), "RAWA Statement on the Terrorist Attacks in the US", Centre for Research on Globalization (CRG), http://globalresearch.ca/articles/RAW109A.html, 16 September 2001

7. Dilip Hiro, "Fallout from the Afghan Jihad", Inter Press Services, 21 November 1995.

8. National Public Radio, Weekend Sunday (NPR) with Eric Weiner and Ted Clark, 16 August 1998.

9. *Ibid.*

10. Dipankar Banerjee, "Possible Connection of ISI With Drug Industry", *India Abroad*, 2 December 1994.

11. *Ibid.*

12. Diego Cordovez and Selig Harrison, *Out of Afghanistan: The Inside Story of the Soviet Withdrawal*, Oxford University Press, New York, 1995. See also the review of Cordovez and Harrison in International *Press Services* (IPS), 22 August 1995.

13. Alfred McCoy, "Drug Fallout: the CIA's Forty Year Complicity in the Narcotics Trade", *The Progressive*, 1 August 1997.

14. *Ibid.*

15. *Ibid.*

16. Douglas Keh, *Drug Money in a Changing World*, Technical document No. 4, 1998, Vienna UNDCP, p. 4. See also United Nations Drug Control Program, Report of the International Narcotics Control Board for 1999, E/INCB/1999/1 United Nations, Vienna 1999, p. 49-51, and Richard Lapper, "UN Fears Growth of Heroin Trade", *Financial Times*, 24 February 2000.

17. BBC, "Afghanistan's Opium Industry", 9 April 2002.

18. Report of the International Narcotics Control Board, op cit, p. 49-51; see also Richard Lapper, *op. cit.*

19. International Press Services, 22 August 1995.

20. Ahmed Rashid, "The Taliban: Exporting Extremism", *Foreign Affairs*, November-December, 1999, p. 22.

21. Quoted in the *Christian Science Monitor*, 3 September 1998.

22. Tim McGirk, "Kabul Learns to Live with its Bearded Conquerors", *The Independent*, London, 6 November 1996.

23. See K. Subrahmanyam, "Pakistan is Pursuing Asian Goals", *India Abroad*, 3 November 1995.

24. Levon Sevunts, "Who's Calling The Shots? Chechen conflict finds Islamic roots in Afghanistan and Pakistan", *The Gazette*, Montreal, 26 October 1999.

25. *Ibid.*

26. *Ibid.*

27. See Vitaly Romanov and Viktor Yadukha, "Chechen Front Moves To Kosovo", *Segodnia*, Moscow, 23 Feb 2000.

28. See, "Mafia linked to Albania's Collapsed Pyramids", *The European*, 13 February 1997. See also Itar-Tass, 4-5 January 2000.

29. BBC, 29 September 1999.

30. See Global Muslim News, http://www.islam.org.au/articles/21/news.htm, December 1997.

31. Mateen Siddiqui, "Differentiating Islam from Militant 'Islamists'" *San Francisco Chronicle*, 21 September 1999.

32. See K. Subrahmanyam, "Pakistan is Pursuing Asian Goals", *India Abroad*, 3 November 1995.

33. Council on Foreign Relations, "Terrorism: Questions and Answers, Harakat ul-Mujahideen, Lashkar-e-Taiba, Jaish-e-Muhammad", http://www.terrorism-answers.com/groups/harakat2.html, Washington 2002.

34. See Murali Ranganathan, "Human Rights Report Draws Flak", *News India*, 16 September 1994.

35. *Ibid.*

36. According to official Chinese sources quoted in UPI, 20 November 2001.

37. *Defense and Security*, 30 May 2001.

Chapter III
Washington Supports International Terrorism

While the "Islamic Jihad"—featured by the Bush administration as "a threat to America"—is blamed for the terrorist attacks on the World Trade Center and the Pentagon, these same Islamic organizations constitute a key instrument of US military-intelligence operations not only in the Balkans and the former Soviet Union, but also in India and China.

While the Mujahideen are busy fighting on behalf of Uncle Sam, the FBI—operating as a US-based Police Force—is waging a domestic war against terrorism, operating in some respects independently of the CIA, which has—since the Soviet-Afghan war—supported international terrorism through its covert operations.

Confronted with the evidence and history of CIA covert operations since the Cold War era, the US Administration can no longer deny its links to Osama. While the CIA admits that Osama bin Laden was an "intelligence asset" during the Cold War, the relationship is said to "go way back" to a bygone era.

According to the CIA, an "intelligence asset"—as distinct from a bona fide "intelligence agent"—need not be committed to the pursuit of US interests. Rather, it is meant to act and/or behave in a way which serves US foreign policy interests.

Intelligence assets are often unaware of the precise functions and roles they are performing on behalf of the CIA on the geopolitical chessboard. In turn, for these covert operations to be "successful", the CIA will use various proxy and front organizations such as Pakistan's military intelligence apparatus.

Most post-September 11 news reports consider that these Osama-CIA links belong to the "bygone era" of the Soviet-Afghan war. They are invariably viewed as *irrelevant* to an understanding of the September 11 crisis. Lost in the barrage of recent history, the role of the CIA, in supporting and developing international terrorist organizations during the Cold War and its aftermath, is casually ignored or downplayed by the Western media.

The 'Blowback' Thesis

A blatant example of post-September 11 media distortion is the "blowback" thesis: "Intelligence assets" are said to "have gone against their sponsors; what we've created blows back in our face".[1] In a display of twisted logic, the US Government and the CIA are portrayed as the ill-fated victims:

> The sophisticated methods taught to the Mujahideen, and the thousands of tons of arms supplied to them by the US—and Britain—are now tormenting the West in the phenomenon known as "blowback", whereby a policy strategy rebounds on its own devisers.[2]

The US media, nonetheless, concedes that "the Taliban's coming to power [in 1996] is partly the outcome of the US support of the Mujahideen—the radical Islamic group—in the 1980s in the war against the Soviet Union".[3] But it also readily dismisses its own factual statements and concludes, in chorus, that the CIA had been tricked by a deceitful Osama. It's like "a son going against his father".

The "blowback" thesis is a fabrication. The CIA has never severed its ties to the "Islamic Militant Network".

'Bosniagate': Replicating the Iran-Contragate Pattern

Remember Oliver North and the Nicaraguan Contras under the Reagan administration, when weapons financed by the drug trade were channeled to "freedom fighters" in Washington's covert war against the Sandinista government? The same pattern was used in the Balkans in the 1990s to arm and equip the Mujahideen fighting in the ranks of the Bosnian Muslim army against the Armed Forces of the Yugoslav Federation.

Pakistan's ISI was used by the CIA as a "go-between"—to channel weapons and Mujahideen mercenaries to the Bosnian Muslim Army in the civil war in Yugoslavia. According to a report by the London-based International Media Corporation:

> Reliable sources report that the United States is now [1994] actively participating in the arming and training of the Muslim forces of Bosnia-Herzegovina in direct contravention of the United Nations accords. US agencies have been providing weapons made in … China (PRC), North Korea (DPRK) and Iran. The sources indicated that … Iran, with the knowledge and agreement of the US Government, supplied the Bosnian forces with a large number of multiple rocket launchers and a large quantity of ammunition. These included 107mm and 122mm rockets from the PRC, and VBR-230 multiple rocket launchers … made in Iran …. It was [also] reported that 400 members of the Iranian Revolutionary Guard (Pasdaran) arrived in Bosnia with a large supply of arms and ammunition. It was alleged that the US Central Intelligence Agency (CIA) had full knowledge of the operation and that the CIA believed that some of the 400 had been detached for future terrorist operations in Western Europe.
>
> During September and October [of 1994], there has been a stream of "Afghan" Mujahideen … covertly landed in Ploce, Croatia (South-West of Mostar) from where they have traveled with false papers … before deploying with the Bosnian Muslim forces in the Kupres, Zenica and Banja Luka areas. These forces have recently [late 1994] experienced a significant degree of military success. They have, according to sources in Sarajevo, been aided by the UNPROFOR Bangladesh battalion, which took over from a French battalion early in September [1994].

The Mujahideen landings at Ploce are reported to have been accompanied by US Special Forces equipped with high-tech communications equipment. …. The sources said that the mission of the US troops was to establish a command, control, communications and intelligence network to coordinate and support Bosnian Muslim offensives—in concert with Mujahideen and Bosnian Croat forces—in Kupres, Zenica and Banja Luka. Some offensives have recently been conducted from within the UN-established safe-havens in the Zenica and Banja Luka regions ….

The US Administration has not restricted its involvement to the clandestine contravention of the UN arms embargo on the region. … It [also] committed three high-ranking delegations over the past two years [prior to 1994] in failed attempts to bring the Yugoslav Government into line with US policy. Yugoslavia is the only state in the region to have failed to acquiesce to US pressure.[4]

'From the Horse's Mouth'

Ironically, the US Administration's undercover military-intelligence operations in Bosnia have been fully documented by the Republican Party. A lengthy Congressional report by the Republican Party Committee (RPC) published in 1997 accuses the Clinton administration of having "helped turn Bosnia into a militant Islamic base" leading to the recruitment, through the "Militant Islamic Network", of thousands of Mujahideen from the Muslim world:

Perhaps most threatening to the SFOR [Stabilization Force in Bosnia-Herzegovina] mission—and more importantly, to the safety of the American personnel serving in Bosnia—is the unwillingness of the Clinton administration to come clean with the Congress and with the American people about its complicity in the delivery of weapons from Iran to the Muslim government in Sarajevo. That policy, personally approved by Bill Clinton in April 1994, at the urging of CIA Director-designate (and then-NSC chief) Anthony Lake and the US ambassador to Croatia Peter Galbraith, has, according to the *Los Angeles Times* (citing classified intelligence community sources), "played a central role in the dramatic increase in Iranian influence in Bosnia". …

Along with the weapons, Iranian Revolutionary Guards and VEVAK intelligence operatives entered Bosnia in large numbers, along with thousands of Mujahideen (holy warriors) from across the Muslim world. Also engaged in the effort were several other Muslim countries (including Brunei, Malaysia, Pakistan, Saudi Arabia, Sudan and Turkey) and a number of radical Muslim organizations. For example, the role of one Sudan-based "humanitarian organization", called the Third World Relief Agency, has been well documented.

The Clinton administration's "hands-on" involvement with the Islamic network's arms pipeline included inspections of missiles from Iran by US Government officials .... [T]he Third World Relief Agency (TWRA), a Sudan-based, phoney humanitarian organization ... has been a major link in the arms pipeline to Bosnia. ... TWRA is believed to be connected with such fixtures of the Islamic terror network as Sheik Omar Abdel Rahman (the convicted mastermind behind the 1993 World Trade Center bombing) and Osama bin Laden, a wealthy Saudi émigré believed to bankroll numerous militant groups.[5]

Complicity of the Clinton Administration

The RPC report confirms unequivocally the complicity of the Clinton administration with several Islamic fundamentalist organizations, including Osama bin Laden's Al Qaeda.

The Republicans wanted to undermine the Clinton administration. However, at a time when the entire country had its eyes riveted on the Monica Lewinsky scandal, they chose not to trigger an untimely "Iran-Bosniagate" affair, which might have unduly diverted public attention away from the Lewinsky scandal.

The Republicans wanted to impeach Bill Clinton "for having lied to the American people" regarding his affair with White House intern Monica Lewinsky. On the more substantive "foreign policy lies" regarding drug running and covert operations in the Balkans, Democrats and Republicans agreed in unison, no doubt pressured by the Pentagon and the CIA, not to "spill the beans".

From Bosnia to Kosovo

The "Bosnian pattern" described in the 1997 Congressional RPC report was replicated in Kosovo with the complicity of NATO and the US State Department. Mujahideen mercenaries from the Middle East and Central Asia were recruited to fight in the ranks of the KLA in 1998-99, largely supporting NATO's war effort.

Confirmed by British military sources, the task of arming and training of the KLA had been entrusted in 1998 to the US Defense Intelligence Agency (DIA) and Britain's Secret Intelligence Services MI6, together with "former and serving members of 22 SAS [Britain's 22nd Special Air Services Regiment], as well as three British and American private security companies".[6]

> "The US DIA approached MI6 to arrange a training program for the KLA", said a senior British military source. "MI6 then sub-contracted the operation to two British security companies, who in turn approached a number of former members of the (22 SAS) regiment. Lists were then drawn up of weapons and equipment needed by the KLA." While these covert operations were continuing, serving members of 22 SAS Regiment, mostly from the unit's D Squadron, were first deployed in Kosovo before the beginning of the bombing campaign in March [1999].[7]

While British SAS Special Forces in bases in Northern Albania were training the KLA, military instructors from Turkey and Afghanistan, financed by the "Islamic jihad", were collaborating in training the KLA in guerrilla and diversion tactics.[8]

> Bin Laden had visited Albania himself. He was one of several fundamentalist groups that had sent units to fight in Kosovo .... Bin Laden is believed to have established an operation in Albania in 1994 .... Albanian sources say Sali Berisha, who was then president, had links with some groups that later proved to be extreme fundamentalists.[9]

Congressional Testimonies on KLA-Osama Links

According to Frank Ciluffo of the Globalized Organized Crime Program, in a testimony presented to the House of Representatives Judicial Committee:

> What was largely hidden from public view was the fact that the KLA raise part of their funds from the sale of narcotics. Albania and

Kosovo lie at the heart of the "Balkan Route" that links the "Golden Crescent" of Afghanistan and Pakistan to the drug markets of Europe. This route is worth an estimated $400 billion a year and handles 80 per cent of heroin destined for Europe.[10]

According to Ralf Mutschke of Interpol's Criminal Intelligence division, also in a testimony to the House Judicial Committee:

> The US State Department listed the KLA as a terrorist organization, indicating that it was financing its operations with money from the international heroin trade and loans from Islamic countries and individuals, among them allegedly Osama bin Laden. Another link to bin Laden is the fact that the brother of a leader in an Egyptian Jihad organization, and also a military commander of Osama bin Laden, was leading an elite KLA unit during the Kosovo conflict.[11]

Madeleine Albright Covets the KLA

These KLA links to international terrorism and organized crime documented by the US Congress, were totally ignored by the Clinton administration. In fact, in the months preceding the bombing of Yugoslavia, Secretary of State Madeleine Albright was busy building a "political legitimacy" for the KLA. The paramilitary army had—from one day to the next—been elevated to the status of a bona fide "democratic" force in Kosovo. In turn, Madeleine Albright forced the pace of international diplomacy: the KLA had been spearheaded into playing a central role in the failed "peace negotiations" at Rambouillet in early 1999. Meanwhile, the KLA developed and reinforced its relationship to the Militant Islamic Network including Osama bin Laden's Al Qaeda.

The US Congress tacitly Endorses State Terrorism

While Congressional transcripts confirmed that the KLA had been working hand in glove with Osama bin Laden's Al Qaeda, this did not prevent the Clinton and later the Bush administration from arming and equipping the KLA. The Congressional documents also confirm that members of the Senate and the House knew the relationship of the Administration to international terrorism. To quote the statement of Rep. John Kasich of the House Armed

Services Committee: "We connected ourselves [in 1998-99] with the KLA, which was the staging point for bin Laden."[12]

Members of Congress were fully cognizant of the links between the US Administration and Al Qaeda. They knew exactly who Osama bin Laden was—a pawn in the hands of the Clinton and, later, the Bush administration. Therefore they also knew that the "campaign against international terrorism", launched in the wake of September 11, implied a hidden agenda. Despite this knowledge, Republicans and Democrats in unison gave their full support to the President to "wage war on Osama".

In 1999, Senator Joe Lieberman stated authoritatively that "fighting for the KLA is fighting for human rights and American values". When making this statement, he knew that the KLA was supported by Osama bin Laden. In the hours following the October 7, 2001 cruise missile attacks on Afghanistan, the same Joe Lieberman called for punitive air strikes against Iraq: "We're in a war against terrorism ... we can't stop with bin Laden and the Taliban." Yet Senator Joe Lieberman, as a member of the Armed Services Committee of the Senate, had access to all the Congressional documents pertaining to KLA-Osama links. In making this statement, he was fully aware that other agencies of the US Government, as well as NATO, had been supporting Al Qaeda.

The War in Macedonia

In the wake of the 1999 war in Yugoslavia, the terrorist activities of the KLA were extended into Southern Serbia and Macedonia. Meanwhile, the KLA—renamed the Kosovo Protection Corps (KPC)—was elevated to United Nations status, implying the granting of "legitimate" sources of funding through the United Nations as well as through bilateral channels, including direct US military aid.

Barely two months after the official inauguration of the KPC under UN auspices in September 1999, KPC-KLA commanders—using UN resources and equipment—were already preparing assaults into Macedonia as a logical follow-up to their terrorist activities in Kosovo. According to the Skopje daily *Dnevnik*, the

KPC had established a "sixth operation zone" in Southern Serbia and Macedonia:

> Sources, who insist on anonymity, claim that the headquarters of the Kosovo Protection Brigades [i.e., linked to the UN-sponsored KPC] have [March 2000] already been formed in Tetovo, Gostivar and Skopje. They are being prepared in Debar and Struga [on the border with Albania] as well, and their members have defined codes.[13]

According to the BBC, "Western special forces were still training the guerrillas", meaning that they were assisting the KLA in opening up "a sixth operation zone" in Southern Serbia and Macedonia.[14]

The Islamic Militant Network and NATO Join Hands in Macedonia

Among the foreign mercenaries fighting in Macedonia in 2001 with the self-proclaimed National Liberation Army (NLA) of Macedonia, were Mujahideen from the Middle East and the Central Asian republics of the former Soviet Union. Also within the KLA's proxy force in Macedonia, were senior US military advisers from a private mercenary outfit on contract to the Pentagon, as well as "soldiers of fortune" from Britain, Holland and Germany. Some of these Western mercenaries had previously fought with the KLA and the Bosnian Muslim Army.

Extensively documented by the Macedonian press and statements made by the Macedonian authorities, the US Government and the "Islamic Militant Network" were working hand in glove in supporting and financing the NLA, which was involved in the terrorist attacks in Macedonia. The NLA is a proxy of the KLA. In turn, the KLA and the UN-sponsored KPC are identical institutions, with the same commanders and military personnel. *KPC Commanders on UN salaries are fighting in the NLA together with the Mujahideen.*

Ironically, while supported and financed by Osama bin Laden's Al Qaeda, the KLA-NLA is also supported by NATO and the United Nations mission to Kosovo (UNMIK). In fact, the "Islamic Militant

Network"—also using Pakistan's ISI as the CIA's "go-between"—still constitutes an integral part of Washington's covert military-intelligence operations in Macedonia and Southern Serbia.

The KLA-NLA terrorists are funded from US military aid and the United Nations peace-keeping budget, as well as by several Islamic organizations, including Osama bin Laden's Al Qaeda. Drug money is also being used to finance the terrorists, with the complicity of the US Government. The recruitment of Mujahideen to fight in the ranks of the NLA in Macedonia was implemented through various Islamic groups.

US military advisers mingle with the Mujahideen within the same paramilitary force; Western mercenaries from NATO countries fight alongside the Mujahideen recruited in the Middle East and Central Asia. And the US media calls this a "blowback" where "intelligence assets" have gone against their sponsors.

But this did not happen during the Cold War. It happened in Macedonia in 2001. And it is confirmed by numerous press reports, eyewitness accounts and photographic evidence as well as official statements by the Macedonian Prime Minister, who has accused the Western military alliance of supporting the terrorists. Moreover, the official Macedonian news agency (MIA) has pointed to the complicity between Washington's envoy Ambassador James Pardew and the NLA terrorists.[15] In other words, the "intelligence assets" are still serving the interests of their US sponsors.

Misleading the American People

A major war in Central Asia, supposedly "against international terrorism", was launched by a government which is harboring international terrorism as part of its foreign policy agenda. In other words, the main justification for waging war has been totally fabricated. The American people have been deliberately and consciously misled by their government.

It is important to remember that this decision to mislead the American people was taken barely a few hours after the terrorist attacks on the World Trade Center. Without supporting evidence, Osama had already been tagged as the "prime suspect". Two days

---

TEXT BOX 3.1

America's Envoy James Pardew

James Pardew started his Balkans career in 1993 as a senior intelligence officer for the Joint Chiefs of Staff, responsible for channelling US aid to the Bosnian Muslim Army. Colonel Pardew had been put in charge of arranging the "air drops" of supplies to Bosnian forces. At the time, these "air drops" were tagged as "civilian aid". It later transpired—confirmed by the Republican Party Committee (RPC) Congressional report—that the US had violated the United Nations arms embargo. And James Pardew played an important role as part of the team of intelligence officials working closely with the Chairman of the National Security Council, Anthony Lake.

Pardew was later involved in the Dayton negotiations (in 1995) on behalf of the US Defense Department. In 1999, prior to the bombing of Yugoslavia, he was appointed "Special Representative for Military Stabilization and Kosovo Implementation" by President Clinton. One of his tasks was to channel support to the Kosovo Liberation Army (KLA), which at the time was also being supported by Osama bin Laden. Pardew was in this regard instrumental in replicating the "Bosnian pattern" in Kosovo and subsequently in Macedonia.

---

later on Thursday the 13th of September—while the FBI investigations had barely commenced—President Bush pledged to "lead the world to victory".

Moreover, the entire US Congress—with only one honest and courageous dissenting voice in the House of Representatives—had endorsed the Administration's decision to go to war. Members of the House and the Senate have access through the various committees to official confidential reports and intelligence documents which prove beyond a shadow of a doubt that agencies of the US Government have strong ties to international terrorism. They cannot say "we did not know". In fact, most of this evidence is in the public domain.

Under the historical resolution of the US Congress adopted by both the House and the Senate on the 14th of September, 2001:

> The President is authorized to use all necessary and appropriate force against those nations, organizations or persons he determines planned, authorized, committed or aided the terrorist attacks that occurred on September 11, 2001, or harbored such organizations or persons, in order to prevent any future acts of international terrorism against the United States by such nations, organizations or persons.[16]

Our analysis confirms that agencies of the US Government, as well as NATO, have, since the end of the Cold War, continued to "harbor such organizations".

Ironically, the text of the September 14 Congressional resolution also constitutes a "blowback" against the US sponsors of international terrorism. The resolution does not exclude the conduct of an "Osamagate" inquiry, as well as appropriate actions against agencies and/or individuals of the US Government (including members of the Clinton and Bush administrations, the CIA and the US Congress) who may have collaborated with Osama bin Laden's Al Qaeda.

Notes

1. United Press International (UPI), 15 September 2001.

2. *The Guardian,* London, 15 September 2001.

3. UPI, *op cit.*

4. International Media Corporation Defense and Strategy Policy, *US Commits Forces, Weapons to Bosnia,* London, 31 October 1994.

5. Congressional Press Release, Republican Party Committee (RPC), US Congress, "Clinton-Approved Iranian Arms Transfers Help Turn Bosnia into Militant Islamic Base", Washington DC, 16 January 1997, available on the website of the Centre of Research on Globalization (CRG) at http://globalresearch.ca/articles/DCH109A.html. The original document is on the website of the US Senate Republican Party Committee (Senator Larry Craig), at http://www.senate.gov/~rpc/releases/1997/iran.htm; see also *Washington Post,* 22 September 1999; emphasis added.

6. *The Scotsman*, Edinburgh, 29 August 1999.

7. *Ibid.*

8. Truth in Media, "Kosovo in Crisis", Phoenix, Arizona, http://www.truthin-media.org/, 2 April 1999.

9. *The Sunday Times*, London, 29 November 1998.

10. US Congress, Testimony of Frank J. Cilluffo, Deputy Director of the Global Organized Crime Program, to the House Judiciary Committee, Washington DC, 13 December 2000.

11. US Congress, Testimony of Ralf Mutschke of Interpol's Criminal Intelligence Division, to the House Judicial Committee, Washington DC, 13 December 2000.

12. US Congress, Transcripts of the House Armed Services Committee, Washington, DC, 5 October 1999, emphasis added.

13. *Macedonian Information Centre Newsletter*, Skopje, 21 March 2000, published by BBC Summary of World Broadcast, 24 March 2000.

14. BBC, 29 January 2001.

15. *Scotland on Sunday*, 15 June 2001. See also UPI, 9 July 2001. For further details see Michel Chossudovsky, "Washington Behind Terrorist Assaults in Macedonia", Centre for Research on Globalization at http://globalresearch.ca/articles/CHO108B.html, August 2001.

16. See *The White House Bulletin*, 14 September 2001.

Chapter IV
Cover-Up or Complicity?

Role of Pakistan's ISI in the September 11 Attacks

As discussed in Chapter III, the US Administration has consciously used international terrorism in the pursuit of its foreign policy objectives by engaging Pakistan's ISI as a "go-between". Ironically, while Pakistan's ISI has supported and abetted international terrorism (including Osama bin Laden's Al Qaeda), the Bush administration, in the wake of September 11, chose to seek the assistance of Pakistan's ISI in its "campaign against international terrorism".

Two days after the terrorist attacks on the World Trade Center and the Pentagon, it was reported that a delegation led by the head of Pakistan's ISI, Lt. Gen. Mahmoud Ahmed, was in Washington for high level talks at the State Department.[1]

Most US media conveyed the impression that Islamabad had put together a delegation at Washington's behest, and that the invitation to the meeting had been transmitted to the Pakistan government "after" the tragic events of September 11.

However this is not what happened.

Pakistan's chief spy, Lt. General Mahmoud Ahmad, "was in the US when the attacks occurred".[2] According to the *New York Times,* "he happened to be [in Washington] on a regular visit of consultations".[3] Not a word was mentioned regarding the nature of his "business" in the US in the week prior to the terrorist attacks. According to *Newsweek*, he was "on a visit to Washington at the time of the attack, and, like most other visitors, is still stuck there", unable to return home because of the freeze on international airline travel.[4]

General Ahmad had in fact arrived in the US on the 4th of September, a full week before the attacks.[5] Bear in mind that the purpose of his meeting at the State Department on the 13th was only made public "after" the September 11 terrorist attacks, when the Bush administration took the decision to formally seek the "cooperation" of Pakistan in its "campaign against international terrorism".

The press reports confirm that Lt. General Mahmoud Ahmad had two meetings with Deputy Secretary of State, Richard Armitage, on the 12th and 13th.[6] After September 11, he also met Senator Joseph Biden, Chairman of the powerful Committee on Foreign Relations of the Senate.

Confirmed by several press reports, however, General Ahmad also had "a regular visit of consultations" with US officials during the week prior to September 11—i.e., meetings with his US counterparts at the CIA and the Pentagon.[7]

The nature of these routine "consultations" was not made public. Were they in any way related to the subsequent "post-September 11 consultations" pertaining to Pakistan's decision to "cooperate with Washington", which were held behind closed doors at the State Department on September 12 and 13? Was the planning of war being discussed between Pakistani and US officials? One can only speculate based on what happened later in Afghanistan.

"The ISI-Osama-Taliban Axis"

On the 9th of September, the leader of the Northern Alliance, Commander Ahmad Shah Masood, was assassinated. The Northern Alliance had informed the Bush administration that the ISI was allegedly implicated in the assassination. The Northern Alliance had confirmed in an official statement that:

> A "Pakistani ISI-Osama-Taliban axis" [was responsible for] plotting the assassination by two Arab suicide bombers .... "We believe that this is a triangle between Osama bin Laden, ISI, which is the intelligence section of the Pakistani army, and the Taliban."[8]

The complicity of the ISI in the "ISI-Osama-Taliban axis" was a matter of public record, confirmed by congressional transcripts and intelligence reports. (See Chapter III.)

The Bush Administration Cooperates with Pakistan's Military-Intelligence

The Bush administration consciously took the decision in "the post-September 11 consultations" at the State Department to directly "cooperate" with Pakistan's ISI, despite its links to Osama bin Laden and the Taliban and its alleged role in the assassination of Commander Massoud, which occurred coincidentally two days before the terrorist attacks.

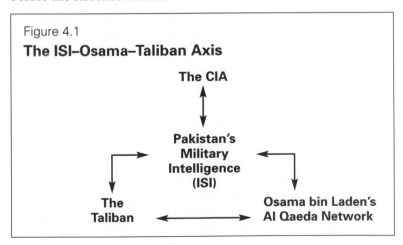

Figure 4.1
The ISI–Osama–Taliban Axis

TEXT BOX 4.1

Schedule of Pakistan's Chief Spy, Lt. General Mahmoud Ahmad, Washington, 4 to 13 September 2001

4 September: Ahmad arrives in the US on an official visit.

4-9 September: He meets his US counterparts including CIA Head, George Tenet.

9 September: Assassination of General Massoud, leader of the Northern Alliance. The Official statement by the Northern Alliance points to the involvement of the ISI-Osama-Taliban axis.

11 September: Terrorist attacks on the WTC and the Pentagon.

12-13 September: Meetings between Lt. General Ahmad and Deputy Secretary of State, Richard Armitage. Agreement on Pakistan's "collaboration" negotiated with the Bush administration.

13 September: Ahmad meets Senator Joseph Biden, Chairman of the Senate Foreign Relations Committee.

Meanwhile, the Western media—in the face of mounting evidence—remained silent on the insidious role of Pakistan's ISI. The assassination of Massoud was mentioned, but its political significance in relation to September 11 and the subsequent decision to go to war against Afghanistan was barely touched upon.
Without discussion or debate, Pakistan was heralded as a "friend" and an ally of America.

In an utterly twisted piece of logic, the US media concluded in chorus that:

> US officials had sought cooperation from Pakistan [precisely] because it is the original backer of the Taliban, the hard-line Islamic leadership of Afghanistan accused by Washington of harboring bin Laden.[9]

"Patterns of Global Terrorism"

Nobody seemed to have noticed the obtrusive and unsubtle falsehoods behind the Administration's "campaign against international terrorism", with perhaps the exception of one inquisitive journalist who questioned Colin Powell at the outset of his State department briefing on Thursday September 13th:

> [Does] the US see Pakistan as an ally or, as the "Patterns of Global Terrorism" pointed out, "a place where terrorist groups get training." Or is it a mixture?[10]

Colin Powell's reply was:

> We have provided to the Pakistani government a specific list of things we think would be useful for them to work on with us, and we'll be discussing that list with the President of Pakistan later this afternoon.[11]

"Patterns of Global Terrorism" referred to by the journalist is a publication of the US State Department.[12] In other words, Colin Powell's evasive response at the Press Conference is refuted by official US Government documents, which confirm unequivocally that the government of President Pervez Musharraf (including Pakistan's Military and Intelligence apparatus) has links to international terrorism:

> Credible reporting indicates that Pakistan is providing the Taliban with material, fuel, funding, technical assistance, and military advisers. Pakistan has not prevented large numbers of Pakistani nationals from moving into Afghanistan to fight for the Taliban. Islamabad also failed to take effective steps to curb the activities of certain madrasas, or religious schools, that serve as recruiting grounds for terrorism.[13]

Behind Close Doors at the State Department

The Bush administration sought, therefore, the "cooperation" of those (including Pakistan's ISI) who were directly supporting and abetting the terrorists. This may seem absurd, but at the same time consistent with Washington's broader strategic and economic objectives in Central Asia and the Middle East.

The meeting behind closed doors at the State Department on September 13, between Deputy Secretary of State, Richard Armitage, and Lt. General Mahmoud Ahmad was shrouded in secrecy. It is noteworthy that President Bush was not even involved in these crucial negotiations: "Deputy Secretary of State Richard Armitage handed over [to ISI chief Mahmoud Ahmad] a list of specific steps Washington wanted Pakistan to take."[14]

> After a telephone conversation between [Secretary of State Colin] Powell and Pakistani President Pervez Musharraf, State Department spokesman Richard Boucher said Pakistan had promised to cooperate.[15]

President George W. Bush confirmed later on September 13, that the Pakistan government had agreed "to cooperate and to participate as we hunt down those people who committed this unbelievable, despicable act on America".[16]

Pakistan's Chief Spy on Mission to Afghanistan

On September 13th, Pakistan President Pervez Musharraf promised Washington that he would send chief spy Lt. General Mahmoud Ahmad to meet the Taliban and negotiate the extradition of Osama bin Laden. This decision was at Washington's behest, most probably agreed upon during the meeting between Dick Armitage and General Mahmoud at the State Department.

Pakistan's chief spy returned immediately to prepare for the delivery of a practically impossible ultimatum:

> At American urging, Ahmad traveled … to Kandahar, Afghanistan. There he delivered the bluntest of demands. Turn over bin Laden without conditions, he told Taliban leader Mohammad Omar, or face certain war with the United States and its allies.[17]

Mahmoud's meetings on two separate occasions with the Taliban were reported as a "failure." Yet this "failure" to extradite Osama was part of Washington's design, providing a pretext for a military intervention which was already in the pipeline.

If Osama had been extradited, the main justification for waging a war "against international terrorism" would no longer hold. And the evidence suggests that this war had been planned well in advance of September 11 in response to broad strategic and economic objectives.

Meanwhile, senior Pentagon and State Department officials had been rushed to Islamabad to put the finishing touches on America's war plans. And on Sunday, October 7th, prior to the onslaught of the bombing of major cities in Afghanistan by the US Air Force, Lt. General Mahmoud Ahmad was removed from his position as head of the ISI in what was described as a routine "reshuffling". It was later reported that he had been appointed to the powerful position of Governor of Punjab bordering India's Western frontier.

The Missing Link

In the days following Lt. General Mahmoud Ahmad's removal, a report published in *The Times of India*, which went virtually unnoticed by the Western media, revealed the links between Lt. General Mahmoud Ahmad and the presumed "ring leader" of the WTC attacks Mohammed Atta. The *Times of India* report constitutes "the missing link" to understanding who was behind the terrorist attacks of September 11:

> While the Pakistani Inter Services Public Relations claimed that former ISI Director-General, Lt.-General Mahmoud Ahmad, sought retirement after being superseded on Monday [8 October], the day the US started bombing Afghanistan, the truth is more shocking. Top sources confirmed here on Tuesday [October 9], that the General lost his job because of the "evidence" India produced to show his links to one of the suicide bombers that wrecked the World Trade Center. The US authorities sought his removal after confirming the fact that $100,000 was wired to WTC hijacker Mohammed Atta from Pakistan by Ahmad Umar Sheikh at the instance of Gen. Mahmoud. Senior government sources have confirmed that India contributed significantly to establishing the link between the money transfer and the role played by the dismissed ISI chief. While they did not provide details, they said that Indian inputs, including Sheikh's mobile phone number, helped the FBI in tracing and establishing the link.
>
> A direct link between the ISI and the WTC attack could have enormous repercussions. The US cannot but suspect whether or not there were other senior Pakistani Army commanders who were in the know of things. Evidence of a larger conspiracy could shake US confidence in Pakistan's ability to participate in the anti-terrorism coalition.[18]

According to FBI files, Mohammed Atta was "the lead hijacker of the first jet airliner to slam into the World Trade Center and, apparently, the lead conspirator".[19]

The Times of India article was based on an official intelligence report of the Delhi government that had been transmitted through official channels to Washington. Agence France Press (AFP) confirms that:

> A highly-placed government source told AFP that the "damning link" between the General and the transfer of funds to Atta was part of evidence which India has officially sent to the US "The evidence we have supplied to the US is of a much wider range and depth than just one piece of paper linking a rogue general to some misplaced act of terrorism," the source said.[20]

The information in the Indian Intelligence report regarding the money transfer by Pakistan's ISI is corroborated by the FBI-led investigation in the wake of September 11. While not mentioning the role of Pakistan's ISI, the FBI nonetheless points to a Pakistan connection and to "the people connected to Osama bin Laden" who are the "money men" behind the terrorists:

> As to September 11th, federal authorities have told ABC News they have now tracked more than $100,000 from banks in Pakistan, to two banks in Florida, to accounts held by suspected hijack ring leader Mohammed Atta. As well, this morning, *Time Magazine* is reporting that some of that money came in the days just before the attack and can be traced directly to people connected to Osama bin Laden. It's all part of what has been a successful FBI effort so far to close in on the hijackers'high commander, the money men, the planners and the mastermind.[21]

Pakistan's Military-Intelligence Agency Behind 9/11?

The revelation by the *Times of India* article (confirmed by the FBI Report) has several implications. The report not only points to the links between ISI Chief General Ahmad (the presumed "Money Man") and terrorist ringleader Mohammed Atta, but it also indicates that other ISI officials might have had contacts with the terrorists. Moreover, it suggests that the September 11 attacks were not an act of "individual terrorism" organized by a single Al Qaeda cell, but rather they were part of a coordinated military-intelligence operation emanating from Pakistan's ISI.

The *Times of India* report also sheds light on the nature of General Ahmad's "business activities" in the US during the week prior to September 11, raising the distinct possibility of ISI contacts with Mohammed Atta in the US in the week "prior" to the attacks on the WTC, precisely at the time when General Mahmoud and his delegation were on a "regular visit of consultations" with US officials. Remember, Lt. General Mahmoud Ahmad arrived in the US on the 4th of September.

Despite the fact that the FBI investigation had uncovered Pakistan's complicity in the September 11 attacks, the Bush administration was, nevertheless, determined to get the support of the Pakistani government in the "war on terrorism".

US Approved Appointee

In assessing the alleged links between the terrorists and the ISI, it should be pointed out that Lt. General Mahmoud Ahmad, as head of the ISI, was a "US-approved appointee". As head of the ISI since 1999, he was in liaison with his US counterparts in the CIA, the Defense Intelligence Agency (DIA) and the Pentagon. One should also bear in mind that Pakistan's ISI remained, throughout the entire post-Cold War era until the present, the launch pad for CIA covert operations in the Caucasus, Central Asia and the Balkans. (See our earlier analysis on this issue.)

In other words, General Mahmoud Ahmad was serving US foreign policy interests. His dismissal on the orders of Washington was not the result of a fundamental political disagreement. Without US support channeled through the Pakistani ISI, the Taliban would not have been able to form a government in 1996. *Jane Defense Weekly* confirms in this regard that "half of Taliban manpower and equipment originate[d] in Pakistan under the ISI," which in turn was supported by the US.[22]

Moreover, the assassination of the leader of the Northern Alliance, General Ahmad Shah Masood,—in which the ISI is alleged to have been implicated—was not at all in contradiction with US foreign policy objectives. Since the late 1980s, the US had consistently sought to sidetrack and weaken Masood, who was perceived as a nationalist reformer, by providing support to both to the Taliban and the Hezb-I-Islami group led by Gulbuddin Hektmayar against Masood. Moreover, Masood was supported by Moscow.

After his assassination, which broadly served US interests, the Northern Alliance became fragmented into different factions. Had Masood not been assassinated, he would have become the head of the post-Taliban government formed in the wake of the US bombings of Afghanistan.

Corroborated by Congressional Transcripts

Corroborated by the House of Representatives International Relations Committee, US support funnelled through the ISI to the Taliban and Osama bin Laden has been a consistent policy of the US Administration since the end of the Cold War. According to Rep. Dana Rohrbacher:

> … [T]he United States has been part and parcel to supporting the Taliban all along, and still is, let me add …. You have a military government [of President Musharraf] in Pakistan now that is arming the Taliban to the teeth …. Let me note that [US] aid has always gone to Taliban areas …. We have been supporting the Taliban, because all our aid goes to the Taliban areas. And when people from the outside try to put aid into areas not controlled by the Taliban, they are thwarted by our own State Department …. At that same moment, Pakistan initiated a major resupply effort, which eventually saw the defeat, and caused the defeat of almost all of the anti-Taliban forces in Afghanistan.[23]

Cover-up and Complicity?

The existence of an "ISI-Osama-Taliban axis" is a matter of public record. The links between the ISI and agencies of the US Government, including the CIA, are also a matter of public record. Pakistan's ISI has been used by successive US Administrations as a "go-between". Pakistan's military-intelligence apparatus constitutes the core institutional support to both Osama's Al Qaeda and the Taliban. Without this institutional support, there would be no Taliban government in Kabul. In turn, without the unbending support of the US Government, there would be no powerful military-intelligence apparatus in Pakistan.

Senior officials in the State Department were fully cognizant of General Mahmoud Ahmad's role. In the wake of September 11, the Bush administration consciously sought the "cooperation" of the ISI which had been aiding and abetting Osama bin Laden and the Taliban.

The Bush administration's relations with Pakistan's ISI—including its "consultations" with General Mahmoud Ahmad in the week prior to September 11—raise the issue of "cover-up" as well as "complicity". While Ahmad was talking to US officials at the CIA and the Pentagon, the ISI allegedly was in contact with the September 11 terrorists.

According to the Indian government intelligence report (referred to in the *Times of India*), the perpetrators of the September 11 attacks had links to Pakistan's ISI, which in turn has links to agencies of the US Government. What this suggests is that key individuals within the US military-intelligence establishment might have known about the ISI contacts with the September 11 terrorist "ring leader" Mohammed Atta and failed to act.

Whether this amounts to complicity on the part of the Bush administration remains to be firmly established. The least one can expect at this stage is an inquiry. But the Bush administration refuses to investigate these ISI links, as well as the money trail, not to mention the precise circumstances of the September 11 attacks.

What is crystal clear, however, is that this war is not a "campaign against international terrorism". It is a war of conquest with devastating consequences for the future of humanity. And the American people have been consciously and deliberately deceived by their government.

Notes

1. *The Guardian,* London, 15 September 2001.

2. Reuters, 13 September 2001.

3. *The New York Times,* 13 September 2001.

4. *Newsweek,* 14 September 2001.

5. *The Daily Telegraph.* London, 14 September 2001.

6. *The New York Times,* September 13th, 2001, confirms the meeting on the 12th of September 2001.

7. *The New York Times,* 13 September 2001.

8. The Northern Alliance's statement was released on 14 September 2001, quoted in Reuters, 15 September 2001.

9. Reuters, 13 September 2001, emphasis added.

10. Journalist's question to Secretary of State Colin Powell, State Department Briefing, Washington DC, 13 September 2001.

11. *Ibid.*

12. See http://www.state.gov/s/ct/rls/pgtrpt/2000/.

13. US State Department, "Patterns of Global Terrorism", State Department, http://www.state.gov/s/ct/rls/pgtrpt/2000, Washington, DC, 2000.

14. Reuters, 13 September 2001.

15. *Ibid.*

16. Remarks in a telephone conversation with New York City Mayor Rudolph Giuliani and New York Governor George Pataki and an exchange with reporters, *Presidential Papers,* 13 September 2001.

17. *The Washington Post,* 23 September 2001.

18. *The Times of India,* Delhi, 9 October 2001.

19. *The Weekly Standard,* Vol. 7, No. 7, October 2001.

20. AFP, 10 October 2001.

21. Statement of Brian Ross reporting on information conveyed to him by the FBI, ABC News, *This Week,* September 30, 2001.

22. Quoted in the *Christian Science Monitor,* 3 September 1998.

23. US House of Representatives: Statement by Rep. Dana Rohrbacher, Hearing of The House International Relations Committee on "Global Terrorism And South Asia", Washington, DC, July 12, 2000.

PART II
War and Globalization

CHAPTER V
War and the Hidden Agenda

Conquest of Oil Reserves and Pipeline Routes

"America's New War" consists in extending the global market system while opening up new "economic frontiers" for US corporate capital. More specifically, the US-led military invasion—in close liaison with Britain—responds to the interests of the Anglo-American oil giants, in alliance with America's "Big Five" weapons producers: Lockheed Martin, Raytheon, Northrop Grumman, Boeing and General Dynamics.

The "Anglo-American axis" in defense and foreign policy is the driving force behind the military operations in Central Asia and Middle East. This rapprochement between London and Washington is consistent with the integration of British and American business interests in the areas of banking, oil and the defense industry. The merger of British Petroleum (BP) and the American Oil Company (AMOCO) into the world's largest oil conglomerate has a direct bearing on the pattern of Anglo-American relations and the close relationship between the US President and the British Prime Minister. In the wake of the 1999 war in Yugoslavia, Britain's giant weapons producer, British Aerospace Systems (BAES), was fully integrated into the US system of defense procurement.

The Planning of War

In fact, the planning of America's New War has been in the "pipeline" for at least three years prior to the tragic events of September 11. At the outset of the 1999 war in Yugoslavia, the "enlargement" of the Western military alliance was proclaimed with the acceptance by NATO of Hungary, Poland and the Czech Republic into its fold. This enlargement was directed against Yugoslavia and Russia.

In April 1999, barely a month into the bombing of Yugoslavia, the Clinton administration announced the planned extension of

---

TEXT BOX 5.1

Military Action against Afghanistan

"A former Pakistani Foreign Secretary [Mr. Naik] was told by senior American officials [during a UN-sponsored international contact group meeting on Afghanistan in mid-July 2001] that military action against Afghanistan would go ahead by the middle of October [2001] …. The wider objective, according to Mr. Naik, would be to topple the Taliban regime …. Mr. Naik was told that Washington would launch its operation from bases in Tajikistan, where American advisers were already in place. Bin Laden would [be] 'killed or captured'.

"He was told that Uzbekistan would also participate in the operation … Mr. Naik was told that if the military action went ahead, it would take place before the snows started falling in Afghanistan, by the middle of October at the latest. He said that he was in no doubt that after the World Trade Center bombings, this pre-existing US plan had been built upon and would be implemented within two or three weeks. And he said it was doubtful that Washington would drop its plan even if bin Laden were to be surrendered immediately by the Taliban."[1]

NATO's dominion into the heartland of the former Soviet Union. Coinciding with the ceremony of NATO's 50th anniversary, the heads of state from Georgia, the Ukraine, Uzbekistan, Azerbaijan and Moldava were in attendance in the plush decorum of the Andrew Mellon Auditorium in Washington. They had been invited to NATO's three day celebration to sign GUUAM (Georgia, Uzbekistan, Ukraine, Azerbaijan and Moldava). GUUAM is a regional military alliance which lies strategically at the hub of the Caspian oil and gas wealth, "with Moldava and the Ukraine offering [pipeline] export routes to the West".[2] Georgia, Azerbaijan and Uzbekistan immediately announced that they would be leaving the Commonwealth of Independent States (CIS)' "security union", which defines the framework of military cooperation between the former Soviet republics, as well their links to Moscow.

The formation of GUUAM (under NATO's umbrella and financed by Western military aid) was intent upon further fracturing the CIS. The Cold War, although officially over, had not yet reached its climax. The members of this new pro-NATO political grouping were not only supportive of the 1999 bombing of Yugoslavia, they had also agreed to "low level military cooperation" with NATO, while insisting that "the group is not a military alliance directed against any third party, namely Moscow".[3] Dominated by Anglo-American oil interests, the formation of GUUAM ultimately purports to exclude Russia from the oil and gas deposits in the Caspian area, as well as isolating Moscow politically.

Militarization of the Eurasian Corridor

Just five days before the bombing of Yugoslavia (19 March 1999), the US Congress adopted the Silk Road Strategy Act, which defined America's broad economic and strategic interests in a region extending from the Mediterranean to Central Asia. The Silk Road Strategy (SRS) outlines a framework for the development of America's business empire along an extensive geographical corridor: (See map page 2.)

The ancient Silk Road, once the economic lifeline of Central Asia and the South Caucasus, traversed much of the territory now within the countries of Armenia, Azerbaijan, Georgia, Kazakhstan, Kirghizstan, Tajikistan, Turkmenistan, and Uzbekistan .... One hundred years ago, Central Asia was the arena for a great game played by Czarist Russia, Colonial Britain, Napoleon's France, and the Persian and the Ottoman Empires. Allegiances meant little during this struggle for empire building, where no single empire could gain the upper hand.

One hundred years later, the collapse of the Soviet Union has unleashed a new great game, where the interests of the East India Trading Company have been replaced by those of Unocal and Total [oil companies], and many other organizations and firms. Today [we are seeing] the interests of a new contestant in this new great game, the United States. The five [former Soviet republics] which make up Central Asia, Kazakhstan, Kirghizstan, Tajikistan, Turkmenistan, and Uzbekistan ... are anxious to establish relations with the United States. Kazakhstan and Turkmenistan possess large reserves of oil and natural gas, both on-shore and off-shore in the Caspian Sea, which they urgently seek to exploit. Uzbekistan [also] has oil and gas reserves.[4]

Under the SRS, US foreign policy consists in undermining and eventually destabilizing its competitors in the oil business including Russia, Iran and China:

Stated US policy goals regarding energy resources in this region include fostering the independence of the States and their ties to the West; breaking Russia's monopoly over oil and gas transport routes; promoting Western energy security through diversified suppliers; encouraging the construction of east-west pipelines that do not transit [through] Iran; and denying Iran dangerous leverage over the Central Asian economies ....

Central Asia would seem to offer significant new investment opportunities for a broad range of American companies which, in turn, will serve as a valuable stimulus to the economic development of the region. Japan, Turkey, Iran, Western Europe, and China are all pursuing economic development opportunities and challenging Russian dominance in the region. It is essential that US policymakers understand the stakes involved in Central Asia as we seek to craft a policy that serves the interests of the United States and US business.[5]

While the SRS sets the stage for incorporating the former Soviet republics into America's business empire, the GUUAM military alliance defines "cooperation" in the area of defense, including the stationing of US troops in the former Soviet republics. Under GUUAM auspices, the US has established a military base in Uzbekistan, which was used as a launch pad for its October 2001 invasion of Afghanistan after the September 11 attacks.

The Silk Road Strategy Act points to the establishment under Washington's protection—i.e., explicitly directed against Moscow—of *"strong political, economic, and security ties among countries of the South Caucasus and Central Asia".*

Also, under the guidance of the US Government, working closely with the IMF and the World Bank, these former Soviet Republics are to establish:

> ... open market economies and open democratic systems in the countries of the South Caucasus and Central Asia [which] will provide positive incentives for international private investment, increased trade, and other forms of commercial interactions.[6]

Backed by US military might, the SRS is to open up a vast geographical region to US corporations and financial institutions. The stated purpose is "to promote political and economic liberalization" including the adoption of "free market reforms" under IMF-World Bank-WTO supervision.

In a region extending from the Black Sea to the Chinese border, the objective of the SRS is to instate a US-controlled "free trade area" composed of eight former Soviet republics. This extensive corridor—which until recently was largely within Moscow's economic and geopolitical orbit—will eventually transform the entire region into a patchwork of American protectorates.

The SRS not only constitutes a continuation of US foreign policy of the Cold War era, but it also designates Israel as America's "partner" in the Silk Road corridor:

Many of the countries of the South Caucasus have secular Muslim governments that are seeking closer alliance with the United States and that have active and cordial diplomatic relations with Israel.[7]

Oil Politics

Afghanistan is, in many regards, strategic. It not only borders the "Silk Road Corridor" linking the Caucasus to China's Western border, it is also at the hub of five nuclear powers: China, Russia, India, Pakistan and Kazakhstan. While the bombing of Afghanistan was still ongoing, an interim "government"—designated by the "international community"—was installed in Kabul on the Bosnia-Kosovo model. The underlying objective, of course, is to militarize Afghanistan with a permanent presence of "peacekeeping troops".

Afghanistan is at the strategic crossroads of the Eurasian oil pipeline and transport routes. It also constitutes a potential land-bridge for the southbound oil pipeline from the former Soviet republic of Turkmenistan to the Arabian Sea across Pakistan, which had initially been negotiated by Unocal with the Taliban government. (For further details see Chapter VI.)

> The former Soviet republics of Central Asia—Turkmenistan, Uzbekistan and especially "the new Kuwait", Kazakhstan—have vast oil and gas reserves. But Russia has refused to allow the US to extract it through Russian pipelines and Iran is considered a dangerous route. That left Afghanistan. The US oil company Chevron—where Mr. Bush's National Security Advisor, Condoleezza Rice, was a director throughout the 1990s—is deeply involved in Kazakhstan. In 1995, another US company, Unocal (formerly Union Oil Company of California), signed a contract to export $8 billion worth of natural gas through a $3 billion pipeline which would go from Turkmenistan through Afghanistan to Pakistan.[8]

The oil and natural gas reserves of "the Eurasian Corridor" are substantial, at least of the same size of those in the Persian Gulf.[9]

> The region of the South Caucasus and Central Asia could produce oil and gas in sufficient quantities to reduce the dependence of the United States on energy from the volatile Persian Gulf region. United

States foreign policy and international assistance should be narrowly targeted to support the economic and political independence as well as democracy building, free market policies, human rights and regional economic integration of the countries of the South Caucasus and Central Asia.[10]

"Political and military conditions" in the region (meaning Russia's presence and influence) have been viewed by both the Clinton and Bush administrations as:

... presenting obstacles to bringing this energy to the global market. ... Both regions are the object of outside states competing for influence there. Not only Russia, but also China, Turkey, Iran, Pakistan and Saudi Arabia are competitively engaged, often in non-constructive ways. ... If we [the US] and our allies cannot manage the second and third sets of realities, we will forego the benefits of the first set of realities. Bringing the oil and gas to market will be sporadic, if not impossible, and far more costly. At the same time, the resulting political instabilities may turn both regions into a cauldron of civil wars and political violence, inevitably drawing in the surrounding states. We already have this pattern in the Persian Gulf region, requiring US military involvement, and we could hardly stand by politically, even if we did so militarily, if conflicts entangle Russia, China, Iran, Turkey, Pakistan and some of the Arab states in the Transcaucasus or Central Asia.[11]

In other words, the *successful* implementation of the SRS requires the concurrent "militarization" of the Eurasian corridor as a means to securing control over extensive oil and gas reserves, as well as "protecting" the pipeline routes on behalf of the Anglo-American oil companies. "[A] successful international oil regime is a combination of economic, political and military arrangements to support oil production and transportation to markets."[12]

In the words of a (former) CIA "policy analyst":

Whoever has control over certain kinds of pipelines and certain kinds of investments in the region does have a certain amount of geopolitical clout. Such clout is something of a commodity itself, even if the physical control of the oil is not. For much of the Third World, this is a newer way of thinking about resources; it's no longer

the old story of Hitler's Germany trying to get to the Caucasus and
use the oil for its own purposes in World War II.[13]

Under the SRS Act, Washington commits itself to *"fostering stability in this region, which is vulnerable to political and economic
pressures from the South, North and East,"* suggesting that "the threat
to stability" is not only from Moscow (to the North) but also from
China (to the East) and Iran and Iraq (to the South). The SRS is also
intended to prevent the former Soviet republics from developing
economic, political and defense ties with China, Iran, Turkey and
Iraq.

Covert Operations on Behalf of the Oil Giants

Under the Bush administration, the US oil giants have gained direct
access to the planning of military and intelligence operations on
their behalf. This has been achieved through the powerful Texas
oil lobby, resulting in the appointment of (former) oil company
executives to key defense and foreign policy positions:

> President George W. Bush's family has been running oil companies
> since 1950. Vice President Dick Cheney spent the late '90s as CEO of
> Haliburton, the world's largest oil services company. National Security
> Advisor Condoleeza Rice sat on the board of Chevron, which graced
> a tanker with her name. Commerce Secretary Donald Evans was the
> CEO of Tom Brown Inc.—a natural gas company with fields in Texas,
> Colorado and Wyoming—for more than a decade. The links don't
> end with personnel. The bin Laden family and other members of
> Saudi Arabia's oil-wealthy elite have contributed mightily to several
> Bush family ventures, even as the American energy industry helped
> put Bush in office. Of the top 10 lifetime contributors to George W.'s
> war chests, six either come from the oil business or have ties to it.[14]

Protecting Multiple Pipelines

In the context of GUUAM and the SRS, Washington has encouraged the formation of pro-US client states strategically located
along oil pipeline routes. The latter are to be "protected" by NATO
under GUUAM and various other military cooperation agree-

ments. The hidden agenda is to eventually cut the Russians off altogether from the Caspian oil and gas fields.

The oil giants are vying for control over the oil reserves of Azerbaijan, as well as strategic pipeline routes out of the Azeri capital Baku on the Caspian coast.

A pro-US regime was installed in Azerbaijan under President Heydar Aliyevich Aliyev in 1993. In the military coup which brought him to power, Aliyev—a former KGB official and Communist party politburo member—was allied to Suret Husseinov, leader of the Jadovov clan.

In 1994 "the Contract of the Century", involving the development of the Charyg oil fields near Baku, was signed with the Western oil consortium led by BP-Amoco. The Aliyev clan was in control of SOCAR, the State Oil Company, which has entered into joint ventures with the oil conglomerates. In addition to the links of the Azeri State to narcotics, there is evidence of a profitable black-market trade in raw materials, including trade of copper, nickel and other metals.

Western financial institutions, including the World Bank, had béen actively involved in opening up the Azeri oil and gas fields to Western transnationals. Generous money payoffs had been channeled to politicians and state officials. The criminalization of the Azeri State had largely facilitated the entry of foreign capital:

> Azerbaijan's leaders are wined and dined on oil company expense accounts, while 600,000 Azeris still live in the most horrendous conditions … .The snake oil companies act as agents of their countries'foreign policies and try to obtain commercial favors from Azeri leaders, who are ready to sell Azerbaijan's resources cheaply and for personal gains …. Over $6 billion in contract "signing bonuses" were paid to the Aliyev regime in Baku—by far more than all aid and investments in Georgia and Armenia combined—yet Azeris still live in refugee camps, worse off than even Georgians and Armenians.[15]

With a view to weakening Moscow's control over Caspian oil, several alternative pipeline routes had been envisaged. The Baku-Supsa pipeline—inaugurated in 1999 during the War in Yugoslavia and protected militarily by GUUAM—totally bypasses Russian territory. The oil is transported by pipeline from Baku to the Georgian port of Supsa, where it is shipped by tanker to the Pivdenny terminal near Odessa in the Ukraine. Both Georgia and the Ukraine are part of the GUUAM military alliance.

This Pivdenny terminal has been financed—in agreement with the (neo-fascist) government of President Leonid Kuchma—by Western loans. From there, the oil can be transported by pipeline "connecting to the already existing southern branch of the Druzhba pipeline, which runs through Slovakia, Hungary and the Czech Republic".[16]

NATO enlargement, announced shortly before the inauguration of the Baku-Supsa route, also ensures the protection of the connecting pipeline routes which transit through Hungarian and Czech territory. In other words, the entire pipeline route out of the Caspian sea basin transits through countries which are under the protection of the Western military alliance.

Chechnya at the Crossroads of Strategic Pipelines
Russia's Soviet era pipeline linked the Azeri port of Baku on the Southern tip of the Caspian Sea, via Grozny, to Tikhoretsk. This pipeline route, controlled by the Russian state, terminates at Novorossiysk, and Chechnya is located at the crossroads of this strategic pipeline route.

During the Soviet era, Novorossiysk was the terminal for both the Kazakh and Azeri pipelines. Since the end of the Cold War and the opening up of the Caspian oil fields to foreign capital, Washington has incorporated the Ukraine and Georgia into its sphere of influence. Their membership in the GUUAM military alliance is crucial to Western pipeline plans, which are intent upon bypassing the Novorossiysk terminal, as well as shunting Moscow's influence over the pipelines crossing its own territory.

In the immediate wake of the Cold War, Washington encouraged the secession of Chechnya from the Russian Federation by providing covert support to the two main rebel factions. As discussed in Chapter II, the Islamic insurgencies in Chechnya were supported by Osama bin Laden's Al Qaeda and Pakistan's ISI.

In 1994, Moscow went to war in order to protect its strategic pipeline route threatened by Chechen rebels. In August 1999 the pipeline was temporarily put out of order when the Chechen rebel army invaded Dagestan, triggering the Kremlin's decision to send federal troops into Chechnya.

The evidence suggests that the CIA was behind the Chechen rebels, using Pakistan's ISI as a "go-between". Washington's "hidden agenda" consisted in weakening the control of the Russian oil companies and the Russian state over the pipeline routes through Chechnya and Dagestan. Ultimately, Washington's objective is to separate Dagestan and Chechnya from the Russian Federation, thereby bringing a large part of the territory between the Caspian Sea and the Black Sea under the "protection" of the Western military alliance.

Under this scenario, Russia would be excluded from the Caspian Sea. All the existing as well as future pipeline routes and transport corridors between the Caspian and Black Seas would be in the hands of the Anglo-American oil giants. The covert operations led by Pakistan's ISI in support of the Chechen rebels once again serve the interests of the Anglo-American oil giants.

The BP-Amoco Consortium

Shouldered by BP-Amoco, a US client government had been installed in Azerbaijan. President Aliyev has established himself by distributing power to various members of his family. In Azerbaijan, a modest $8 billion investment is estimated to yield profits of more than $40 billion to Western oil companies.[17] BP-Amoco was particularly anxious to shunt competing bids from Russia's Lukoil. The Anglo-American consortium led by BP-Amoco also included Unocal, McDermott and Pennzoil, together with Turkey's TPAO. Unocal was also the main player in the pipeline project across Afghanistan to the Arabian Sea. (See Chapter VI.)

The BP-Amoco consortium owns 60 per cent of the shares in the Azerbaijani International Operating Corporation (AIOC). In

1997, in a separate venture, Vice President Al Gore was instrumental in the signing of a major oil deal with SOCAR allowing Chevron (now allied with Texaco) to acquire control over vast oil reserves in the southern Caspian Sea.[18] Chevron is also involved in the Northern Caspian region of Kazakhstan through its joint venture Tengizchevroil. In other words, prior to the 2000 Presidential elections, both George W. Bush and Al Gore, the two opposing candidates, had already made commitments to competing oil conglomerates in the Caspian Sea basin.

Europe versus Anglo-America:
The Clash of Competing Oil Interests

The Anglo-American oil giants, supported by US military might, are directly competing with Europe's oil giant Total-Fina-Elf—associated with Italy's ENI, which is a big player in Kazakhstan's wealthy North East Caspian Kashagan oil fields. The stakes are high: Kashagan is reported to have deposits "so large as to even surpass the size of the North Sea oil reserves".[19]

The competing EU-based consortium, however, lacks a significant stake and leverage in the main pipeline routes out of the Caspian Sea basin and back (via the Black Sea and through the Balkans) to Western Europe. The key pipeline corridor projects are largely in the hands of their Anglo-American rivals.

The Franco-Belgian consortium Total-Fina-Elf, in partnership with Italy's ENI, also has sizeable investments in Iran. Total had established, together with Russia's Gazprom and Malaysia's Petronas, a joint venture with the National Iranian Oil company (NIOC). Predictably, Washington has, on several occasions, attempted to break France's deal with Tehran on the grounds that it openly contravened the Iran-Libya Sanctions Act.

What this suggests is that Europe's largest oil conglomerate, dominated by French and Italian oil interests in association with their Iranian and Russian partners, are potentially on a collision course with the dominant Anglo-American oil consortia, which in turn are backed by Washington.

Russia's Oil Transnationals

Russia's major oil groups, while establishing strong ties to the Franco-Italian consortium, have, nonetheless, also entered into joint ventures with the Anglo-American groups.

While Russia's oil companies are supported by the Russian state and military against Western encroachment, several of Russia's major oil giants (including Lukoil and the State-owned company Rosneft) are participating in the Anglo-American pipeline projects as junior partners.

The Anglo-American oil companies are intent upon eventually taking over the Russian oil companies and excluding Russia from the Caspian Sea basin. At the same time, the Anglo-American groups are clashing with the Franco-Italian consortium, which in turn has ties to Russian and Iranian oil interests.

The militarization of the Eurasian corridor is an integral part of Washington's foreign policy agenda. In this regard, America's quest to control the Eurasian pipeline corridors on behalf of the Anglo-American oil giants is not only directed against Russia, it is also intended to weaken competing European oil interests in the Transcaucasus and Central Asia.

Notes

1. George Arney, "US planned attack on Taliban", BBC, 18 September 2001.

2. *Financial Times*, London, 6 May 1999, p. 2.

3. *Ibid.*

4. US Congress, Hearing On US Interests In The Central Asian Republics, House of Representatives, Subcommittee on Asia and the Pacific, Committee on International Relations, Washington, DC, http://commdocs.house.gov/committees/intlrel/hfa48119.000/hfa48119_0f.htm, Washington DC, 12 February 1998.

5. *Ibid.*

6. US Congress, Silk Road Strategy Act, 106th Congress, 1st Session, S. 579, "To amend the Foreign Assistance Act of 1961 to target assistance to support the economic and political independence of the countries of the South Caucasus and Central Asia", US Senate, Washington DC, March 10, 1999.

7. *Ibid.*

8. Lara Marlowe, "US efforts to make peace summed up by 'oil'", *Irish Times,* 19 November 2001.

9. Lt.-Gen. William E. Odom, USA, Ret, "US Policy Toward Central Asia and the South Caucasus", *Caspian Crossroads Magazine,* Volume 3, Issue No.1, Summer 1997.

10. *Ibid.*

11. *Ibid.*

12. Robert V. Baryiski, "The Caspian Oil Regime: Military Dimensions", *Caspian Crossroads Magazine,* Volume 1, Issue No. 2, Spring 1995.

13. Graham Fuller, "Geopolitical Dynamics of the Caspian Region", *Caspian Crossroads Magazine,* Volume 3, Issue No.2, Fall 1997

14. Damien Caveli, "The United States of Oil", Salon.com, 19 November 2001.

15. The Great Game. Aliyev.com, http://www.aliyev.com/aliyev/fact_07.htm, 9 January 2000.

16. Bohdan Klid, *Ukraine's Plans to Transport Caspian Sea and Middle East Oil to Europe,* Canadian Institute of Ukrainian Studies, University of Alberta, Edmonton, undated. See also Energy Information Administration at http://www.eia.doe.gov/emeu/cabs/russpip.html.

17. See Richard Hottelet, "Tangled Web of an Oil Pipeline" *The Christian Science Monitor,* 1 May 1998.

18. PR News Wire, 1 August 1997.

19. Richard Giragosian, "Massive Kashagan Oil Strike Renews Geopolitical Offensive In Caspian", *The Analyst,* Central Asia-Caucasus Institute, Johns Hopkins University, Paul H. Nitze School of Advanced International Studies, 7 June, 2000.

CHAPTER VI
The Trans-Afghan Pipeline

Washington's Silk Road Strategy consists in not only excluding Russia from the westbound oil and gas pipeline routes out of the Caspian Sea basin, but also in securing Anglo-American control over strategic southbound and eastbound routes.

This strategy consists in isolating and eventually "encircling" the former Soviet republics by simultaneously taking control of both westbound and east/southbound corridors. In this regard, Washington's strategy in support of the oil giants is also to prevent the former republics from entering into pipeline ventures (or military cooperation agreements) with Iran and China.

> According to the Washington-based Heritage Foundation, a conservative public policy organization, the American diplomatic dance with the Taliban was partly an attempt to prevent the construction of a pipeline through Iran and to reduce Russian leverage over Turkmenistan and Kazakhstan.[1]

Backed by the Clinton administration, Unocal, the California-based oil giant, developed a plan in 1995 to build an oil and gas pipeline route from Turkmenistan, through Afghanistan and

Pakistan, to the Arabian Sea. Unocal is also involved in the west-bound Baku-Ceyan pipeline project out of Azerbaijan across Turkey and Georgia, together with BP, which has a majority stake in the consortium.

The CentGas Consortium

By transiting through Afghanistan, Unocal's CentGas pipeline project was meant to bypass the more direct southbound route across Iran. Unocal's design was to develop a dual pipeline system that would also transport Kazakhstan's huge oil reserves in the Tenghiz Northern Caspian region to the Arabian Sea.

Although the Russian oil giant Gazprom was part of the CentGas consortium, its participation was insignificant.[2] The hidden agenda was also to weaken Gazprom, which controls the Northbound gas pipeline routes out of Turkmenistan, and undermine the agreement between Russia and Turkmenistan, which handled the export of Turkmen gas through the network of Russian pipelines.

After Unocal had completed a first round of negotiations with Turkmenistan's President Niyazov, it opened talks with the Taliban.[3] In turn, the Clinton administration decided to back the installation of a Taliban government in Kabul in 1996, as opposed to the Northern Alliance, which was backed by Moscow:

> Impressed by the ruthlessness and willingness of the then-emerging Taliban to cut a pipeline deal, the State Department and Pakistan's ISI agreed to funnel arms and funding to the Taliban in their war against the ethnically Tajik Northern Alliance. As recently as 1999, US taxpayers paid the entire annual salary of every single Taliban government official.[4]

Meanwhile, the Russians were providing logistical support and military supplies to General Massoud's Northern Alliance out of military bases in Tajikistan. When Kabul finally fell to the Taliban with the military backing of America's ally Pakistan, in September 1996, State Department spokesman Glyn Davies said the US found "nothing objectionable" in the steps taken by the Taliban to impose

Islamic law. Senator Hank Brown, a supporter of the Unocal project, said "the good part of what has happened is that one of the factions at least seems capable of developing a government in Kabul." Unocal's Vice-President, Martin Miller, called the Taliban's success a "positive development".[5]

> When the Taliban took Kabul in 1996, Washington said nothing. Why? Because Taliban leaders were soon on their way to Houston, Texas, to be entertained by executives of the oil company, Unocal .... A US diplomat said, "The Taliban will probably develop like the Saudis did." He explained that Afghanistan would become an American oil colony, there would be huge profits for the West, no democracy and the legal persecution of women. "We can live with that", he said.[6]

Washington's endorsement of the Taliban regime instead of the Northern Alliance was part of the "Big Game" and the added rivalry between Russian and US conglomerates for control over oil and gas reserves, as well as pipeline routes out of Kazakhstan and Turkmenistan. In early 1997, Taliban officials met at Unocal's Texas office:

> [Unocal's Barry] Lane says he wasn't involved in the Texas meetings and doesn't know whether then-Governor George W. Bush, an ex-oil man, ever had any involvement. Unocal's Texas spokesperson for Central Asia operations, Teresa Covington, said the consortium delivered three basic messages to the Afghan groups. "We gave them the details on the proposed pipelines. We also talked to them about the projects'benefits, such as the transit fees that would be paid," she says. "And we reinforced our position the project could not move forward until they stabilized their country and obtained political recognition from the US and the international community."
>
> Covington says the Taliban were not surprised by that demand .... In December 1997, Unocal arranged a high-level meeting in Washington, DC, for the Taliban with Clinton's undersecretary of state for South Asia, Karl Inderforth. The Taliban delegation included Acting Minister for Mines and Industry Ahmad Jan, Acting Minister for Culture and Information, Amir Muttaqi, Acting Minister for Planning, Din Muhammad and Abdul Hakeem Mujahid, their permanent UN delegate.[7]

Two months following these negotiations, in February 1998, Unocal Vice President for International Relations, John Maresca, in a statement to the House Committee on International Relations, called for "the need for multiple pipeline routes for Central Asian oil and gas resources". (See Chapter V.) Implied in his statement, US foreign policy in the region was to be geared towards destabilizing the north, west and southbound pipeline routes controlled by Russia, as well as competing pipelines through Iran:

> [A] chief technical obstacle [or more likely political obstacle] which we in the industry face in transporting oil is the region's existing pipeline infrastructure. Because the region's pipelines were constructed during the Moscow-centred Soviet period, they tend to head north and west toward Russia. There are no connections to the south and east. ...
>
> The key question then, is how the energy resources of Central Asia can be made available to nearby Asian markets .... One obvious route south would cross Iran, but this is foreclosed for American companies because of US sanctions legislation. The only other possible route is across Afghanistan, which has of course its own unique challenges. The country has been involved in bitter warfare for almost two decades, and is still divided by civil war. From the outset, we have made it clear that construction of the pipeline we have proposed across Afghanistan could not begin until a recognized government is in place that has the confidence of governments, lenders, and our company.
>
> Unocal foresees a pipeline which would become part of a regional system that would gather oil from existing pipeline infrastructure in Turkmenistan, Uzbekistan, Kazakhstan and Russia. The 1,040-mile long oil pipeline would extend south through Afghanistan to an export terminal that would be constructed on the Pakistan coast. This 42-inch diameter pipeline would have a shipping capacity of one million barrels of oil per day. The estimated cost of the project, which is similar in scope to the trans-Alaska pipeline, is about $2.5 billion.
>
> Without peaceful settlement of the conflicts in the region, cross-border oil and gas pipelines are not likely to be built. We urge the Administration and the Congress to give strong support to the UN-

led peace process in Afghanistan. The US Government should use its influence to help find solutions to all of the region's conflicts.[8]

The Unocal-Bridas Feud

There was something else behind the Unocal pipeline project, which mainstream reports failed to mention. The Taliban had also been negotiating with an Argentinean oil group, Bridas Energy Corporation, and were "playing one company against the other".[9] Bridas belonged to the wealthy and powerful Bhulgeroni family. Carlos Bhulgeroni is a close friend of former Argentine President Carlos Menem, whose government was instrumental in implementing in 1990—under advice from the World Bank—a comprehensive deregulation of Argentina's oil and gas industry. This deregulation contributed to the enrichment of the Bhulgeroni family.

In 1992—several years prior to Unocal's involvement—Bridas Energy Corporation had obtained gas exploration rights in Eastern Turkmenistan, and the following year it was awarded the Keimir oil and gas block in Western Turkmenistan. Washington considered this an encroachment. It responded to Bridas'inroads into Central Asia by sending former Secretary of State Alexander Haig to lobby for "increased US investments" in Turkmenistan.[10] A few months later, Bridas was prevented from exporting oil from the Keimir block.

Unocal and Bridas were clashing in their attempts to gain political control. While Bridas had a head start in its negotiations with Turkmen officials, Unocal had the direct support of the US Government, which was acting both overtly (through diplomatic channels) as well as covertly to undermine Bridas Energy Corp.

In August 1995, at the height of the Afghan civil war, Bridas representatives met up with Taliban officials to discuss the pipeline project. Meanwhile, Turkmen President Saparmurat Niyasov had been invited to New York (October 1995) to sign an agreement with Unocal and its CentGas consortium partner, Delta Oil Corporation of Saudi Arabia. The agreement was signed by President Niyazov of Turkmenistan and John F. Imle, Jr., President of Unocal, and witnessed by Badr M. Al-Aiban, CEO of Delta Oil Corporation.

Bridas and the Taliban

In February 1996, Bridas Energy Corporation of Argentina and the Taliban provisional government signed a preliminary agreement. Washington responded through its embassy in Islamabad, urging Pakistan's Prime Minister Benazir Bhutto to dump Bridas and grant exclusive rights to Unocal.[11] Meanwhile, the Clinton administration had funnelled, through Pakistan's ISI, military aid to advancing Taliban forces. This support was a crucial factor in the Taliban's takeover of Kabul in September 1996. Following the installation of a hard-line Islamic government, Unocal confirmed that "it will give aid to Afghan warlords once they agree to form a council to supervise the project".[12]

Back in Texas, Bridas Energy Corporation filed a $15 billion lawsuit against Unocal, accusing it of dirty tricks and interference in:

> ... secretly contacting the Turkmen deputy prime minister for oil and gas [in 1996] about its own pipeline plan. According to a Bridas source, the Turkmen government then made an overnight decision to cut off the export of oil from Bridas'Keimir field on the Caspian Sea. The company also alleges that the deputy prime minister demanded that Bridas, with its cash flow strangled, renegotiate its concession. "We found written evidence that Unocal was behind the curtains," the Bridas source said.[13]

BP-Amoco Enter the Pipeline Saga

Facing pending financial difficulties, 60 per cent of Bridas shares were sold in August 1997 to the American Oil Company (Amoco), leading to the formation of the Pan American Energy Corporation. The bidders in the Bridas merger were Amoco and Union Texas Petroleum of the United States, France's Total, Royal Dutch Shell, Spain's Endesa and a consortium including Spain's Repsol and US Mobil.

For Amoco, which later merged with BP in 1998, Bridas was a prize acquisition, which was facilitated by Chase Manhattan and Morgan Stanley. Former National Security adviser, Zbigniew Brzezinski, was a consultant to Amoco. Arthur Andersen—the accounting firm implicated in the 2002 Enron scandal—was put in charge of "post-merger integration".[14]

BP-Amoco is the main player in the Westbound pipeline routes out of the Caspian Sea basin including the controversial Baku-Ceyan pipeline project through Georgia and Turkey. By acquiring Bridas, the BP-led consortium gained a direct stake in the east and southbound pipeline negotiations.

Unocal is both a "rival" as well as a consortium "partner" of BP. In other words, BP controls the westbound pipeline consortium in which Unocal has a significant stake. With Bridas in the hands of BP-Amoco, however, it is unlikely that a future trans-Afghan pipeline will proceed without the consent and/or participation of BP:

> Recognizing the significance of the merger, a Pakistani oil company executive hinted, "If these [Central Asian] countries want a big US company involved, Amoco is far bigger than Unocal."[15]

Following the takeover of Bridas by Amoco, Bridas'successor company, Pan American Energy Corporation, continued to actively negotiate with the Taliban. But the dynamics of these negotiations had been fundamentally modified. Pan American Energy was negotiating on behalf of its Chicago-based parent company Amoco. Moreover, the Clinton administration had abandoned its dirty tricks and was now backing Amoco's subsidiary.

Meanwhile, in August 1998, Amoco and BP announced their decision to unite their global operations leading to the formation (together with Atlantic Ritchfield) of the world's largest oil company.

The Bridas-Unocal rivalry had evolved towards "a fall-out" between two major US corporations (Unocal and BP-Amoco), which were also "partners" in the westbound pipeline projects. Both Unocal and BP-Amoco have extensive links to seats of political power, not only in the White House and Congress, but also with the military and intelligence establishment in charge of covert operations in Central Asia. Both companies contributed generously to the Bush presidential campaign.

The merger between BP and Amoco (leading to the integration of British and American oil interests) had no doubt also contributed to the development of closer political ties between the British and US Governments. Responding to the merger of American and British interests in oil, banking and the military-industrial complex, Britain's new Labour government, under Prime Minister Tony Blair, has become America's unconditional ally.

The US Embassy Bombings
In the course of 1998, talks between Taliban and Unocal officials had stalled. The honeymoon was over. Then came the East African US Embassy bombings, allegedly by Osama bin Laden's Al Qaeda, and the launching of cruise missiles against targets in Afghanistan.

The official suspension of negotiations with the Taliban was announced by Unocal in August 1998 in the immediate wake of the punitive actions against Afghanistan and Sudan, ordered by President Clinton. Whether the 1997 takeover of Bridas by Amoco and the subsequent merger of BP-Amoco (also in August 1998) had a bearing on Unocal's decision remains unclear. Nonetheless, "the Big Game" had evolved: Unocal was now competing against the world's largest oil company, BP-Amoco.

The Texas Court Case: BP-Amoco (Bridas) versus Unocal
Two months later in this evolving saga, in October 1998, a Texas court dismissed the (formerly Argentinian-owned) Bridas' US$15 billion lawsuit against Unocal "for preventing them developing gas fields in Turkmenistan".[16] It turned out that the court ruling was in fact against Bridas'parent company, BP-Amoco, which had, a year earlier, acquired a controlling stake in Bridas.

In all likelihood, there was a mutual understanding between Unocal and BP-Amoco, which are consortium partners in the Caspian Sea basin. Moreover, while Zbigniew Brzezinski, a former National Security Adviser (in a Democratic administration), was acting as a consultant for Amoco, Henry Kissinger, a former Secretary of State (in a Republican administration), was advising Unocal Corporation.

The acquisition of Bridas by BP-Amoco suggests that BP will, in all likelihood, be a major player in future pipeline negotiations, most probably in an agreement with Unocal.

Unocal Withdraws But Only Temporarily

While Unocal had formally withdrawn from the CentGas consortium in the wake of the cruise missile attacks on Afghanistan and the Sudan, BP-Amoco's subsidiary, Pan American Energy, (the successor company to Bridas), continued to actively negotiate with Afghan, Russian, Turkmen and Kazakh officials regarding the trans-Afghan pipeline project.

Meanwhile, a turnaround had occurred in US foreign policy under the Clinton administration towards Bridas: No more dirty tricks against a company which is now owned by one of America's largest oil conglomerates! Visibly, in the last two years of the Clinton administration, Unocal's rival in the pipeline negotiations, BP-Amoco, had the upper hand.

Despite Unocal's temporary withdrawal, the CentGas consortium was not disbanded. Unocal's partner, Delta Oil Corporation of Saudi Arabia, in CentGas continued to negotiate with the Taliban.

George W. Bush Enters the White House

The evolving pipeline saga gained a new momentum upon George W. Bush's accession to the White House in January 2001.

At the very outset of the Bush administration, Unocal (which had withdrawn in 1998 from pipeline negotiations under the Clinton administration) reintegrated the CentGas Consortium and resumed its talks with the Taliban (in January 2001), with the firm backing, this time, of senior officials of the Bush administration, including Deputy Secretary of State, Richard Armitage. Dick Armitage had previously been a lobbyist for Unocal in the Burma/Myanmar Forum, which is a Washington-based group funded by Unocal.[17]

These negotiations with the Taliban occurred only a few months before the September 11 attacks:

Laila Helms [daughter of Senator Jesse Helms], who was hired as the public relations agent for the Taliban government, brought Rahmatullah Hashimi, an advisor to Mullah Omar, to Washington as recently as March 2001. Helms was uniquely positioned for the job through her association with her uncle Richard Helms, former chief of the CIA and former Ambassador to Iran. One of the negotiating meetings was held just one month before September 11, on August 2, when Christina Rocca, in charge of Asian Affairs at the State Department, met Taliban Ambassador to Pakistan, Abdul Salem Zaef, in Islamabad.

Rocca has had extensive connections with Afghanistan, including supervising the delivery of Stinger missiles to the Mujahideen in the 1980s. At the CIA, she had been in charge of contacts with Islamist fundamentalist guerrilla groups.[18]

Unocal 'Appoints' Interim Government in Kabul

In the wake of the bombing of Afghanistan, the Bush administration designated Hamid Karzai as head of the interim government in Kabul. While highlighting Karzai's patriotic struggle against the Taliban, what the media failed to mention is that Karzai had collaborated with the Taliban government. He had also been on Unocal's payroll.

In fact, since the mid-1990s, Hamid Karzai, who later became President, had acted as a consultant and lobbyist for Unocal in negotiations with the Taliban. His appointment—visibly on behalf of the US oil giants—had been casually rubber-stamped by the "international community" at the November 2001 Bonn conference, held under UN auspices.

According to the Saudi newspaper *Al-Watan:*

> Karzai has been a Central Intelligence Agency covert operator since the 1980s. He collaborated with the CIA in funneling US aid to the Taliban as of 1994 "when the Americans had—secretly and through the Pakistanis [specifically the ISI]—supported the Taliban's assumption of power."[19]

"Coincidentally, President Bush's Special Envoy to Kabul, Zalmay Khalizad, had also worked for Unocal. He had drawn up the risk analysis for the pipeline in 1997, lobbied for the Taliban and took part in negotiations with them."[20] Khalizad had occupied the position of Special Advisor to the State Department during the Reagan administration, "lobbying successfully for accelerated US military aid to the Mujahideen".

He later became Undersecretary of Defense in the Bush Senior Cabinet.[21] When George W. was inaugurated in January 2001, Khalizad was appointed to the National Security Council. While Clinton's foreign policy had provided support to US oil interests in Central Asia, under the Republicans oil company officials were brought into the inner sphere of political decision-making.

The 'Reconstruction' of Afghanistan

Washington had set the stage. According to a World Bank representative in Kabul, "reconstruction in Afghanistan [was] going to open up a whole range of opportunities."[22]

Two days after the bombing of Afghanistan commenced, on October 9, the US Ambassador to Pakistan, Wendy Chamberlain, met with Pakistani officials regarding the trans-Afghan pipeline. The pipeline, according to the report, was slated to "open up new avenues of multi-dimensional regional cooperation, particularly in light of recent geopolitical developments [bombing of Afghanistan] in the region".[23]

With Afghanistan under US military occupation, the role of Hamid Karzai as the country's President is to "broker" the pipeline deal on behalf of the Anglo-American oil giants with the firm backing of the Bush administration.

In the immediate wake of the October 2001 bombing raids, the media reported that "two small companies", Chase Energy and Caspian Energy Consulting (acting on behalf of major oil interests), had contacts with the governments of Turkmenistan and Pakistan to revive the pipeline deal. While the identity of the oil companies behind these "small firms" was not mentioned, it just so happens that the President of Caspian Sea Consulting, S. Rob Sobhani, had been a consultant to BP-Amoco in Central Asia. Sobhani also sits on the Council of Foreign Relations'"Caspian Sea

Discourse", together with representatives of major oil companies, the George Soros Open Society Institute, the CIA and the Heritage Foundation (a Republican party think tank).

According to S. Rob Sobhani:

> It is absolutely essential that the US make the pipeline the center-piece of rebuilding Afghanistan .... The State Department thinks it's a great idea, too. Routing the gas through Iran would be avoided, and the Central Asian republics wouldn't have to ship through Russian pipelines.[24]

According to Joseph Noemi, CEO of Chase Energy, September 11, and the "War on Terrorism" are a blessing in disguise for Afghanistan:

> If the United States'presence continues in the region, [September 11] is probably the best thing that could have happened here for the Central Asian republics .... This region, in terms of oil economics, is the frontier for this century ... and Afghanistan is part and par-cel of this.[25]

Notes

1. *Knight Ridder News*, 31 October 2001.

2. Jim Crogan, "The Oil War", *LA Weekly*, 30 November 2001.

3. *Ibid.*

4. Ted Rall, "It's About Oil", *San Francisco Chronicle*, 2 November 2001, p. A25.

5. Ishtiaq Ahmad, "How America Courted Taliban", *Pakistan Observer*, 20 October 2001.

6. John Pilger, "This War is a Fraud", *Daily Mirror*, 29 October 2001.

7. Jim Crogan, "Pipeline Payoff to Afghanistan War", *California CrimeTimes*, November 2001, http://www.californiacrimetimes.com/. See also Jim Crogan, "The Oil War: Unocal's once-grand plan for Afghan pipelines", *LA Weekly*, 30 November-6 December 2001.

8. US Congress, Hearing on US Interests in the Central Asian Republics, House of Representatives, Subcommittee on Asia and the Pacific, Committee on International Relations, Washington, DC, http://commdocs.house.gov/committees/intlrel/hfa48119.000/hfa48119_0f.htm.

9. See Karen Talbot, "US Energy Giant Unocal Appoints Interim Government in Kabul", *Global Outlook*, No. 1, Spring 2002, p. 70.

10. "Timeline of Competition Between Unocal and Bridas", *World Press Review*, December 2001, www.worldpress.org.

11. *Ibid.*

12. *Ibid.*

13. Alexander Gas and Oil Connections, http://www.gasandoil.com/goc/company/cnc75005.htm, 12 August 1997

14. Larry Chin, "Unocal and the Afghanistan Pipeline", *Online Journal*, 6 March 2002, Centre for Research on Globalization (CRG), http://www.globalresearch.ca/articles/CHI203A.html, 6 March 2002.

15. *Ibid.*

16. *Timeline, op. cit.*

17. Larry Chin, *op. cit.*

18. See Karen Talbot, "US Energy Giant Unocal Appoints Interim Government in Kabul", *Global Outlook*, No. 1, Spring 2002. p. 70.

19. Karen Talbot, *op. cit.* and BBC Monitoring Service, 15 December 2001.

20. Karen Talbot, *op. cit.*

21. Patrick Martin, "Unocal Advisor Named Representative to Afghanistan", World Socialist Web Site, 3 January 2002.

22. Statement of William Byrd, World Bank Acting Country Manager for Afghanistan, 27 November 2001.

23. Quoted in Larry Chin, "The Bush administration's Afghan Carpet", Centre for Research on Globalization (CRG), http://www.globalresearch.ca/articles/CHI203B.html, 13 March 2002.

24. Daniel Fisher, "Kabuled Together", *Forbes Online*, 4 February 2002, http://www.forbes.com.

25. *Knight Ridder News*, 30 October 2001.

CHAPTER VII
America's War Machine

The 1999 war in Yugoslavia—which coincided with the formation of GUUAM and NATO enlargement into Eastern Europe—marked an important turnaround in East-West relations.

Aleksander Arbatov, Deputy Chairman of the Defense Committee of the Russian State Duma US-Russian Relations, described the war in Yugoslavia as the "worst, most acute, most dangerous juncture since the US-Soviet Berlin and Cuban missile crises".[1] According to Arbatov:

> START II is dead, co-operation with NATO is frozen, co-operation on missile defense is out of the question, and Moscow's willingness to co-operate on non-proliferation issues is at an all-time low. Moreover, anti-US sentiment in Russia is real, deep and more widespread than ever, and the slogan describing NATO action—"today Serbia, tomorrow Russia," is deeply planted in Russians'minds.[2]

Despite President Boris Yeltsin's conciliatory statements at the 1999 G-8 Summit in Cologne, Russia's military establishment had openly expressed its distrust of the US: "The bombing of Yugoslavia could turn out in the very near future to be just a rehearsal for similar strikes on Russia."[3]

Mary-Wynne Ashford, co-President of the International Physicians for the Prevention of Nuclear War (IPPNW), warned that, whereas Russia was moving towards integration with Europe, they (the Russians) now:

> ... perceive their primary threat [to be] from the West. Officials in [Russia's] Foreign Affairs (Arms Control and Disarmament) told us [the IPPNW] that Russia has no option but to rely on nuclear weapons for its defense, because its conventional forces are inadequate .... [T]he changes in Russia's attitude toward the West, its renewed reliance on nuclear weapons with thousands on high alert and its loss of confidence in international law leave us vulnerable to catastrophe .... This crisis makes de-alerting nuclear weapons more urgent than ever. To those who say the Russian threat is all rhetoric, I reply that rhetoric is what starts wars.[4]

Post 1999 Military Buildup

Meanwhile, in Washington, a major build-up of America's military arsenal was in the making. The underlying objective was to achieve a position of global military hegemony. Defense spending in 2002 was hiked up to more than $300 billion, an amount equivalent to the entire Gross Domestic Product of the Russian Federation (approximately $325 billion). An even greater increase in US military spending was set in motion in the wake of the October 2001 bombing of Afghanistan:

> More than one-third of the $68 billion allocated for new weapons in the 2003 budget is for Cold War-type weapons. Several billion dollars are allocated for cluster bomb systems that have been condemned by human rights groups around the world. There is no rationale for this level of military spending other than a clear intent for the United States to be the New World Empire, dominating the globe economically and militarily, including the militarization of space.[5]

In the largest military buildup since the Vietnam War, the Bush administration plans to increase military spending by $120 billion over a five-year period, "bringing the 2007 military budget to an astounding $451 billion".[6]

This colossal amount of money allocated to America's war machine does not include the enormous budget of the Central Intelligence Agency (CIA) allocated from both "official" and undisclosed sources to finance its covert operations. The official budget of the CIA is in excess of $30 billion (10 per cent of Russia's GDP). This amount excludes the multi-billion dollar earnings from narcotics accruing to CIA shell companies and front organizations.[7]

From the overall defense budget, billions of dollars have been allocated to "refurbishing America's nuclear arsenal". A new generation of "cluster missiles"—with multiple nuclear warheads—has been developed, capable of delivering (from a single missile launch) up to 10 nuclear warheads directed at 10 different cities. These missiles are now targeted at Russia. In this context, Washington has clung to its "first strike" nuclear policy, which in principle is intended to deal with "rogue states" but, in fact, is largely directed against Russia and China.

Meanwhile, the US have also developed a new generation of "tactical nuclear weapons" or "mini-nukes" to be used in conventional war theatres. Already during the Clinton administration, the Pentagon was calling for the use of the "nuclear" B61-11 bunker buster bomb, suggesting that because it was "underground", there was no toxic radioactive fallout which could affect civilians:

> Military officials and leaders of America's nuclear weapon laboratories are urging the US to develop a new generation of precision low-yield nuclear weapons … which could be used in conventional conflicts with Third World nations.[8]

America's War Economy

The military buildup initiated during the Clinton administration has gained a new momentum. September 11 and Bush's "war on terrorism" are used as an excuse for expanding America's military machine and fuelling the growth of the military-industrial complex.

A new "legitimacy" has unfolded. Increased military spending is said to be required "to uphold freedom" and defeat "the axis of evil":

It costs a lot to fight this war. We have spent more than a billion dollars a month—over $30 million a day—and we must be prepared for future operations. Afghanistan proved that expensive precision weapons defeat the enemy and spare innocent lives, and we need more of them. We need to replace aging aircraft and make our military more agile, to put our troops anywhere in the world quickly and safely .... My budget includes the largest increase in defense spending in two decades—because while the price of freedom and security is high, it is never too high. Whatever it costs to defend our country, we will pay.[9]

Since September 11, 2001, billions of dollars have been channeled towards developing new advanced weapons systems, including the F22 Raptor fighter plane and the Joint Fighter (JF) program.

The Strategic Defense Initiative ("Star Wars") not only includes the controversial "Missile Shield", but also a wide range of "offensive" laser-guided weapons with striking capabilities anywhere in the world, not to mention instruments of weather and climatic warfare under the High Altitude Auroral Research Program (HAARP). The latter has the ability of destabilizing entire national economies through climatic manipulations, without the knowledge of the enemy, at minimal cost and without engaging military personnel and equipment as in a conventional war.[10]

Long-term planning pertaining to advanced weapons systems and the control of outer space is outlined in a US Space Command document released in 1998, entitled "Vision for 2020". The underlying objective consists in:

... dominating the space dimension of military operations to protect US interests and investment .... The emerging synergy of space superiority with land, sea and air superiority will lead to Full Spectrum Dominance.[11]

Nuclear Weapons in the Wake of September 11

In the wake of September 11, the "war on terrorism" is also being used by the Bush administration to redefine the assumptions underlying the use of nuclear weapons. The concept of "nuclear deterrence" has been scrapped. "They're trying desperately to find new uses for nuclear weapons, when their uses should be limited to deterrence."[12]

In early 2002, a secret Pentagon report confirmed the Bush administration's intent to use nuclear weapons against China, Russia, Iraq, North Korea, Iran, Libya and Syria. The secret report, leaked to the *Los Angeles Times,* states that nuclear weapons "could be used in three types of situations: against targets able to withstand non-nuclear attack; in retaliation for attack with nuclear,

---

TEXT BOX 7.1
America's Tactical Nuclear Weapons

In the 2002 war in Afghanistan, the US Air Force was using GBU-28 "bunker buster bombs" capable of creating large scale underground explosions. The official story was that these bombs were intended to target "cave and tunnel complexes" in mountainous areas in southern Afghanistan, which were used as hideaways by Osama bin Laden. Dubbed by the Pentagon "the Big Ones", the GBUs (guided bomb units) are 5000-lb laser guided bombs with improved BLU-113 warheads capable of penetrating several metres of reinforced concrete. The BLU-113 is the most powerful conventional "earth penetrating warhead" ever created.

While the Pentagon's "Big Ones" are classified as "conventional weapons", the official statements fail to mention that the same "bunker buster bombs" launched from a B-52, a B-2 stealth bomber, or an F-16 aircraft can also be equipped with a nuclear device. The B61-11 is the "nuclear version" of its "conventional" BLU-113 counterpart.

The nuclear B61-11 is categorized as a "deep earth penetrating bomb" capable of "destroying the deepest and most hardened of underground bunkers, which the conventional warheads are not capable of doing." Secretary of Defense Donald Rumsfeld has stated that while the 'conventional' bunker buster bombs "'are going to be able to do the job' .... He did not rule out the eventual use of nuclear weapons."[14]

---

biological or chemical weapons; or in the event of surprising military developments".[13]

> With a Strangelovian genius, they cover every conceivable circumstance in which a president may wish to use nuclear weapons—planning in great detail for a war they hope never to wage.
>
> In this top-secret domain, there has always been an inconsistency between America's diplomatic objectives of reducing nuclear arsenals and preventing the proliferation of weapons of mass destruction on

---

The Bush administration needs a justification, as well as public support, for the use of tactical nuclear weapons as part of its "war against international terrorism". It is also anxious to test its "low yield" B61-11 bombs.

First, it is saying that these "low yield" nuclear weapons do not affect civilians, therefore justifying their being used in the same way as conventional weapons. Second, the Administration is hinting that the use of nuclear bunker busters may be justified as part of "the campaign against international terrorism", because Osama bin Laden's Al Qaeda network possesses nuclear capabilities and could use them against us. America's tactical nuclear weapons are said to be "safe" in comparison to those of Osama bin Laden's Al Qaeda. Administration statements suggest, in this regard, that a "low-yield" earth penetrating tactical nuclear weapon such as the B61-11 would "limit collateral damage" and therefore be relatively safe to use.[15]

These new buzzwords are being spread by the US media to develop public support for the use of tactical nuclear weapons. Yet, the scientific evidence on this issue is unequivocal: the impacts on civilians of the "low yield" B61-11 would be devastating "because of the large amount of radioactive dirt thrown out in the explosion, the hypothetical 5-kiloton weapon ... would produce a large area of lethal fallout".[16]

---

the one hand, and the military imperative to prepare for the unthinkable on the other.

Nevertheless, the Bush administration plan reverses an almost two-decade-long trend of relegating nuclear weapons to the category of weapons of last resort. It also redefines nuclear requirements in hurried post-September 11 terms.[17]

While identifying a number of "rogue states", the not-so-hidden agenda of the Bush administration is to deploy and use nuclear weapons against Russia and China in the context of America's expansionary policy into Central Asia, the Middle East and the Far East:

> The report says the Pentagon should be prepared to use nuclear weapons in an Arab-Israeli conflict, in a war between China and Taiwan or in an attack from North Korea on the south. They might also become necessary in an attack by Iraq on Israel or another neighbour, it said.
>
> The report says Russia is no longer officially an "enemy". Yet it acknowledges that the huge Russian arsenal, which includes about 6,000 deployed warheads and perhaps 10,000 smaller "theatre" nuclear weapons, remains of concern.
>
> Pentagon officials have said publicly that they were studying the need to develop theatre nuclear weapons, designed for use against specific targets on a battlefield, but had not committed themselves to that course.[18]

The thrust of this secret report, presented to the US Congress in early 2002, has been endorsed by the Republican Party:

> [C]onservative analysts insisted that the Pentagon must prepare for all possible contingencies, especially now, when dozens of countries, and some terrorist groups, are engaged in secret weapons'development programs .... They argued that smaller weapons have an important deterrent role because many aggressors might not believe that the US forces would use multi-kiloton weapons that would wreak devastation on surrounding territory and friendly populations.
>
> We need to have a credible deterrence against regimes involved in international terrorism and development of weapons of mass destruction," said Jack Spencer, a defense analyst at the conservative

Heritage Foundation in Washington. He said the contents of the report did not surprise him and represent "the right way to develop a nuclear posture for a post-Cold War world".[19]

Encircling China

In the wake of the 1999 war in Yugoslavia, the Clinton administration boosted its military support to Taiwan against China, leading to a significant military buildup in the Taiwan Straits. Taiwan's Air Force had been previously equipped with some 150 F16A fighter planes from Lockheed Martin. In this regard, the Clinton administration had argued that military aid to Taiwan was required to maintain "a military balance with the People's Republic of China" as part of Washington's policy of "peace through deterrence".[20]

US-built Aegis destroyers equipped with state-of-the-art surface-to-air missiles, ship-to-ship missiles, and Tomahawk cruise missiles were delivered to Taiwan to boost its naval capabilities in the Taiwan Straits.[21] Beijing responded to this military buildup by taking delivery in 2000, of its first Russian-built guided missile destroyer, the Hangzhou, equipped with SS-N-22 Sunburn anti-ship missiles, "capable of penetrating the state-of-the-art defenses of a US or Japanese naval battle group".[22]

Military assumptions have been radically changed since September 11. The Bush administration has scrapped the "peace through deterrence" doctrine. The post-September 11 military buildup in the Taiwan Straits is an integral part of Washington's overall military planning, which now consists in deploying "on several fronts".

Supported by the Bush administration, Taiwan has been "conducting active research aimed at developing a tactical ballistic missile capable of hitting targets in mainland China. … The alleged purpose of these missiles is to degrade the PLA's (People's Liberation Army) strike capability, including missile infrastructure and non-missile infrastructure (airfields, harbors, missile sites, etc.)."[23] In turn, US military presence in Pakistan and Afghanistan (and in several former Soviet republics), on China's western border, are being coordinated with Taiwan's naval deployment in the South China Sea.

China has been encircled: The US military is present in the South China Sea and the Taiwan Straits, in the Korean Peninsula and the Sea of Japan, as well as in the heartland of Central Asia and on the Western border of China's Xinjiang-Uigur autonomous region. "Temporary" US military bases have been set up in Uzbekistan (which is a member of the GUUAM agreement with NATO), in Tajikistan and in Kyrgyztan, where airfields and military airport facilities have been made available to the US Air Force.

Using Nuclear Weapons Against China
In early 2002, the Bush administration confirmed its intent to use nuclear weapons against China if there was a confrontation in the Taiwan Straits:

> China, because of its nuclear forces and "developing strategic objec-
> tives", is listed as "a country that could be involved in an immediate
> or potential contingency". Specifically, the NPR lists a military con-
> frontation over the status of Taiwan as one of the scenarios that
> could lead Washington to use nuclear weapons.[24]

The Anglo-American Axis
The 1999 war in Yugoslavia contributed to reinforcing strategic, military and intelligence ties between Washington and London. After the war in Yugoslavia, US Defense Secretary William Cohen and his British counterpart, Geoff Hoon, signed a "Declaration of Principles for Defense Equipment and Industrial Cooperation" so as to "improve cooperation in procuring arms and protecting tech-nology secrets", while at the same time "easing the way for more joint military ventures and possible defense industry mergers".[25]

Washington's objective was to encourage the formation of a "trans-Atlantic bridge across which DoD [US Department of Defense] can take its globalization policy to Europe ....Our aim is to improve interoperability and war fighting effectiveness via closer industrial linkages between US and allied companies."[26]

In the words of President Clinton's Defense Secretary William Cohen:

> [The agreement] will facilitate interaction between our respective [British and American] industries so that we can have a harmonized approach to sharing technology, working cooperatively in partnership arrangements and, potentially, mergers as well.[27]

The agreement was signed in 1999 shortly after the creation of British Aerospace Systems (BAES) resulting from the merger of British Aerospace (BAe) with GEC Marconi. British Aerospace was already firmly allied to America's largest defense contractors Lockheed Martin and Boeing.[28]

The hidden agenda behind the Anglo-American "trans-Atlantic bridge" is to eventually displace the Franco-German military conglomerates and ensure the dominance of the US military industrial complex (in alliance with Britain's major defense contractors).

Moreover, this integration in the area of defense production has been matched by increased cooperation between the CIA and Britain's MI6 in the sphere of intelligence and covert operations, not to mention the joint operations of British and US Special Forces.

The United States and Germany

The British military-industrial complex has become increasingly integrated into that of the US. In turn, significant rifts have emerged between Washington and Berlin. Franco-German integration in aerospace and defense production is ultimately directed against US dominance in the weapons market. The latter hinges upon the partnership between America's Big Five and Britain's defense industry under the trans-Atlantic bridge agreement.

Since the early '90s, the Bonn government has encouraged the consolidation of Germany's military industrial complex dominated by Daimler, Siemens and Krupp. Several important mergers in Germany's defense industry took place in response to the megamergers between America's aerospace and weapons producers.[29]

By 1996 Paris and Bonn had already set up a joint armaments agency with the mandate "to manage common programs [and] award contracts on behalf of both governments".[30] Both countries had stated that they "did not want Britain to join the agency".

France and Germany also now control Airbus industries, which is competing against America's Lockheed-Martin. (Britain's BAES owns the remaining 20 per cent.) The Germans are also collaborating in the Ariane Space satellite-launching program in which Deutsche Aerospace (DASA) is a major shareholder.

In late 1999, in response to the "alliance" of British Aerospace with Lockheed Martin, France's Aerospatiale-Matra merged with Daimler's DASA, forming the largest European defense conglomerate. The following year the European Aeronautic Defense and Space Co. (EADS) was formed, integrating DASA, Matra and Spain's Construcciones Aeronauticas, SA. EADS and its Anglo-American rivals are competing for the procurement of weapons to NATO's new Eastern European members. (Europe's third largest defense contractor is Thomson, which in recent years has several projects with US weapons producer Raytheon.)

While EADS still cooperates with Britain's BAES in missile production and has business ties with the US "Big Five", including Northrop Grumman, the Western defense and aerospace industry tends to be split into two distinct groups: EADS dominated by France and Germany on the one hand, the Anglo-US "Big Six", which includes the US Big Five contractors (Lockheed Martin, Raytheon, General Dynamics, Boeing and Northrop Grumman) plus Britain's powerful BAES on the other.

Integrated into US Department of Defense procurement under the Atlantic bridge arrangement, BAES was the Pentagon's fifth largest defense contractor in 2001. Under the Anglo-American "transatlantic bridge", BAES operates freely in the US market through its subsidiary BAE Systems North America.[31]

Franco-German Integration in Nuclear Weapons

The Franco-German alliance in military production under EADS opens the door for the integration of Germany (which does not officially possess nuclear weapons) into France's nuclear weapons program. In this regard, EADS already produces a wide range of bal-

listic missiles, including the M51 nuclear-tipped ballistic subma-
rine-launched ICBMs for the French Navy.[32] What this means is
that Germany, through its alliance with France, is a de facto nuclear
power.

Euro versus Dollar:
Rivalry Between Competing Business Conglomerates

The European common currency system has a direct bearing on
strategic and political divisions. London's decision not to adopt
the common European currency is consistent with the integration
of British financial and banking interests with those of Wall Street,
as well as the Anglo-American alliance in the oil industry (as in
BP-Amoco) and weapons production ("Big Five" plus BAES). In
other words, this shaky relationship between the British pound
and the US dollar is an integral part of the new Anglo-American
axis.

What is at stake is the rivalry between two competing global
currencies: the Euro and the US dollar, with Britain's pound being
torn between the European and the US-dominated currency systems. Thus two rival financial and monetary systems are competing worldwide for control over money creation and credit. The
geopolitical and strategic implications are far-reaching because
they are also marked by splits in the Western defense industry and
the oil business.

In both Europe and America, monetary policy, although formally under state jurisdiction, is largely controlled by the private
banking sector. The European Central Bank based in Frankfurt—
although officially under the jurisdiction of the European Union—
is, in practice, overseen by a handful of private European banks,
including Germany's largest banks and business conglomerates.

The US Federal Reserve Board is formally under state supervision—marked by a close relationship to the US Treasury. Unlike
the European Central Bank, the 12 Federal Reserve banks (of which
the Federal Reserve Bank of New York is the most important) are
controlled by their shareholders, which are private banking institutions. In other words, "the Fed" as it is known in the US, which

is responsible for monetary policy and hence money creation for the nation, is actually controlled by private financial interests.

Currency Systems and 'Economic Conquest'

In Eastern Europe, in the former Soviet Union and in the Balkans, extending into Central Asia, the dollar and the Euro are competing with one another. Ultimately, control over national currency systems is the basis upon which countries are colonized. While the US dollar prevails throughout the Western Hemisphere, the Euro and the US dollar are clashing in the former Soviet Union, Central Asia, Sub-Saharan Africa and the Middle East.

In the Balkans and the Baltic States, central banks largely operate as colonial style "currency boards" invariably using the Euro as a proxy currency. What this means is that German and European financial interests are in control of money creation and credit. In other words, the pegging of the national currency to the Euro— rather than to the US dollar—means that both the currency and the monetary system will be in the hands of German-EU banking interests.

More generally, the Euro dominates in Germany's hinterland: Eastern Europe, the Baltic States and the Balkans, whereas the US dollar tends to prevail in the Caucasus and Central Asia. In GUUAM countries (which have military cooperation agreements with Washington) the dollar tends (with the exception of the Ukraine) to overshadow the Euro.

The "dollarization" of national currencies is an integral part of America's SRS. The SRS consists of first destabilizing and then replacing national currencies with the American greenback over an area extending from the Mediterranean to China's Western border. The underlying objective is to extend the dominion of the Federal Reserve System—namely, Wall Street—over a vast territory.

What we are dealing with is an "imperial" scramble for control over national currencies. Control over money creation and credit is an integral part of the process of economic conquest, which in turn is supported by the militarization of the Eurasian corridor.

While American and German-EU banking interests are clashing over the control of national economies and currency systems, they seem to have agreed on "sharing the spoils"—i.e., establishing their respective "spheres of influence". Reminiscent of the policies of "partition" in the late 19th century, the US and Germany have agreed upon the division of the Balkans: Germany has gained control over national currencies in Croatia, Bosnia and Kosovo, where the Euro is legal tender. In return, the US has established a permanent military presence in the region (i.e., the Bondsteel military base in Kosovo).

Cross-cutting Military Alliances

The rift between Anglo-American and Franco-German weapons producers—including the rifts within the Western military alliance—seem to have favored increased military cooperation between Russia on the one hand, and France and Germany on the other.

In recent years, both France and Germany have entered into bilateral discussions with Russia in the areas of defense production, aerospace research and military cooperation. In late 1998, Paris and Moscow agreed to undertake joint infantry exercises and bilateral military consultations. In turn, Moscow has been seeking German and French partners to participate in the development of its military industrial complex.

In early 2000, Germany's Defense Minister, Rudolph Sharping, visited Moscow for bilateral consultations with his Russian counterpart. A bilateral agreement was signed pertaining to 33 military cooperation projects, including the training of Russian military specialists in Germany.[33] This agreement was reached outside the framework of NATO, and without prior consultation with Washington.

Russia also signed a "long term military cooperation agreement" with India in late 1998, which was followed a few months later by a defense agreement between India and France. The agreement between Delhi and Paris included the transfer of French military technology, as well as investment by French multinationals in India's defense industry. The latter investment includes facilities for the production of ballistic missiles and nuclear warheads, in which the French companies have expertise.

This Franco-Indian agreement has a direct bearing on Indo-Pakistani relations. It also impinges upon US strategic interests in Central and South Asia. While Washington has been pumping military aid into Pakistan, India is being supported by France and Russia.

Visibly, France and the US are on opposite sides of the India-Pakistan conflict.

With Pakistan and India at the brink of war, in the immediate wake of September 11, 2001, the US Air Force had virtually taken control of Pakistan's air space, as well as several of its military facilities. Meanwhile, barely a few weeks into the 2001 bombing of Afghanistan, France and India conducted joint military exercises in the Arabian Sea. Also in the immediate wake of September 11, India took delivery of large quantities of Russian weapons, under the Indo-Russian military cooperation agreement.

Moscow's New National Security Doctrine

US post-Cold War era foreign policy had designated Central Asia and the Caucasus as a "strategic area". Yet this policy no longer consisted in containing the "spread of communism", but rather in preventing Russia and China from becoming competing capitalist powers. In this regard, the US had increased its military presence along the entire 40th parallel, extending from Bosnia and Kosovo to the former Soviet republics of Georgia, Azerbaijan, Turkmenistan and Uzbekistan, all of which had entered into bilateral military agreements with Washington.

The 1999 war in Yugoslavia and the subsequent outbreak of war in Chechnya in September 1999 were crucial turning points in Russian-American relations. They also marked a rapprochement between Moscow and Beijing and the signing of several military cooperation agreements between Russia and China.

US covert support to the two main Chechen rebel groups (through Pakistan's ISI) was known to the Russian government and military. (For further details, see Chapter II.) However, it had never previously been made public or raised at the diplomatic level. In November 1999, the Russian Defense Minister, Igor Sergueyev, formally accused Washington of supporting the Chechen rebels. Following a meeting held behind closed doors with Russia's military high command, Sergueyev declared that:

> "The national interests of the United States require that the military conflict in the Caucasus [Chechnya] be a fire, provoked as a result of outside forces," while adding that "the West's policy constitutes a challenge launched to Russia with the ultimate aim of weakening her international position and of excluding her from geo-strategic areas".[34]

In early 2000, in the wake of the Chechen war, a new "National Security Doctrine" was formulated and signed into law by President Vladimir Putin. Barely acknowledged by the international media, a critical shift in East-West relations had occurred. The document reasserted the building of a strong Russian state, the concurrent growth of the military and the reintroduction of state controls over foreign capital.

The document carefully spelled out what it described as "fundamental threats" to Russia's national security and sovereignty. More specifically, it referred to "the strengthening of military-political blocs and alliances" (namely GUUAM), as well as to "NATO's eastward expansion" while underscoring "the possible emergence of foreign military bases and major military presences in the immediate proximity of Russian borders".[35]

The document confirmed that "international terrorism is waging an open campaign to destabilize Russia". While not referring explicitly to CIA covert activities in support of armed terrorist groups, such as the Chechen rebels, it nonetheless called for appropriate "actions to avert and intercept intelligence and subversive activities by foreign states against the Russian Federation".[36]

Undeclared War Between Russia and America

The cornerstone of US foreign policy was to encourage—under the disguise of "peace-keeping" and "conflict resolution"—the formation of small pro-US states, which lie strategically at the hub of the Caspian Sea basin, which contains vast oil and gas reserves:

> The US must play an increasingly active role in conflict resolution in the region. The boundaries of the Soviet republics were intentionally drawn to prevent secession by the various national communities of the former USSR and not with an eye towards possible independence .... Neither Europe, nor our allies in East Asia, can defend our [US] mutual interests in these regions. If we [the US] fail to take the lead in heading off the kinds of conflicts and crises that are already looming there, that will eventually exacerbate our relations with Europe and possibly Northeast Asia. It will encourage the worst kind of political developments in Russia. This linkage, or interconnectedness, gives the Transcaucasus and Central Asia a strategic importance to the United States and its allies that we overlook at huge risk. To put it another way, the fruits accruing from ending the Cold War are far from fully harvested. To ignore the Transcaucasus and Central Asia could mean that a large part of that harvest will never be gathered.[37]

Russia's Military Industrial Complex

Alongside the articulation of Moscow's National Security doctrine, the Russian State was planning to regain economic and financial control over key areas of Russia's military industrial complex. For instance, the formation of "a single corporation of designers and manufacturers of all anti-aircraft complexes" was envisaged in cooperation with Russia's defense contractors.[38]

This proposed "re-centralization" of Russia's defense industry, in response to national security considerations, was also motivated by the merger of major Western competitors in the area of military procurement. The development of new production and scientific capabilities was also contemplated, based on enhancing Russia's military potential as well as its ability to compete with its Western rivals in the global weapons market.

The National Security Doctrine also "eases the criteria by which Russia could use nuclear weapons ... which would be permissible if the country's existence were threatened".[39]

> Russia reserves the right to use all forces and means at its disposal, including nuclear weapons, in case an armed aggression creates a threat to the very existence of the Russian Federation as an independent sovereign state.[40]

In response to Washington's "Star Wars" initiative, Moscow had developed "Russia's Missile and Nuclear Shield". The Russian government announced in 1998 the development of a new generation of intercontinental ballistic missiles, known as Topol-M (SS-27). These new single-warhead missiles (based in the Saratov region) are currently in "full combat readiness", against a "pre-emptive first strike" from the US, which (in the wake of 9/11) constitutes the Pentagon's main assumption in an eventual nuclear war. "The Topol M is lightweight and mobile, designed to be fired from a vehicle. Its mobility means it is better protected than a silo-based missile from a pre-emptive first strike."[41]

Following the adoption of the National Security Document (NSD) in 2000, the Kremlin confirmed that it would not exclude "a first-strike use" of nuclear warheads "if attacked even by purely conventional means".[42]

Political 'Turnaround' under President Vladimir Putin

The foreign policy directions of the Putin Administration remain unclear. There are significant divisions within both the political establishment and the military. On the diplomatic front, President Putin has sought a "rapprochement" with Washington and the Western Military Alliance in the "war on terrorism".

In the wake of 9/11, a significant turnaround in Russian foreign policy, largely orchestrated by President Putin, has occurred. The Putin Administration, acting against the Russian Duma, has, nonetheless, accepted the process of "NATO Enlargement" into the Baltic states (Latvia, Lithuania and Estonia) implying the establishment of NATO military bases on Russia's western border.

Meanwhile, Moscow's military cooperation agreement signed with Beijing after the 1999 war in Yugoslavia was virtually on hold:

> China is obviously watching with deep concern Russia surrendering these positions. China is also concerned by the presence of the US Air Force close to its borders in Uzbekistan, Tajikistan and the Kyrghyz Republic. ... Everything that Mr. Putin has earned through the spectacular improvement of Russia's relations with China, India, Vietnam, Cuba and some other countries collapsed nearly overnight. What has surfaced is a primitive Gorbachev concept of "common human values"—i.e., the subordination of Russia's interests to those of the West.[43]

Ironically, the Russian President was supporting America's "war on terrorism", which is ultimately directed against Moscow. Washington's hidden agenda is to dismantle Russia's strategic and economic interests in the Eurasian corridor and close down or take over its military facilities, while transforming the former Soviet republics (and eventually the Russian Federation) into American protectorates:

> It becomes clear that the intention to join NATO, expressed by Mr. Putin in an offhand manner last year [2000], reflected a long matured idea of a far deeper (i.e., in relation to the positions previously taken by Gorbachev or Yeltsin) integration of the Russian Federation into the "international community". In fact, the intention is to squeeze Russia into the Western economic, political and military system. Even as a junior partner. Even at the price of sacrificing an independent foreign policy.[44]

Notes

1. Quoted in Mary-Wynne Ashford, "Bombings Reignite Nuclear War Fears", *The Victoria Times-Colonist.* 13 May 1999, p. A15. Mary-Wynne Ashford is co-president of the Nobel Peace Prize winning IPPNW.

2. Quoted in Mary-Wynne Ashford, *op. cit.*

3. According to Viktor Chechevatov, a Three-star General and Commander of ground forces in Russia's Far East, quoted in *The Boston Globe,* 8 April 1999, emphasis added.

4. Ashford, *op. cit.*

5. Douglas Mattern, "The United States of Enron-Pentagon, Inc", Centre for Research on Globalization, http://www.globalresearch.ca/articles/MAT202A.html, February 2002.

6. *Ibid.*

7. See "Intelligence Funding and the War on Terror", CDI Terrorism Project at http://www.cdi.org/terrorism/intel-funding-pr.cfm, 2 February 2002. See also Patrick Martin, "Billions for War and Repression: Bush Budget for a Garrison State", World Socialist Website (WSWS), http://www.wsws.org/articles/2002/feb2002/mili-f06.shtml, 6 February 2002.

8. Federation of American Scientists (FAS) at http://www.fas.org/faspir/2001/.

9. George W. Bush, *State of the Union Address*, 29 January 2002.

10. For further details on HAARP, see Michel Chossudovsky, "Washington's New World Order Weapons Have the Ability to Trigger Climate Change", Centre for Research on Globalization at globalresearch.ca, http://globalresearch.ca/articles/CHO201A.html, January 2002.

11. See Bob Fitrakis, "Chemtrails Outlaw", Centre for Research on Globalization (CRG), http://www.globalresearch.ca/articles/FIT203A.html, 6 March 2002. See also Air University of the US Air Force, AF 2025 Final Report, http://www.au.af.mil/au/2025/.

12. John Isaacs, President of the Council for a Livable World quoted in Paul Richter, "US Works Up Plan for Using Nuclear Arms", *Los Angeles Times*, 9 March 2002.

13. Paul Richter, "US Works Up Plan for Using Nuclear Arms", *Los Angeles Times*, 9 March 2002.

14. Quoted in *The Houston Chronicle*, 20 October 2001.

15. Cynthia Greer, *The Philadelphia Inquirer*, 16 October 2000.

16. *Ibid.*

17. William Arkin, "Secret Plan Outlines the Unthinkable", *Los Angeles Times*, 9 March 2002.

18. *Ibid.*

19. *Ibid.*

20. *Mother Jones*, "Taiwan wants bigger Slingshot", http://www.mojones.com/arms/taiwan.html, 2000.

21. Deutsche Press Agentur, 27 February 2000.

22. Japan Economic Newswire, March 4, 2000.

23. AFP, 12 December 2001.

24. William Arkin, *op. cit.*

25. Reuters, 5 February 2000.

26. For further details see Vago Muradian, "Pentagon Sees Bridge to Europe", *Defense Daily*, Vol. 204, No. 40, 1 December 1999.

27. *Ibid.*

28. *Ibid.* See also Michel Collon's analysis in *Poker Menteur*, Editions EPO, Brussels, 1998, p. 156.

29. *Ibid.*, p. 156.

30. "American Monsters, European Minnows: Defense Companies." *The Economist*, 13 January 1996.

31. British Aerospace Systems'home page at: http://www.BAESystems.com/globalfootprint/northamerica/northamerica.htm.

32. "BAES, EADS Hopeful that Bush will broaden Transatlantic Cooperation", *Defense Daily International*, 29, 2001.

33. Interfax, 1 March 2000.

34. See *The New York Times*, 15 November 1999; see also the article of Steve Levine, *The New York Times*, 20 November 1999.

35. To consult the document, see Federation of American Scientists (FAS), http://www.fas.org/nuke/guide/russia/doctrine/gazeta012400.htm.

36. *Ibid.*

37. Joseph Jofi, *Pipeline Diplomacy: The Clinton Administration's Fight for Baku-Ceyhan*, Woodrow Wilson Case Study, No. 1. Princeton University, 1999.

38. Mikhail Kozyrev, "The White House Calls for the Fire", *Vedomosti*, Nov. 1, 1999, p.1.

39. See Andrew Jack, "Russia Turns Back Clock", *Financial Times*, London, 15 January 2000, p.1.

40. Quoted in Nicolai Sokov, "Russia's New National Security Concept: The Nuclear Angle", Centre for Non Proliferation Studies, Monterrey, http://cns.miis.edu/
pubs/reports/sokov2.htm, January 2000.

41. BBC, "Russia Deploys New Nuclear Missiles", London, 27 December 1998.

42. Stephen J. Blank, "Nuclear Strategy and Nuclear Proliferation in Russian Commission to Assess the Ballistic Missile Threat to the United States", Appendix III: *Unclassified Working Papers*, Federation of American Scientists (FAS),

http://www.fas.org/irp/threat/missile/rumsfeld/toc-3.htm. Washington DC, undated.

43. V. Tetekin, "Putin's Ten Blows", Centre for Research on Globalization (CRG) http://globalresearch.ca/articles/TET112A.html, 27 December 2001.

44. *Ibid.*

CHAPTER VIII
The American Empire

> We are on the verge of global transformation.
> All we need is the right major crisis and the
> nations will accept the New World Order.
>
> *David Rockefeller*
> *Statement to the United Nations*
> *Business Council, 1994*

War Without Borders

In the aftermath of September 11, 2001, the world is at an important crossroads in its history. The "campaign against terrorism"
constitutes a "war of conquest" with devastating consequences for
the future of humanity.

America's New War is not confined to Central Asia. Using the
"war on terrorism" as a pretext, the Bush administration had
announced already in 2001, the extension of US military operations into new frontiers, including Iraq, Iran and North Korea.
While accusing these countries of developing "weapons of mass
destruction", Washington has not excluded itself from using nuclear
weapons as part of the "war on terrorism".

Moreover, Israel, which now possesses an arsenal of at least 200
thermonuclear weapons with a sophisticated delivery system, "has
made countless veiled nuclear threats against the Arab nations".[1]

The ongoing war waged by Israel against the Palestinian people
is part and parcel of America's New War strategy. The 2003 invasion of Iraq could trigger a broader war throughout the Middle

East in which Israel would be aligned with the Anglo-American military axis.

In 2001, military planners at the Pentagon had drawn up a "blueprint for a two-pronged invasion of Iraq involving up to 100,000 US troops".[2] Gun boats were on standby in the Gulf of Oman. "Military contingency plans [were] being refined for Somalia, Sudan, Iraq, Indonesia and Yemen. ... Special forces and US intelligence agencies are active overtly and covertly in all of these countries with local militias or militaries."[3] Meanwhile, Britain had been asked by the US "to help prepare military strikes against Somalia in the next phase of the global campaign against Osama bin Laden's Al Qaeda".[4]

The War on Afghanistan was Illegal

In launching the war on Afghanistan in October 2001, the Bush administration—with the full support and military backing of Britain, and with the prior consent of member governments of the Western military alliance—is in blatant violation of international law:

> This war is illegal because it is a flagrant violation of the express words of the Charter of the United Nations. ... In fact, it is not only illegal, it's criminal. It is what the Nuremberg Tribunal called "the supreme crime", the crime against peace.[5]

In turn, these same political leaders, responsible for thousands of civilian deaths in Afghanistan, have launched a process within their respective countries, which recasts—in the framework of the "anti-terrorist legislation"—the *legal definition* of "terrorism" and "war crimes".

In other words, the actual protagonists of state terrorism— namely, our elected politicians—can now arbitrarily decide, through their "legally constituted" secret tribunals, "who are the war criminals" and "who are the terrorists". Ironically, the "elite war criminals"—using the powers of high office—decide who can be prosecuted. Moreover, by derogating the Rule of Law and setting up kangaroo courts, their own "hands are clean"—i.e., they will not be prosecuted on charges of war crimes: they cannot be blamed since these military tribunals will ultimately decide if an accused person should be executed.

The American Empire

The onslaught of the US-led war also coincides with a worldwide depression, leading to the impoverishment of millions of people. While the civilian economy plummets, extensive financial resources are funneled towards America's war machine. The most advanced weapons systems are being developed by America's military-industrial complex with a view to achieving a position of global military and economic dominance, not only in relation to China and Russia, but also in relation to the European Union, which Washington considers as an encroachment upon America's global hegemony.

Behind America's "war on terrorism" is the militarization of vast regions of the world, leading to the consolidation of what is best described as the "American Empire". Since the 1999 war in Yugoslavia, an Anglo-American military axis has developed, based on a close coordination between Britain and the US in defense, foreign policy and intelligence. Israel is the launch pad of the Anglo-American axis in the Middle East. The objective behind this war is to "re-colonize" not only China and the countries of the former Soviet block, but also Iran, Iraq and the Indian peninsula.

War and globalization go hand in hand. The powers of the Wall Street financial establishment, the Anglo-American oil giants and the US-U.K. defense contractors are undeniably behind this process, which consists in extending the frontiers of the global market system. Ultimately, the purpose of "America's New War" is to transform sovereign nations into open territories (or "free trade areas"), both through "military means", as well as through the imposition of deadly "free market" reforms.

Defined under Washington's 1999 SRS, America's war is intent upon destroying an entire region, which, in the course of history, was the cradle of ancient civilizations linking Western Europe to the Far East. In turn, covert support to Islamic insurgencies (channeled by the CIA through Pakistan's ISI) in the former Soviet Union, the Middle East, China and India has been used by Washington as an instrument of conquest—ie. by deliberately destabilizing national societies and fostering ethnic and social divisions.

More generally, war and "free market" reforms *destroy civilization* by forcing national societies into abysmal poverty.

America's NATO Partners

While significant divisions have emerged within the Western military alliance, America's NATO partners including Germany, France and Italy, have nonetheless endorsed the 2001 US-U.K.-led military operation into Afghanistan. Despite their differences, Europe and America appear to be united in the planned "re-colonization" and "partition" of a broad geographic area extending from Eastern Europe and the Balkans to China's Western frontier.

Within this broad region, "spheres of influence" have nonetheless been agreed upon largely between Germany and America. This "partition" must be understood in historical terms. It is, in some regards, similar to the agreement reached between the European powers at the Berlin Conference pertaining to the partition and territorial conquest of Africa in the late 19th century. Similarly, colonial policy in China's treaty ports in the years leading up to the First World War was carefully coordinated and agreed upon by the same imperialist powers.

The Military-Intelligence Apparatus

While civilian state institutions increasingly assume the role of a façade, elected politicians in most Western "democracies" (including the US, Britain and Canada) increasingly play a nominal role in decision-making. Under this evolving totalitarian system, the institutions of civilian government are being superseded by the military-intelligence-police apparatus (see Chapter XXI). In the US, the CIA has come to play the role of a de facto "parallel government" in charge of formulating and implementing US foreign policy.

Moreover, the intelligence apparatus in the US has been integrated into the workings of the financial system. Senior military and intelligence officials in the US have become full-fledged "partners" in a number of lucrative business undertakings.

As mentioned earlier, the CIA's official budget is in excess of $30 billion a year. This colossal amount does not include the multi-billion dollar revenues and proceeds of CIA covert operations. Documented by Alfred McCoy, the CIA has, since the Vietnam war, used the flow of dirty money from the drug trade to finance its covert operations conducted in the context of Washington's foreign policy initiatives.[6]

In other words, the extensive accumulation of money wealth from the proceeds of the drug trade has transformed the CIA into a powerful financial entity. The latter operates through a web of corporate shells, banks and financial institutions wielding tremendous power and influence.

These CIA-sponsored "corporations" have, over time, been meshed into the mainstay of the business and corporate establishment, not only in weapons production and the oil business, but also in banking and financial services, real estate, etc. In turn, billions of narco-dollars are channeled—with the support of the CIA—into the spheres of "legitimate" banking, where they are used to finance bona fide investments in a variety of economic activities.

In other words, CIA covert activities play a crucial undercover role in ensuring the appropriation of drug money by powerful financial and banking interests. In this regard, Afghanistan is strategic because it is the world's largest producer of heroin. The Taliban government was crushed on the orders of the Bush administration because it had (under United Nations guidance) curbed opium production by more than 90 per cent. (See Chapter XVI.) The bombing of Afghanistan served to restore the multi-billion dollar drug trade, which is protected by the CIA. Immediately following the installation of the US puppet government, under President

Hamid Karzai, opium production soared, regaining its historic levels. (See Chapter XVI.)

War: A Money Making Operation

The military-intelligence community has also developed its own money-making operations in the areas of mercenaries services, defense procurement, intelligence, etc. Key individuals in the Bush administration, including Vice-President Dick Cheney through his company, Haliburton, have links to these various business undertakings.

Under the New World Order, the pursuit of profit hinges upon political "manipulations", the bribing of officials and the routine exercise of covert intelligence operations on behalf of powerful corporate interests. The US-sponsored paramilitary armies in different parts of the world are trained and equipped by private mercenary outfits on contract to the Pentagon.

Ultimately, the conduct of war, rather than being controlled by the state, is subordinated to the pursuit of private economic interests.

While interfacing with Wall Street, intelligence agencies, including the CIA, have also developed undercover ties with powerful criminal syndicates involved in the drug trade. These syndicates, through the process of money laundering, have also invested heavily in legitimate business undertakings.

Under the New World Order, the demarcation between "organized capital" and "organized crime" is blurred. In other words, the restructuring of global trade and finance tends to favor the concurrent "globalization" of the criminal economy, which is intricately tied into the corporate establishment. In turn, the state apparatus is criminalized. Amply documented, senior policy-makers in the Bush administration in charge of foreign policy have links to various drug cartels.[7]

Dollarization and the Big Picture

While securing corporate control over extensive oil reserves and pipeline routes along the Eurasian corridor on behalf of the Anglo-American oil giants, Washington's ultimate objective is to eventually destabilize and then colonize both China and Russia. This means the takeover of their national financial systems and the control over monetary policy, leading eventually to the imposition of the US dollar as the national currency. This objective has, in part, already been achieved in parts of the former Soviet Union where the US dollar has become a de facto national currency.

While the US has established a permanent military presence on China's Western frontier, China's banking system has also been "opened up" to Western banks and financial institutions following China's accession to the World Trade Organization (WTO) in October 2001. The tendency in China is towards the demise of the state banking system, which provides credit to thousands of industrial enterprises and agricultural producers. Ironically, the system of state credit has sustained China's role as the West's largest "industrial colony", producer of cheap labour-manufactured goods for the European and American markets.

This deregulation of state credit has triggered a deadly wave of bankruptcies, which in all likelihood will devastate China's economic landscape. In turn, the restructuring of China's financial institutions could lead, within a matter of years, to the destabilization of its national currency, the Renminbi, through speculative assaults, opening the door to a broader process of economic and political "colonization" by Western capital.

In other words, the outright manipulation of currency markets by "institutional speculators", similar to that of the 1997 Asian crisis, also constitutes a powerful instrument, which contributes to the fracturing of national economies. In this regard, financial warfare applies complex speculative instruments encompassing the gamut of derivative trade, forward foreign exchange transactions, currency options, hedge funds, index funds, etc. Speculative instruments have been used with the ultimate purpose of capturing financial wealth and acquiring control over productive assets. In the words of Malaysia's former Prime Minister Mahathir Mohamad: "This deliberate devaluation of the currency of a country by currency traders purely for profit is a serious denial of the rights of independent nations."[8]

TEXT BOX 8.1

Financial Warfare: An Instrument of Conquest

In Korea, Indonesia and Thailand the vaults of the central banks were pillaged by institutional speculators, while the monetary authorities sought, in vain, to prop up their ailing currencies. The speculative assaults waged against these countries constitute a "dress rehearsal" for the application of a similar process directed against China's national currency, the Renminbi.

In 1997, more than $100 billion of Asia's hard currency reserves were confiscated and transferred (in a matter of months) into private financial hands. In the wake of the currency devaluations, real earnings and employment plummeted virtually overnight, leading to mass poverty in countries which had, in the post-war period, registered significant economic and social progress.

The financial scam in the foreign exchange market had destabilised national economies, thereby creating the preconditions for the subsequent plunder of the Asian countries' productive assets by "vulture foreign investors".

The Demise of Central Banking

This worldwide crisis marks the demise of central banking, meaning the derogation of national economic sovereignty and the inability of the national state to control money creation on behalf of society. In other words, privately held money reserves in the hands of "institutional speculators" far exceed the limited capabilities of the world's central banks. The latter, acting individually or collectively, are no longer able to fight the tide of speculative activity.

Monetary policy is in the hands of private creditors who have the ability to freeze state budgets, paralyse the payments process, thwart the regular disbursement of wages to millions of workers (as in the former Soviet Union) and precipitate the collapse of production and social programs. As the crisis deepens, speculative raids on central banks are extending into China, Latin America and the Middle East with devastating economic and social consequences.[9]

Together with the liberalization of trade and the deregulation of agriculture and industry (in accordance with WTO rules), China is heading towards massive unemployment and social unrest. In turn, the US-sponsored covert operations in Tibet and the Xinjiang-Uigur Autonomous Region, in support of secessionist movements, contribute to fostering political instability, which in turn tends to support the "dollarization" process.

More generally, the deregulation of national banking institutions has created havoc worldwide. Washington's foreign policy agenda consists in eventually encroaching upon the Euro and imposing the US dollar as a "global currency" (in overt confrontation with the powerful banking interests behind the European currency system). "Militarization" of vast regions of the world (e.g., where the dollar and the Euro are competing) tends to support the "dollarization" process. In other words, "dollarization" and "free trade"—supported by US militarization—constitute two essential pillars of the American Empire.

Militarization and Dollarization of the Western Hemisphere

In the Western hemisphere, Wall Street has already extended its control by displacing or taking over existing national financial institutions. With the help of the IMF, Washington is also bullying Latin American countries into accepting the US dollar as their national currency. The greenback has already been imposed on five Latin American countries including Ecuador, Argentina, Panama, El Salvador and Guatemala.

The economic and social consequences of "dollarization" have been devastating. In these countries, Wall Street and the US Federal Reserve system directly control monetary policy. The entire structure of public expenditure is controlled by US creditors.

"Militarization" and "dollarization" are the essential building blocks of the American Empire. In this regard, "Plan Colombia", financed by US military aid, constitutes the basis for militarizing the Andean region of South America in support of "free trade" and "dollarization".

Meanwhile, the same Anglo-American oil companies (Chevron-Texaco, BP, Exxon-Mobil), which are vying for control over the oil wealth of the former Soviet Union, are also present in the Andean region of South America. Under the disguise of the "war on drugs" or the "war on terrorism", US foreign policy has led to the militarization of both of these regions. The hidden agenda is to protect both the oil pipelines and the powerful financial interests behind the multibillion dollar drug trade. In Colombia, many of the paramilitary groups "responsible for hundreds of murders and thousands of disappearances" are financed by US military assistance under Plan Colombia.[10]

In turn, Plan Colombia is implemented in close liaison with the imposition of IMF "guidelines". In Colombia, for example, the IMF's economic medicine has led to the destruction of domestic industry and agriculture. More generally, the militarization of the continent is an integral part of the "Free Trade" Agenda. The Free Trade Area of the Americas (FTAA) initiative is being negotiated alongside a "parallel" military cooperation protocol signed by 27 countries of the Americas (the Declaration of Manaus), which virtually puts the entire hemisphere under the military control of the US.

Already in Latin America, the economic and social consequences of "dollarization" have been devastating. The current economic and social crisis in Argentina is the direct result of "dollarization" imposed by Wall Street and the US Federal Reserve system, which directly control monetary policy. The entire structure of Argentinean public expenditure is controlled by US creditors.

Real wages have collapsed, social programs have been destroyed and large sectors of the population have been driven into abysmal poverty. The Argentinean pattern, engineered by Wall Street, will undoubtedly be replicated elsewhere as the "invisible fist" of the American Empire extends its reach to other regions of the world.

Notes

1. John Steinbach, "Israeli Weapons of Mass Destruction: A Threat to Peace", DC Iraq Coalition, March 2002, Centre for Research on Globalization (CRG), http://www.globalresearch.ca/articles/STE203A.html, 3 March 2002.

2. Iain Bruce, "Pentagon Draws up Plans for Invasion of Iraq", *The Herald* (Scotland) January 31, 2002.

3. *Florida Times-Union*, Jacksonville, 17 February 2002.

4. Deirdre Griswold, "Will Somalia be next? US targets another Poor Country", *Workers World*, December 2001, Centre for Research on Globalization (CRG), http://globalresearch.ca/articles/GRI112A.html, 13 December 2001.

5. Michael Mandel, "This War is Illegal and Immoral: It will not Prevent Terrorism", Science Peace Forum & Teach-In, December 9, 2001, Centre for Research on Globalization, http://globalresearch.ca/articles/MAN112A.html, Dec. 2001.

6. Alfred McCoy, *op. cit.*

7. For further details see Michel Chossudovsky, "Globalization and the Criminalization of Economic Activity", *Covert Action Quarterly*, No. 58, Fall 1996; Michel Chossudovsky, "Financial Scams and the Bush Family", Centre for Research on Globalization (CRG), http://www.globalresearch.ca/articles/CHO202C.html, 18 February 2002.

8. Quoted in Michel Chossudovsky, "Financial Warfare", Third World Network, Penang, http://www.twnside.org.sg/title/trig-cn.htm. 1999.

9. Michel Chossudovsky, "Financial Warfare", *op. cit.*

10. See Kim Alphandary, "Colombia War: 'Highest Priority'", Centre for Research on Globalization (CRG), http://www.globalresearch.ca/articles/ALP204A.html, 5 April 2002.

CHAPTER IX
Disarming the New World Order

The "war on terrorism" is a lie. Amply documented, the pretext to wage this war is totally fabricated.

Realities have been turned upside down.

Acts of war are heralded as "humanitarian interventions" geared towards restoring "democracy".

Military occupation and the killing of civilians are presented as "peace-keeping operations".

The derogation of civil liberties—by imposing the "anti-terrorist legislation"—is portrayed as a means to providing "domestic security" and upholding civil liberties.

Meanwhile, expenditures on health and education are curtailed to finance the military-industrial complex and the police state.

Under the American Empire, millions of people around the world are being driven into abysmal poverty, and countries are being transformed into open territories.

US protectorates are installed with the blessing of the "international community".

"Interim governments" are formed. Political puppets designated by America's oil giants are casually endorsed by the United Nations, which increasingly performs the role of a rubber-stamp for the US Administration.

When viewed historically, "September 11" is the biggest fraud in American history.

Totalitarian State

We are fast moving towards a totalitarian system in which the institutions of war, police repression and economic policy (i.e., "strong economic medicine") interface with one another.

This system relies on the manipulation of public opinion. The "fabricated realities" of the Bush administration must become indelible truths, which form part of a broad political and media consensus. In this regard, the corporate media is an instrument of this totalitarian system. It has carefully excluded, from the outset, any real understanding of the September 11 crisis.

Millions of people have been misled regarding the causes and consequences of September 11.

While the Bush administration implements a "war on terrorism", the evidence (including mountains of official documents) amply confirms that successive US Administrations have supported, abetted and harbored international terrorism.

This fact, in itself, must be suppressed because if it ever trickles down to the broader public, the legitimacy of the "war on terrorism" collapses "like a deck of cards". In the process, the legitimacy of the main actors behind this system is threatened, so they enact new laws to protect themselves:

> We are becoming a banana republic here in the United States, with "disappeared" people, which was the phenomenon that we all saw down in Latin American dictatorships in the 1970s and 1980s, with the support, by the way, of the United States Government.[1]

Disarming the New World Order

Militarization, covert intelligence operations and outright war support the extension of the "free market" economy into new frontiers. The development of America's war machine supports an unprecedented accumulation of private wealth into fewer and fewer hands, which threatens the future of humanity.

The dangers of a possible Third World War must be addressed and understood. To disarm the New World Order, the inner features of this totalitarian system must be revealed and fully understood. This understanding must not be confined to a handful of writers and critics, it must be shared by all our fellow citizens, whose lives are directly affected by the "war on terrorism".

An understanding of this system is required to develop cohesive mass movements, which will reverse the tide and prevent the onslaught of a World War.

The workings of global capitalism and of the "free market" economy are intricately tied to the corridors of power. The powers behind this system are those of the global banks and financial institutions, the military-industrial complex, the oil and energy giants, the biotech-pharmaceutical conglomerates and the powerful media and communications giants, which fabricate the news and overtly distort the course of world events.

To effectively disarm this system, it is not sufficient to call for the "democratization" of the financial system, coupled with "reforms" of global institutions (such as the IMF, World Bank, WTO and the UN). These "reforms" do not change the workings of global capitalism, nor do they in any way upset the underlying power structures. In fact, the New World Order not only allows, but actively encourages this type of cosmetic "reform", which provides the illusion that "the globalizers" are somehow committed to progressive change.

Sustaining the Illusion of Democracy

The Bush administration requires "legitimacy" in the eyes of public opinion, namely, that in launching the "war on terrorism", it is acting in the best interests of society, with the full endorsement of the American people and with the backing of the "international community".

To effectively build this "legitimacy", the Bush administration not only needs to uphold the falsehoods behind the "war on terrorism", it also needs to sustain the illusion that constitutional democracy continues to prevail.

Sustaining the "freedom and democracy rhetoric" is part of the process of building a totalitarian State. While "legitimate dissent" is encouraged, democracy requires that "civil liberties be balanced against public safety":

> Our response to the threat of terrorism, in the context of systemic vulnerability, will have an impact both on the cost of providing security and on the civil liberties prized in many communities.[2]

Fabricating Dissent

To convey the illusion of democracy, "the globalizers" must "fabricate dissent". In other words, they must create, covet and finance their own political opposition. In order to appear legitimate, they must actively encourage the type of "criticism" which does not challenge "their right to rule".

This libertarian "counter-discourse"—which serves to disarm a genuine mass movement against war and globalization—constitutes part of the foundations of this evolving totalitarian system. Leaders of trade union confederations and mainstream NGOs, together with selected "academics" and critics, are invited to participate in policy formulation together with bankers, corporate executives and politicians.

The ploy is to selectively handpick civil society leaders "whom we can trust" and integrate them into a "dialogue". The idea is to cut them off from their rank and file, make them feel that they are "global citizens" acting on behalf of their fellow citizens, but make them act in a way which serves the interests of the corporate establishment:

> Business, government and civil society leaders must have the creativity to forge new institutional arrangements for a more inclusive global economy.[3]

This ritual of "civil society participation" serves several important functions. In the US it requires these "progressive" leaders to accept the fundamental premise that the Bush administration is waging a campaign against international terrorism in response to the events of September 11. In the words of Edward Herman and David Peterson, "this ['leftist accommodation'] … of leaning over backwards to downplay the US terrorist role, merges into a serious misreading of ongoing events".[4]

Once the fundamental premise that the US Administration is committed to curbing international terrorism is accepted, these leftist intellectuals and civil society critics are invited to express their "reservations" regarding America's conduct of the war, the impacts on civilians or their humanitarian concerns regarding the derogation of the Rule of Law.

In this ritual, the main justification for waging the war, which is a complete falsehood, is never questioned despite documented evidence that the "war on terrorism" is a fabrication. For instance, numerous NGOs have accused the Bush administration for having breached the 1949 Geneva Convention on the treatment of prisoners of war, yet these same organizations have failed to question the overall legitimacy of the Bush administration's "war on terrorism".

While the "globalizers" are subjected to "constructive criticism", their legitimate right to rule remains unchallenged. What this "left accommodation" and "civil society mingling" does is to reinforce the clutch of the military-intelligence elites and the corporate establishment, while weakening the real protest movement.

More importantly, "left accommodation" splits up the protest movement. It divides the anti-war movement from the anti-globalization movement. It prevents the development of a broader movement against the American Empire. The large trade unions and the mainstream non-governmental organizations, by failing to denounce the falsehoods behind the "war on terrorism", have contributed unwittingly to the failure of a real opposition movement being mounted against the New World Order.

In the words of AFL-CIO president John Sweeney: "We are all angry; let our anger be directed at the real enemy. The terrorists and those who supported them must be brought to justice."[5]

Building Meaningful Mass Movements

We are at the juncture of one of the most important social struggles in world history, requiring an unprecedented degree of solidarity and commitment. America's New War, which includes the "first strike" use of nuclear weapons, threatens the future of humanity as we know it. This is by no means an overstatement.

Some people believe that this New World Order can be changed by developing "new ideas" (or "paradigms") regarding "alternative forms of economic and social organization" and that government policy will somehow adjust and encompass these new concepts. This viewpoint—which is fashionable among civil society advocates—calls for dialogue, debate and discussion with elected politicians concerning reforms and "alternatives".

More importantly, this left accommodation does not question the legitimacy of the elected politicians who have unequivocally endorsed the "war on terrorism". It often trivializes the seriousness of the post-September 11 crisis. It fails to recognize that the US is involved in a war of conquest. It does not address the relationship between the objectives of war and global capitalism. In other words, it dares not look behind the curtain to see who is really driving the hidden agenda. Nor does it address the fact that Western heads of state and heads of government, in endorsing America's war, have blatantly violated international law and are also responsible—together with the Bush administration—for crimes against humanity.

Establishing an "alternative economic and social system" through an abstract set of principles does not, in itself, address the nature of the World Order and the power structures which underlie it.

The abstract formulation of "an alternative" does not ensure that meaningful change will be forthcoming and that the workings of contemporary capitalism will be modified. These workings—which are the result of complex manoeuvers between the business elites and the military-intelligence establishment—cannot be undone simply by formulating a new paradigm, or by calling for a more "Just World" or by presenting demands and/or petitions to the G-7 political leaders who are, themselves, the lackeys of the New World Order.

To bring about meaningful change, the balance of power within society must be modified.

The backbone of this system is militarization, which in turn endorses and enforces the capitalist market system. One cannot disarm the "invisible fist" of the "free market" without concurrently dismantling the military and intelligence apparatus which supports it. Military bases must be closed down; the war machine—including the production of advanced weapons systems—must be dismantled, implying a dramatic shift into civilian production.

Disarming the New World Order also requires a transformation of the structures of ownership, namely the disempowering of banks, financial institutions and transnational corporations, as well as a radical overhaul of the state apparatus. All these issues are complex and will require careful debate and analysis in the years ahead.

The first priority, in this regard, is to stall the privatization of collective assets, infrastructure, public utilities (including water and electricity), state institutions (such as hospitals and schools), the commons, communal lands, etc.

Yet it should be understood that this process—which in itself requires a meaningful debate on policy alternatives—cannot commence unless the falsehoods which provide "legitimacy" to war and globalization are fully revealed and understood by all.

This struggle requires breaking the legitimacy of the system and those who rule in our name. Politicians who are war criminals must be removed. The judicial system must be transformed. The banking system must be overhauled, etc. But none of this is possible as long as citizens continue to blindly uphold the neoliberal agenda.

The legitimacy of the New World Order system must be undone.

Social Movements

At the present juncture, social movements are in a state of disarray. Labour leaders and leftist politicians have been co-opted.

Against this background, the anti-globalization protest movement seems to have coalesced around the "Counter-Summit" or

"People's Summit", held in parallel to various "official" venues such as the G-7, G-8 meetings, or those of the Bretton Woods institutions: namely the World Bank and IMF and also the annual World Economic Forum, usually held in Davos, Switzerland.

These international venues—while bringing together activists from around the world—tend to be dominated by a handful of intellectuals and civil society organizers which set the agenda. The same personalities travel to these various international venues which, over the years, have become heavily ritualized.

The Funding of Dissent

These international conferences and teach-ins are often financed by government grants and donations from the large private foundations (Ford Foundation, MacArthur Foundation, etc.).

This "funding of dissent" plays a key role. It essentially circumscribes the boundaries of dissent. In other words, one cannot meaningfully question the legitimacy of the governments and business corporations while, at the same time, expecting them to foot the bill. The "funding of dissent" ensures that these organizations will criticize the system without going against their government and corporate sponsors. In other words, they will not take a lead in the development of a meaningful mass movement.

Many of the organizations involved have, in the process, become "lobbyists", often funded by governments or intergovernmental organizations. Demands, petitions and declarations are formulated to little avail, largely with respect to issues of debt cancellation, environmental standards and macro-economic reform, etc.

The Ritual of the Counter-Summit

The organization of international counter-summits cannot constitute the basis of this struggle. To effectively "disarm the American Empire", we must move to a higher plane by launching mass movements in our respective countries, grassroots movements—integrated nationally and internationally—which reveal the hidden face of the New World Order and bring the message of what globalization and militarization are doing to ordinary people.

Ultimately, these are the grassroots forces which must be mobilized to challenge those who threaten our collective future.

Existing mass organizations such as trade unions and non-governmental organizations, whose leaders have visibly been co-opted, must be "democratized" and reappropriated by their grass-roots. In other words, these organizations must be rebuilt from within.

This process should take place in all sectors of organized labour (industrial workers, farmers, teachers, public sector employees, professionals, etc.), eventually leading to the transformation of the national and international labour confederations. In other words, within these various organizations, leadership structures must be democratized, while setting an agenda of struggle and resistance against war and globalization.

Other sectors of society, including small and medium-sized businesses and independent producers, whose existence is threatened by the global corporations, must also address these issues within their respective organizations.

Of critical importance, this democratization process must also proceed from within the security, police and military forces with a view to effectively disarming the Empire's repressive apparatus. To succeed, dissident voices within the military, intelligence and police sectors must be fully integrated into the broader struggle.

Grass Roots Organizations
Concurrently, what is also required in each of our countries is the formation of a powerful network of local level councils in neighborhoods, work places, schools, universities, etc. which integrate millions of citizens. These national networks would in turn be integrated into a broad international movement.

The first priority for these grass-roots councils would be to break the legitimacy of global capitalism by informing, educating and sensitizing fellow citizens regarding the nature of the New World Order—i.e., uncovering the falsehoods and media lies, taking a firm position against the "war on terrorism", establishing the links between globalization and militarization, debating the concrete impacts of deadly macroeconomic reforms, etc.

The councils and their respective networks, operating nationally and internationally, would eventually become increasingly politicized, constituting the basis for organized resistance and transformation. In turn, the councils could develop, under certain circumstances, into a de facto system of parallel government.

The struggle must be broad-based and democratic, encompassing all sectors of society at all levels, in all countries, uniting in a major thrust: workers, farmers, independent producers, small businesses, professionals, artists, civil servants, members of the clergy, students and intellectuals.

The anti-war, anti-globalization, environmentalist, civil rights and anti-racism coalitions must unite. "Single issue" groups must join hands in a common understanding on how the New World Order is threatening our collective future on this planet.

This global struggle directed against the American Empire is fundamental, requiring a degree of solidarity and internationalism unprecedented in world history.

The global economic system feeds on social divisiveness between and within countries. Unity of purpose and worldwide coordination among diverse groups and social movements is crucial. A major thrust is required which brings together social movements in all major regions of the world, in common pursuit of and commitment to the elimination of poverty and a lasting world peace.

Notes

1. Christopher Bollyn, "In the Name of Security, Thousands Denied Constitutional Rights", *American Free Press*, 29 November 2001.

2. 2002 World Economic Forum, http://www.weforum.org/.

3. In the words of Ed Mayo, Executive Director of the New Economics Foundation at the 2002 New York World Economic Forum, at http://www.weforum.org, February 2002.

4. Edward Herman and David Peterson, "Who Terrorizes Whom", *Global Outlook*, No. 1, Spring 2002, p. 47.

5. Statement by John Sweeney, President of the AFL-CIO, 14 September 2001, http://www.aflcio.org/publ/press2001/pr0916.htm.

CHAPTER X

Political Deception:
The Missing Link Behind 9/11

A Red Herring is a fallacy in which an irrelevant topic is presented in order to divert attention from the original issue.

On May 16th 2002, *The New York Post* dropped what appeared to be a bombshell: "Bush Knew." Hoping to score politically, the Democrats jumped on the bandwagon, pressuring the White House to come clean on two "top-secret documents" made available to President Bush prior to September 11, concerning "advance knowledge" of Al Qaeda attacks. Meanwhile, the US media had already coined a new set of buzzwords: "Yes, there were warnings" and "clues" of possible terrorist attacks, but "there was no way President Bush could have known" what was going to happen. The Democrats agreed to "keep the cat in the bag" by saying: "Osama is at war with the US" and the FBI and the CIA knew something was cooking but "failed to connect the dots". In the words of House Minority Leader, Richard Gephardt:

> This is not blame-placing .... We support the President on the war against terrorism—have and will. But we've got to do better in preventing terrorist attacks.[1]

The media's spotlight on "foreknowledge" and "FBI lapses" served to distract public attention from the broader issue of political deception. Not a word was mentioned concerning the role of the CIA, which throughout the entire post-Cold War era, has aided and abetted Osama bin Laden's Al Qaeda as part of its covert operations.

Of course they knew! The foreknowledge issue is a red herring. The "Islamic Militant Network" is a creation of the CIA. (See Chapter II.) In standard CIA jargon, Al Qaeda is categorized as an "intelligence asset". Support to terrorist organizations is an integral part of US foreign policy. Al Qaeda continues to participate in CIA covert operations in different parts of the world. (See Chapter IV.)

While individual FBI agents are often unaware of the CIA's role, the relationship between the CIA and Al Qaeda is known at the top levels of the FBI. Members of the Bush administration and the US Congress are fully cognizant of these links.

The foreknowledge issue, focussing on "FBI lapses", is an obvious smokescreen. While the whistleblowers serve to underscore the weaknesses of the FBI, the role of successive US Administrations (since the presidency of Jimmy Carter), in supporting the "Islamic Militant Base", is simply not mentioned.

Fear and Disinformation Campaign

The Bush administration—through the personal initiative of Vice President Dick Cheney—chose not only to foreclose the possibility of a public inquiry, but also to trigger a fear and disinformation campaign:

> I think that the prospects of a future attack on the US are almost a certainty .... It could happen tomorrow, it could happen next week, it could happen next year, but they will keep trying. And we have to be prepared.[2]

What Cheney is really telling us is that our "intelligence asset", which we created, is going to strike again. Now, if this "CIA creature" were planning new terrorist attacks, you would expect that the CIA would be first to know about it. In all likelihood, the CIA also controls the "warnings" emanating from CIA sources on "future terrorist attacks" on American soil.

Carefully Planned Intelligence Operation

The 9/11 terrorists did not act on their own volition. The suicide hijackers were instruments in a carefully planned intelligence operation. The evidence confirms that Al Qaeda is supported by Pakistan's ISI. Amply documented, the ISI owes its existence to the CIA. (See Chapter III.)

The Missing Link

The FBI confirmed in late September 2001, in an interview with ABC News, that the 9/11 ringleader, Mohammed Atta, had been financed from unnamed sources in Pakistan. The FBI had information on the money trail. They knew exactly who was financing the terrorists. Less than two weeks later, the findings of the FBI were confirmed by Agence France Presse (AFP) and the *Times of India*, quoting an official Indian intelligence report (which had been dispatched to Washington). As mentioned in Chapter IV, according to these two reports, the money used to finance the 9/11 attacks had allegedly been "wired to WTC hijacker Mohammed Atta from Pakistan, by Ahmad Umar Sheikh, at the instance of [ISI Chief] General Mahmoud [Ahmad]".[3] According to the AFP (quoting the intelligence source):

> The evidence we have supplied to the US is of a much wider range and depth than just one piece of paper linking a rogue general to some misplaced act of terrorism.[4]

Pakistan's Chief Spy Visits Washington

Now, it just so happens that General Mahmoud Ahmad, the alleged "money man" behind 9/11, was in the US when the attacks occurred. (See Chapter IV.) He arrived on the 4th of September, one week before 9/11, on what was described as a routine visit of consultations with his US counterparts. According to Pakistani journalist Amir Mateen (in a prophetic article published on September 10):

> ISI Chief Lt-Gen. Mahmoud's week-long presence in Washington has triggered speculation about the agenda of his mysterious meet-

ings at the Pentagon and National Security Council. Officially, he is on a routine visit in return for CIA Director George Tenet's earlier visit to Islamabad. Official sources confirm that he met Tenet this week. He also held long parleys with unspecified officials at the White House and the Pentagon. But the most important meeting was with Marc Grossman, US Under Secretary of State for Political Affairs. One can safely guess that the discussions must have centred around Afghanistan ... and Osama bin Laden. What added interest to his visit is the history of such visits. Last time Ziauddin Butt, Mahmoud's predecessor, was here, during Nawaz Sharif's government, the domestic politics turned topsy-turvy within days.[5]

Nawaz Sharif was overthrown by General Pervez Musharaf. General Mahmoud Ahmad, who became the head of the ISI, played a key role in the military coup.

Condoleezza Rice's Press Conference

In the course of Condoleezza Rice's May 16, 2002 press conference (which took place barely a few hours after the publication of the "Bush Knew" headlines in *The New York Post*), an accredited Indian journalist asked a question on the role of General Mahmoud Ahmad:

Q: *Dr. Rice?*
Ms RICE: Yes?
Q: *Are you aware of the reports at the time that the ISI chief was in Washington on September 11th, and on September 10th, $100,000 was wired from Pakistan to these groups here in this area? And why was he here? Was he meeting with you or anybody in the Administration?*
Ms RICE: I have not seen that report, and he was certainly not meeting with me.[6]

Although there is no official confirmation, in all likelihood General Mahmoud Ahmad met Dr. Rice during the course of his official visit. Moreover, she must have been fully aware of the $100,000 transfer to Mohammed Atta, which had been confirmed by the FBI.

Lost in the barrage of media reports on "foreknowledge", this crucial piece of information on the ISI's role in 9/11 implicates key members of the Bush administration including: CIA Director

George Tenet, Secretary of State Colin Powell, Deputy Secretary of State Richard Armitage and Under-Secretary of State Marc Grossman, as well as Senator Joseph Biden (Democrat), Chairman of the powerful Senate Foreign Relations Committee (who met General Ahmad on the 13th of September). "According to Biden, [Ahmad] pledged Pakistan's cooperation."[7] (See Text box 10.1.)

Mysterious 9/11 Breakfast Meeting on Capitol Hill

On the morning of September 11, General Mahmoud Ahmad, the alleged "money-man" behind the 9/11 hijackers, was at a breakfast meeting on Capitol Hill hosted by Senator Bob Graham (Democrat) and Representative Porter Goss, Chairmen of the Senate and House Intelligence committees respectively. Also present at this meeting

---

TEXT BOX 10.1

General Mahmoud Ahmad and the Bush Administration

Confirmed by official sources (quoted by the mainstream media) Pakistan's chief spy General Mahmoud Ahmad met the following members of the Bush administration and the US Congress, during his visit to D.C. (4 to 13 September 2001):

- Secretary of State Colin Powell (12-13 September);
- Deputy Secretary of State Richard Armitage (13 September);
- Under-Secretary of State Marc Grossman (before 11 September);
- CIA Director George Tenet (before 11 September);
- Senator Bob Graham, Chairman of Senate Intelligence Committee (11 September);
- Senator John Kyl, member of the Senate Intelligence Committee (11 September);
- Representative Porter Goss, Chairman of the House Intelligence Committee (11 September);
- Senator Joseph Biden, Chairman of Foreign Relations Committee (13 September).

was Pakistan's ambassador to the US Maleeha Lodhi. The report confirms that other members of the Senate and House Intelligence committees were present.

> When the news [of the attacks on the World Trade Center] came, the two Florida lawmakers who lead the House and Senate intelligence committees were having breakfast with the head of the Pakistani intelligence service. Rep. Porter Goss, R-Sanibel, Sen. Bob Graham and other members of the House Intelligence Committee were talking about terrorism issues with the Pakistani official when a member of Goss'staff handed a note to Goss, who handed it to Graham. "We were talking about terrorism, specifically terrorism generated from Afghanistan," Graham said.
>
> Mahmoud Ahmed, director general of Pakistan's intelligence service, was "very empathetic, sympathetic to the people of the United States," Graham said.
>
> Goss could not be reached Tuesday. He was whisked away with much of the House leadership to an undisclosed "secure location". Graham, meanwhile, participated in late-afternoon briefings with top officials from the CIA and FBI.[8]

While trivializing the importance of the 9/11 breakfast meeting, the *Miami Herald* (16 September 2001) confirms that General Ahmad also met with Secretary of State Colin Powell in the wake of the 9/11 attacks:

> Graham said the Pakistani intelligence official with whom he met, a top general in the government, was forced to stay all week in Washington because of the shutdown of air traffic. "He was marooned here, and I think that gave Secretary of State Powell and others in the administration a chance to really talk with him," Graham said.[9]

With the exception of the Florida press (and Salon.com, 14 September 2001), not a word was mentioned in the US media's September coverage of 9/11 concerning this mysterious breakfast meeting.

Eight months later, on the 18th of May 2002, two days after the "Bush Knew" headline hit the tabloids, the *Washington Post* published an article on Porter Goss, entitled: "A Cloak But No Dagger; An Ex-Spy Says He Seeks Solutions, Not Scapegoats for 9/11."

Focussing on his career as a CIA agent, the article largely served to underscore the integrity and commitment of Porter Goss to waging a "war on terrorism". Yet in an isolated paragraph, the article acknowledged the mysterious 9/11 breakfast meeting with ISI Chief Mahmoud Ahmad, while also confirming that "Ahmad ran a spy agency notoriously close to Osama bin Laden and the Taliban":

> Now the main question facing Goss, as he helps steer a joint House-Senate investigation into the Sept. 11 attacks, is why nobody in the far-flung intelligence bureaucracy—13 agencies spending billions of dollars—paid attention to the enemy among us. Until it was too late.
>
> Goss says he is looking for solutions, not scapegoats. "A lot of nonsense," he calls this week's uproar about a CIA briefing that alerted President Bush, five weeks before Sept. 11, that Osama bin Laden's associates might be planning airline hijackings.
>
> None of this is news, but it's all part of the finger-pointing," Goss declared yesterday in a rare display of pique. "It's foolishness." [This statement comes from the man who was having breakfast with the alleged "money-man" behind 9/11 on the morning of September 11.] …
>
> Goss has repeatedly refused to blame an "intelligence failure" for the terror attacks. As a 10-year veteran of the CIA's clandestine operations wing, Goss prefers to praise the agency's "fine work" .…
>
> On the morning of Sept. 11, Goss and Graham were having breakfast with a Pakistani general named Mahmud Ahmad—the soon-to-be-sacked head of Pakistan's intelligence service. Ahmad ran a spy agency notoriously close to Osama bin Laden and the Taliban.[10]

While *The Washington Post* acknowledges the links between ISI Chief Mahmoud Ahmad and Osama bin Laden, it failed to dwell on the more important question: What were Rep. Porter Goss and Senator Bob Graham and other members of the Senate and House intelligence committees doing, together with the alleged money-man behind 9/11, at breakfast on Capitol Hill on the morning of September 11?

Neither does it acknowledge the fact, amply documented by media reports, that "the money-man" behind the hijackers had been entrusted by the Pakistani government to discuss the precise terms of Pakistan's "collaboration" in the "war on terrorism" in meetings held at the State department on the 12th and 13th of September 2001.

When the "foreknowledge" issue hit the street on May 16, 2002, "Chairman Porter Goss said an existing congressional inquiry has so far found 'no smoking gun' that would warrant another inquiry."[11] This statement points to an obvious "cover-up".

The Investigation and Public Hearings on 'Intelligence Failures'
In a piece of bitter irony, Rep. Porter Goss and Senator Bob Graham—the men who hosted the mysterious September 11 breakfast meeting with the alleged "hijackers'high commander" (to use the FBI's expression)—had been put in charge of the investigation and public hearings on "intelligence failures".

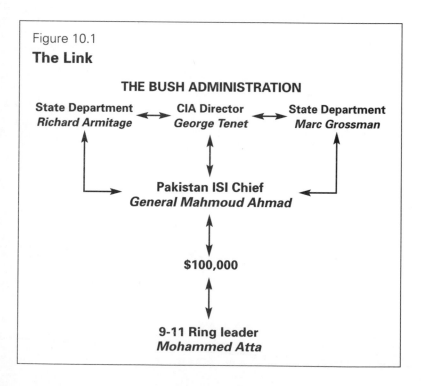

Figure 10.1
The Link

THE BUSH ADMINISTRATION

State Department   CIA Director   State Department
Richard Armitage ⟷ *George Tenet* ⟷ *Marc Grossman*

Pakistan ISI Chief
General Mahmoud Ahmad

$100,000

9-11 Ring leader
Mohammed Atta

Meanwhile, Vice President Dick Cheney had expressed anger on a "leak" emanating from the intelligence committees regarding "the disclosure of National Security Agency intercepts of messages in Arabic on the eve of the attacks. The messages ... were in two separate conversations on Sept. 10 and contained the phrases 'Tomorrow is zero hour'and 'The match is about to begin.'The messages were not translated until September 12."[12]

Red Carpet Treatment for the Alleged "Money Man" behind 9/11

The Bush administration had not only provided red carpet treatment for the alleged "money man" behind the 9/11 attacks, it had also sought his "cooperation" in the "war on terrorism". The precise terms of this "cooperation" were agreed upon between General Mahmoud Ahmad, representing the Pakistani government, and Deputy Secretary of State Richard Armitage in meetings at the State Department on September 12 and 13. In other words, the Administration decided in the immediate wake of 9/11 to seek the "cooperation" of Pakistan's ISI in "going after Osama", despite the fact (documented by the FBI) that the ISI was financing and abetting the 9/11 terrorists. Contradictory? One might say that it's like *asking the Devil to go after Dracula.*

The CIA Overshadows the Presidency

Dr. Rice's statement regarding the ISI chief at her May 16 2002 press conference is an obvious cover-up.

While General Ahmad was talking to US officials at the CIA and the Pentagon, he had allegedly also been in contact (through a third party) with the September 11 terrorists.

But this conclusion is, in fact, the tip of the iceberg. Everything indicates that CIA Director George Tenet and ISI Chief General Mahmoud Ahmad had established a close personal working relationship. As mentioned in Chapter IV, General Mahmoud had arrived a week prior to September 11 for consultations with George Tenet.

Bear in mind that the CIA's George Tenet also has a close personal relationship with President Bush. Prior to September 11,

Tenet would meet the President nearly every morning, at 8:00 a.m. sharp, for about half an hour.[13]

A document, known as the President's Daily Briefing, or PDB, "is prepared at Langley by the CIA's analytical directorate, and a draft goes home with Tenet each night. Tenet edits it personally and delivers it orally during his early morning meeting with Bush."[14] This practice of "oral intelligence briefings" is unprecedented. Bush's predecessors at the White House received a written briefing:

> With Bush, who liked oral briefings and the CIA director in atten-
> dance, a strong relationship had developed. Tenet could be direct,
> even irreverent and earthy.[15]

The Decision to Go To War

At meetings of the National Security Council and in the "War Cabinet" on September 11, 12 and 13, CIA Director George Tenet played a central role in gaining the Commander-in-Chief's approval to the launching of the "war on terrorism".

George W. Bush's Timeline—September 11 (from 9:45 a.m. in the wake of the WTC-Pentagon Attacks to midnight):

Circa 9:45 a.m: Bush's motorcade leaves the Booker Elementary School in Sarasota, Florida.

9:55 a.m: President Bush boards "Air Force One" bound for Washington.[16] Following what was noted as a "false report" that Air Force One would be attacked, Vice-President Dick Cheney had urged Bush (10:32 a.m.) by telephone not to land in Washington. Following this conversation, the plane was diverted (10:41 a.m.) (on orders emanating from Washington) to Barksdale Air Force Base in Louisiana. A couple of hours later (1:30 p.m.), after a brief TV appearance, the President was transported to Offut Air Force base in Nebraska at US Strategic Command Headquarters.

3:30 p.m: A key meeting of the National Security Council (NSC) was convened, with members of the NSC communicating with the President from Washington by secure video.[17] In the course of this NSC video-conference, CIA Director George Tenet fed unconfirmed information to the President. Tenet stated that "he was virtually certain that bin Laden and his network were behind the attacks …."[18]

The President responded to these statements, quite spontaneously, off the cuff, with little or no discussion and with an apparent misunderstanding of their implications. In the course of this video-conference (which lasted for less than an hour), the NSC was given the mandate by the Commander-in-Chief to prepare for the "war on terrorism". Very much on the spur of the moment, the "green light" was given by video conference from Nebraska. In the words of President Bush: "We will find these people. They will pay. And I don't want you to have any doubt about it."[19]

4:36 p.m: (One hour and six minutes later … Air Force One departed for Washington. Back in the White House that same evening (9:00 p.m.) a second meeting of the full NSC took place together with Secretary of State Colin Powell, who had returned to Washington from Peru. The NSC meeting (which lasted for half an hour) was followed by the first meeting of the "war cabinet". The latter was made up of a smaller group of top officials and key advisers.

9:30 p.m: At the war cabinet: "Discussion turned around whether bin Laden's Al Qaeda and the Taliban were one and the same thing. Tenet said they were."[20] By the end of that historic meeting of the war cabinet (11:00 p.m.), the Bush administration had decided to embark upon a military adventure which threatens the future of humanity.

Did Bush Know?
Did Bush, with his minimal understanding of foreign policy issues, know all the details regarding General Mahmoud and the "ISI connection"? Did Tenet and Cheney distort the facts, so as to get the Commander-in-Chief's "thumbs up" for a military operation which was already in the pipeline?

Notes

1. Quoted in AFP, 18 May 2002.

2. Fox News, 18 May 2002.

3. *The Times of India*, Delhi, 9 October 2001.

4. AFP, 10 October 2001.

5. Amir Mateen, "ISI Chief's Parleys continue in Washington", News Pakistan, 10 September 2001.

6. Federal News Service, 16 May 2002. Note that in the White House and CNN transcripts of Dr. Rice's press conference, the words "ISI chief" were transcribed respectively by a blank "—" and "(inaudible)". Federal News Service Inc. which is a transcription Service of official documents provided a correct transcription, with a minor error in punctuation, which we corrected. The White House transcript is at: http://www.whitehouse.gov/news/releases/2002/05/20020516-13.html. All three transcripts were verified by the author and are available on Nexus. Federal News Service documents are also available for a fee at http://www.fnsg.com/ For details on the transcripts, see Appendix.

7. *New York Times*, 14 September 2002.

8. Stuart News Company Press Journal (Vero Beach, FL), September 12, 2001).

9. *Miami Herald*, 16 September 2001.

10. *Washington Post*, 18 May 2002.

11. White House Bulletin, 17 May 2002.

12. *Miami Herald*, 21 June 2002.

13. The Commercial Appeal, Memphis, 17 May 2002.

14. *Washington Post*, 17 May 2002.

15. *Washington Post*, 29 January 2002.

16. *Washington Post*, 27 January 2002.

17. *Ibid.*

18. *Ibid.*

19. *Ibid.*

20. *Ibid.*

Appendix to Chapter X
Doctoring Official Transcripts

Excerpts from the transcripts of Dr. Condoleezza Rice's press conference of May 16, 2002
Below are excerpts from the transcripts of the same Condoleezza Rice press conference from CNN, the White House (FDCH) and Federal News Service. The latter is the source quoted in Chapter X. The other two sources (CNN and the White House) were manipulated.

CNN SHOW: "Inside Politics" 16:00, May 16, 2002
Transcript # 051600CN.V15:
QUESTION: Are you aware of the reports at the time that (*inaudible*) was in Washington on September 11. And on September 10, $100,000 was wired from Pakistan to these groups here in this area? And while he was here, was he meeting with you or anybody in the administration?

RICE: I have not seen that report, and he was certainly not meeting with me.

FDCH Federal Department and Agency Documents, May 16, 2002, Agency, White House:
QUESTION: Dr. Rice, are you aware of the reports at the time that (*inaudible*) was in Washington on September 11th, and on September 10th, $100,000 was wired to Pakistan to this group here in this area? And while he was here was he meeting with you or anybody in the administration?

DR. RICE: I have not seen that report, and he was certainly not meeting with me.

Federal News Service, May 16, 2002, Special White House Briefing:
QUESTION: Are you aware of the reports at the time that *the ISI chief* was in Washington on September 11th, and on September 10th, $100,000 was wired from Pakistan to these groups here in this area? And why he was here? Was he meeting with you or anybody in the administration?

MS. RICE: I have not seen that report, and he was certainly not meeting with me.

Notice the difference between the three transcripts. Both the White House and CNN exclude the identity of the "ISI chief" to the extent that the transcripts are totally unintelligible.

PART III
The Disinformation Campaign

CHAPTER XI
War Propaganda:
Fabricating an Outside Enemy

The US intelligence apparatus has created its own terrorist organizations. And at the same time, it creates its own terrorist warnings concerning the terrorist organizations which it has itself created. In turn, it has developed a cohesive multibillion dollar counterterrorism program "to go after" these terrorist organizations.

Counterterrorism and war propaganda are intertwined. The propaganda apparatus feeds disinformation into the news chain. The terror warnings must appear to be "genuine". The objective is to present the terror groups as "enemies of America".

One of the main objectives of war propaganda is to *fabricate an enemy*. As anti-war sentiment grows and the political legitimacy of the Bush Administration falters, doubts regarding the existence of this illusive "outside enemy" must be dispelled.

Propaganda purports not only to drown the truth but to kill the evidence on how this "outside enemy", namely Osama bin Laden's Al Qaeda was fabricated and transformed into "Enemy Number One". The entire National Security doctrine centers on the existence of an "outside enemy", which is threatening the Homeland.

The "Office of Disinformation"

Waged from the Pentagon, the State Department and the CIA, a fear and disinformation campaign was launched. The blatant distortion of the truth and the systematic manipulation of all sources of information is an integral part of war planning.

In the wake of 9/11, Secretary of Defense Donald Rumsfeld created the Office of Strategic Influence (OSI), or "Office of Disinformation" as it was labeled by its critics:

> The Department of Defense said they needed to do this, and they were going to actually plant stories that were false in foreign countries—as an effort to influence public opinion across the world.[1]

And, all of a sudden, the OSI was formally disbanded following political pressures and "troublesome" media stories that "its purpose was to deliberately lie to advance American interests."[2] "Rumsfeld backed off and said this is embarrassing."[3] Yet despite this apparent about-turn, the Pentagon's Orwellian disinformation campaign remained functionally intact:

> "[T]he secretary of defense is not being particularly candid here. Disinformation in military propaganda is part of war.[4]

Rumsfeld in fact later confirmed in a November 2002 press interview that while the OSI no longer exists in name, the "Office's intended functions are [still] being carried out".[5]

A number of government agencies and intelligence units—with links to the Pentagon—are involved in various components of the propaganda campaign.

Realities are turned upside down. Acts of war are heralded as "humanitarian interventions" geared towards "regime change" and "the restoration of democracy".

Military occupation and the killing of civilians are presented as "peace-keeping". The derogation of civil liberties—in the context of the so-called "anti-terrorist legislation"—is portrayed as a means to providing "domestic security" and upholding civil liberties. And underlying these manipulated realties, "Osama bin Laden" and "Weapons of Mass Destruction" statements, which circulated profusely in the news chain, were upheld as the basis for understanding World events.

The twisting of public opinion at home and around the World had become an integral part of the War agenda. In the months leading up to the March 2003 invasion of Iraq, the Bush Administration and its indefectible British ally had multiplied the "warnings" of future Al Qaeda terrorist attacks.

War propaganda is pursued at all stages: before, during the military operation as well as in its cruel aftermath. The enemy has to appear genuine: thousands of news stories and editorials linking Al Qaeda to the Baghdad government were planted in the news chain.

War propaganda serves to conceal the real causes and consequences of war.

Shortly after the OSI had been officially disbanded amidst controversy, the *New York Times* confirmed that the disinformation campaign was running strong and that the Pentagon was:

> considering issuing a secret directive to American military to conduct covert operations aimed at influencing public opinion and policymakers in friendly and neutral nations .... The proposal has ignited a fierce battle throughout the Bush administration over whether the military should carry out secret propaganda missions in friendly nations like Germany .... The fight, one Pentagon official said, is over 'the strategic communications for our nation, the message we want to send for long-term influence, and how we do it. ... "We have the assets and the capabilities and the training to go into friendly and neutral nations to influence public opinion. We could do it and get away with it. That doesn't mean we should."[6]

Feeding Disinformation into the News Chain

To sustain "the War on Terrorism" agenda these fabricated realities, funneled on a day to day basis into the news chain, must become indelible truths which form part of a broad political and media consensus. In this regard, the corporate media—although acting independently of the military-intelligence apparatus—is an instrument of this evolving totalitarian system.

In close liaison with the Pentagon and the CIA, the State Department had also set up its own "soft-sell" (civilian) propaganda unit, headed by Undersecretary of State for Public Diplomacy and Public Affairs Charlotte Beers, a powerful figure in the advertising industry. Working in liaison with the Pentagon, Beers was appointed to head the State Department's propaganda unit in the immediate wake of 9/11. Her mandate was "to counteract anti-Americanism abroad."[7] Her office at the State Department was to:

> ensure that public diplomacy (engaging, informing, and influencing key international audiences) is practiced in harmony with public affairs (outreach to Americans) and traditional diplomacy to advance US interests and security and to provide the moral basis for US leadership in the world.[8]

The Role of the CIA

The most powerful component of the Fear and Disinformation Campaign rests with the CIA, which secretly subsidizes authors, journalists and media critics, through a web of private foundations and CIA sponsored front organizations. The CIA also influences the scope and direction of many Hollywood productions. Since 9/11, one third of Hollywood productions are war movies:

> Hollywood stars and scriptwriters are rushing to bolster the new message of patriotism, conferring with the CIA and brainstorming with the military about possible real-life terrorist attacks.[9]

"The Sum of All Fears" directed by Phil Alden Robinson, which depicts the scenario of a nuclear war, had received the endorsement and support of both the Pentagon and the CIA.[10]

Disinformation is routinely "planted" by CIA operatives in the newsroom of major dailies, magazines and TV channels. Outside public relations firms are often used to create "fake stories":

> A relatively few well-connected correspondents provide the scoops, that get the coverage in the relatively few mainstream news sources,

where the parameters of debate are set and the "official reality" is consecrated for the bottom feeders in the news chain.[11]

Covert disinformation initiatives under CIA auspices are also funneled through various intelligence proxies in other countries. Since 9/11, they have resulted in the day-to-day dissemination of false information concerning alleged "terrorist attacks".

A routine pattern of reporting had emerged. In virtually all of the reported cases of terrorist incidents (Britain, France, Indonesia,

---

TEXT BOX 11.1

The Secret Downing Street Memo

"The intelligence and facts were being fixed around the policy"

SECRET AND STRICTLY PERSONAL—UK EYES ONLY
DAVID MANNING
From: Matthew Rycroft
Date: 23 July 2002
S 195/02
cc: Defense Secretary, Foreign Secretary, Attorney-General, Sir Richard Wilson, John Scarlett, Francis Richards, CDS, C, Jonathan Powell, Sally Morgan, Alastair Campbell

Iraq: Prime Minister's Meeting, 23 July

C [head of British Intelligence MI-6, Sir Richard Dearlove] reported on his recent talks in Washington. There was a perceptible shift in attitude. Military action was now seen as inevitable. ...

Bush wanted to remove Saddam, through military action, justified by the conjunction of terrorism and WMD. But the intelligence and facts were being fixed around the policy.

... The NSC had no patience with the UN route, and no enthusiasm for publishing material on the Iraqi regime's record. There was little discussion in Washington of the aftermath after military action.

Excerpts from the "Secret Downing Street Memo" to Prime Minister Tony Blair, leaked in May 2005 to the *London Times*.

India, Philippines, etc.) the alleged terrorist groups are identified as having "links to Al Qaeda", without of course acknowledging the fact (amply documented by intelligence reports and official documents) that Al Qaeda is US intelligence asset.

The Doctrine of "Self Defense"

The propaganda campaign is geared towards sustaining the illusion that "America is under attack". Relayed not only through the mainstream media but also through a number of alternative Internet media sites, these fabricated realities continue to portray the war in Afghanistan and Iraq as bona fide acts of self-defense, while carefully concealing the broad strategic and economic objectives of the war.

In turn, the propaganda campaign develops a *casus belli*, a justification, a political legitimacy for waging war. The "official reality" (conveyed profusely in George W's speeches) rests on the broad "humanitarian" premise of a so-called "preemptive", namely "defensive war", "a war to protect freedom":

> We're under attack because we love freedom. ... And as long as we love freedom and love liberty and value every human life, they're going to try to hurt us.[12]

The National Security Strategy (NSS) includes two essential building blocks:
- The preemptive "defensive war" doctrine,
- The "war on terrorism" against Al Qaeda.

The objective is to present "preemptive military action"—meaning war as an act of "self-defense" against two categories of enemies, "rogue States" and "Islamic terrorists":

> The war against terrorists of global reach is a global enterprise of uncertain duration. ... America will act against such emerging threats before they are fully formed.
>   ... Rogue States and terrorists do not seek to attack us using conventional means. They know such attacks would fail. Instead, they rely on acts of terror and, potentially, the use of weapons of mass destruction.

... The targets of these attacks are our military forces and our civilian population, in direct violation of one of the principal norms of the law of warfare. As was demonstrated by the losses on September 11, 2001, mass civilian casualties is the specific objective of terrorists and these losses would be exponentially more severe if terrorists acquired and used weapons of mass destruction.

The United States has long maintained the option of preemptive actions to counter a sufficient threat to our national security. The greater the threat, the greater is the risk of inaction—and the more compelling the case for taking anticipatory action to defend ourselves. ... To forestall or prevent such hostile acts by our adversaries, the United States will, if necessary, act preemptively.[13]

In early 2005, the Pentagon called for the development of a more "pro-active" notion of preemptive warfare, where military operations could also be launched not only against a "declared enemy" but also against countries, which are not openly hostile to America, but which are considered strategic from the point of view of US interests. (See Chapter XIX.)

How is War Propaganda carried out?

Two sets of eye-popping statements emanating from a variety of sources (including official National Security statements, media, Washington-based think tanks, etc.) are fed on a daily basis into the news chain. Some of the events (including news regarding presumed terrorists) were blatantly fabricated by the intelligence agencies. (See chapters XIX and XX.)

However, once the core assumptions of the disinformation campaign have been embedded in the news chain, both the printed press and network TV establish their own self-sustaining routine of fabricating the news.

Disinformation relies on a pattern of reporting which tends to dismiss the substance behind the news. In the months leading up to the March 2003 invasion of Iraq, the disinformation campaign centered on two simple and catchy "buzzwords", which were used profusely to justify US military action:

- **Buzzword no. 1.** "Osama bin Laden's Al Qaeda" (Osama) is behind most news stories regarding the "war on terrorism" including "alleged", "future", "presumed" and "actual" terrorist attacks.
- **Buzzword no. 2.** "Weapons of Mass Destruction" (WMD) statements were used profusely to justify the "pre-emptive war" against the "State sponsors of terror"—i.e., countries such as Iraq, Iran and North Korea which allegedly possess WMD. Amply documented in the case of Iraq, a large body of news on WMD and biological attacks, were fabricated.

In the wake of the invasion of Iraq, "WMD" and "Osama bin Laden" statements continued to be used. They have become part of the day to day debate, embodied in routine conversations between citizens. Repeated ad nauseam, they penetrate the inner consciousness of people, molding their individual perceptions on current events. Through deception and manipulation, this shaping of the minds of entire populations sets the stage—under the façade of a functioning democracy—for the installation of a de facto Police State.

In turn, the disinformation regarding alleged "terrorist attacks" or "weapons of mass destruction" instills an atmosphere of fear, which mobilizes unswerving patriotism and support for the State, and its main political and military actors.

Repeated in virtually every national news report, this stigmatic focus on WMD and Osama/Al Qaeda essentially serves as a dogma, to blind people on the causes and consequences of America's war of conquest, while providing a simple, unquestioned and authoritative justification for "self defense".

In the months leading up to the 2003 invasion of Iraq, both in speeches by President Bush and Prime Minister Tony Blair, as well as in the news, WMD statements were carefully blended into Osama statements. UK Defense Minister Jack Straw had warned in early 2003 "that 'rogue regimes' such as Iraq were the most likely source of WMD technology for groups like Al Qaeda."[14] Also, two months before the March 2003 invasion, a presumed Al Qaeda cell "with links to Iraq" had been discovered in Edinburgh, allegedly involved in the use of biological weapons against people in the UK.

The hidden agenda of "the links to Iraq" statement is blatantly obvious. Its objective was to discredit Iraq in the months leading up to the war: the so-called "State sponsors of terror" are said to support Osama bin Laden. Conversely, Osama is said to collaborate with Iraq in the use of "weapons of mass destruction".

Prior to the 2003 invasion as well as in its wake, several thousand news reports had woven an "Osama connection" into the WMD stories.

The WMD pretext for waging the war was finally dismissed, shortly before Bush's Second Term inauguration in January 2005, by which time the justification for having waged the war on Iraq was no longer considered an issue. The media spin behind WMD was

---

TEXT BOX 11.2
The Secret Crawford-Iraq Memo from British Foreign Secretary Jack Straw to Prime Minister Tony Blair

SECRET AND PERSONAL PM/02/019/PRIME MINISTER
CRAWFORD/IRAQ

If 11 September had not happened, it is doubtful that the US would now be considering military action against Iraq. In addition, there has been no credible evidence to link Iraq with UBL [Osama bin Laden] and Al Qaida. Objectively, the threat from Iraq has not worsened as a result of 11 September. What has however changed is the tolerance of the international community (especially that of the US), the world having witnessed on September 11 just what determined evil people can these days perpetuate.

(Jack Straw)
Foreign and Commonwealth Office, March 2002

Excerpt of Secret-Personal Memo to Prime Minister Tony Blair from British Foreign Secretary Jack Straw, The "Secret and Personal" Crawford-Iraq Memo, 25 March 2002.

never questioned, to the extent that the elimination of WMD is still regarded by public opinion as a central objective of US foreign policy.

While Iraq was the main target of the propaganda campaign, North Korea was also described, without a shred of evidence, as possibly having links to Al Qaeda:

> Skeptics will argue that the inconsistencies don't prove the Iraqis have continued developing weapons of mass destruction. It also leaves Washington casting about for other damning material and charges, including the midweek claim, again unproved, that Islamic extremists affiliated with Al Qaeda took possession of a chemical weapon in Iraq last November or late October.[15]
>
> North Korea has admitted it lied about that and is brazenly cranking up its nuclear program again. Iraq has almost certainly lied about it, but won't admit it. Meanwhile Al Qaeda, although dispersed, remains a shadowy, threatening force, and along with other terrorist groups, a potential recipient of the deadly weaponry that could emerge from Iraq and North Korea.[16]
>
> Britain's Prime Minister Tony Blair listed Iraq, North Korea, the Middle East and Al Qaeda among "difficult and dangerous" problems Britain faced in the coming year.[17]

The WMD-Osama statements were used profusely by the mainstream media. In the wake of 9/11, these stylized statements had become an integral part of day to day political discourse, permeating the workings of international diplomacy and the functioning of the United Nations.

Secretary of State Colin Powell underscored this relationship in his presentation to the Davos World Economic Forum, barely two months before the invasion as well as in his historic February 5, 2003 speech at the UN Security Council:

> Evidence that is still tightly held is accumulating within the administration that it is not a matter of chance that terror groups in the Al Qaeda universe have made their weapons of choice the poisons, gases and chemical devices that are signature arms of the Iraqi regime.[18]

Meanwhile, "anti-terrorist operations" directed against Muslims, including arbitrary mass arrests, had been stepped up:

> The US and Western interests in the Western world have to be prepared for retaliatory attacks from sleeper cells the second we launch an attack in Iraq.[19]

The Smallpox Vaccination Program

In the context of these emergency measures, preparations for compulsory smallpox vaccination were initiated in 2003 in response to a presumed threat of a biological weapons attack on US soil. The vaccination program—which had been the object of intense media propaganda—contributed to creating an atmosphere of insecurity:

> A few infected individuals with a stack of plane tickets—or bus tickets, for that matter—could spread smallpox infection across the country, touching off a plague of large proportions. ... It is not inconceivable that a North Korea or an Iraq could retain smallpox in a hidden lab and pass the deadly agent on to terrorists.[20]

The hidden agenda was clear. How best to discredit the antiwar movement and maintain the legitimacy of the State? Create conditions which instill fear and hatred, present the rulers as "guardians of the peace" committed to weeding out terrorism and preserving democracy. In the words of British Prime Minister Tony Blair, echoing almost verbatim the US propaganda dispatches:

> I believe it is inevitable that they [the terrorists] will try in some form or other [to wage attacks] .... I think we can see evidence from the recent arrests that the terrorist network is here as it is around the rest of Europe, around the rest of the world.... The most frightening thing about these people is the possible coming together of fanaticism and the technology capable of delivering mass destruction.[21]

Mass Arrests

The mass arrests of Muslims and Arabs on trumped up charges since September 11, 2001 is not motivated by security considerations.

Their main function is to provide "credibility" to the fear and propaganda campaign.

Each arrest, amply publicized by the corporate media and repeated day after day, "gives a face" to this illusive enemy. It also serves to obscure the fact that Al Qaeda is a creature of the CIA. In other words, the propaganda campaign performs two important functions.

First, it must ensure that the enemy is considered a "real threat".

Second, it must distort the truth—i.e., it must conceal "the relationship" between this fabricated enemy and its creators within the military-intelligence apparatus. The nature and history of Osama bin Laden's Al Qaeda and the Islamic brigades since the Soviet-Afghan war must be suppressed or distorted.

"Possible" or "Future" Terrorist Attacks based on "Reliable Sources"

The propaganda campaign exhibits a consistent pattern. The objective is to instill credibility and legitimacy focusing on supposedly "reliable sources" of information.

The same concepts appear simultaneously in hundreds of media reports:

- These concepts refer to "*reliable sources*", a "*growing body of evidence*"—e.g., government or intelligence or FBI.
- They invariably indicate that the terrorist groups involved "*have ties to bin Laden*" or Al Qaeda, or are "*sympathetic to bin Laden*",
- The reports often point to the possibility of terrorist attacks, "*sooner or later*" or "*in the next two months*".
- The reports often raise the issue of so-called "*soft targets*", pointing to the likelihood of civilian casualties.
- They indicate that future terrorist attacks could "*take place in a number of allied countries*" (including Britain, France, Germany in which public opinion is strongly opposed to the US-led war on terrorism).
- They confirm the need by the US and its allies to initiate "*preemptive*" *actions* directed against these various terrorist organizations and/or the *foreign governments which harbor the terrorists.*

- They often point to the likelihood that these *"terrorist groups possess WMD" including biological and chemical weapons (as well as nuclear weapons)*. The links to *Iraq and "rogue states"* are also mentioned.
- The reports also include warnings regarding *"attacks on US soil", "attacks against civilians in Western cities"*.
- They point to efforts undertaken by the police authorities to apprehend the alleged terrorists.
- The arrested individuals are in virtually all cases Muslims and/or Arabs.
- The reports are also used to justify the Homeland Security legislation as well as the "ethnic profiling" and mass arrests of presumed terrorists.

"Sooner or Later"

This pattern of disinformation in the Western media applies the usual catch phrases. (In the press excerpts below, catch phrases are in italics):

> Published reports, along with new information *obtained from US intelligence and military sources,* point to *a growing body of evidence* that terrorists *associated with and/or sympathetic to Osama bin Laden* are planning a significant attack *on US soil.*
>
> Also *targeted are allied countries* that have joined the worldwide hunt for the radical Muslim cells hell-bent on unleashing new waves of terrorist strikes. ... The US Government's activation of antiterrorist forces comes as the FBI issued a warning Nov. 14 that a "spectacular" new terrorist attack *may be forthcoming—sooner rather than later.* ...
>
> Elsewhere, the Australian government issued an unprecedented warning to its citizens that Al Qaeda terrorists there might launch *attacks within the next two months.*[22]
>
> Although [former] CIA Director George Tenet said in recent congressional testimony that "an attempt to conduct *another attack on US soil* is certain," a trio of former senior CIA officials doubted the chance of any "spectacular" terror *attacks on US soil.*[23]
>
> Germans have been skittish since the terrorist attacks in the United States, *fearing that their country is a ripe target for terrorism.* Several

of the hijackers in the Sept. 11 attacks plotted their moves in Hamburg.[24]

On Dec. 18 [2002], a senior government official, speaking on condition of anonymity, briefed journalists about *the 'high probability'of a terrorist attack happening "sooner or later".* ... [H]e named hotels and shopping centres as potential *"soft targets"* .... The official also specifically mentioned: a *possible chemical attack* in the London subway, the unleashing of smallpox, the poisoning of the water supply and strikes against "postcard targets" such as Big Ben and Canary Warf.

The "sooner or later" alert followed a Home Office warning at the end of November that said Islamic radicals might use *dirty bombs or poison gas* to inflict huge casualties on British cities. This also made big headlines but the warning was quickly retracted in fear that it would cause public panic.[25]

The message yesterday was that these terrorists, however obscure, are trying—and, *sooner or later,* may break through London's defenses. It is a city where tens of thousands of souls [live]. ... Experts have repeatedly said that the UK, with its bullish support for the US and its war on terror, is a genuine and realistic target for terror groups, including the Al Qaeda network led by 11 September mastermind Osama bin Laden.[26]

Quoting Margaret Thatcher: "Only America has the reach and *means to deal with Osama bin Laden or Saddam Hussein* or the other wicked psychopaths who will *sooner or later* step into their shoes."[27]

According to a recent US State Department alert: "Increased security at official US facilities *has led terrorists to seek softer targets such as residential areas, clubs, restaurants, places of worship, hotels, schools, outdoor recreation events, resorts, beaches and planes."*[28]

Actual Terrorist Attacks

To be effective, the fear and disinformation campaign cannot solely rely on unsubstantiated warnings of future attacks. It requires a credible system of terror alerts, actual arrests of alleged terror suspects (on trumped up charges) as well as "real" terrorist occurrences or "incidents", which provide credibility to the "war on terrorism".

Propaganda endorses the need to implement "emergency measures" as well as implement retaliatory military actions. The triggering of "war pretext incidents" is part of the Pentagon's assumptions. (See Chapter XIX.)

Notes

1. Interview with Steve Adubato, Fox News, 26 December 2002.

2. *Air Force Magazine*, January 2003, emphasis added.

3. Adubato, *op. cit.* emphasis added.

4. *Ibid*, emphasis added.

5. Quoted in Federation of American Scientists (FAS), Secrecy News, 27 November 2002 http://www.fas.org/sgp/news/secrecy/2002/11/112702.html, Rumsfeld's November 2002 press interview can be consulted at:

http://www.fas.org/sgp/news/2002/11/dod111802.html.

6. *New York Times*, 16 December 2002.

7. *Sunday Times*, London, 5 January 2003.

8. See US State Department at http://www.state.gov/r/

9. Ros Davidson, "Stars earn their Stripes", *The Sunday Herald* (Scotland), 11 November 2001.

10. See Samuel Blumenfeld, "Le Pentagone et la CIA enrôlent Hollywood", *Le Monde*, 24 July 2002.

11. Chaim Kupferberg, "The Propaganda Preparation for 9/11", Centre for Research on Globalization, June 2002, p.19, http://www.globalresearch.ca/articles/KUP206A.html

12. Remarks by President Bush in Trenton, New Jersey, Welcome Army National Guard Aviation Support Facility, Trenton, New Jersey, 23 September 2002.

13. National Security Strategy, White House, 2002, http://www.whitehouse.gov/nsc/nss.html

14. Agence France Presse (AFP), 7 January 2003.

15. *Insight on the News*, 20 January 2003.

16. *Christian Science Monitor*, 8 January 2003

17. Agence France Presse (AFP), 1 January 2003

18. *The Washington Post*, 25 January 2003.

19. *Ibid.*

20. *Chicago Sun*, 31 December 2002.

21. Reuters, 21 February 2003

22. *Insight on the News*, 3 February 2003.

23. United Press International (UPI), 19 December 2002.

24. *New York Times*, 6 January 2003.

25. *Toronto Star*, 5 January 2003.

26. *The Scotsman*, 8 January 2003.

27. United Press International (UPI), 10 December 2002.

28. States News Service, State Department Advisory, similar texts published on several dates, 2002-2005.

Chapter XII
9/11 and the Iran-Contra Scandal

The Bush administration accuses people of having links to Al Qaeda. This is the national security doctrine behind the anti-terrorist legislation and Homeland Security. It is not only part of the Administration's disinformation campaign, it is also used to arrest thousands of people on trumped up charges.

Ironically, several key members of the Bush Administration who were the architects of the anti-terrorist agenda, played a key role in supporting and financing Al Qaeda.

Secretary of State Colin Powell, who casually accused Baghdad and other foreign governments of "harboring" Al Qaeda, played an indirect role, during the Reagan administration, in supporting and financing Al Qaeda.

Both Colin Powell and his Deputy Richard Armitage, were implicated, having operated behind the scenes, in the Iran-Contra scandal during the Reagan Administration, which involved the illegal sale of weapons to Iran to finance the Nicaraguan Contra paramilitary army:

> [Coronel Oliver] North set up a team including [Richard] Secord; Noel Koch [Armitage's deputy], then assistant secretary at the Pentagon responsible for special operations; George Cave, a former CIA station chief in Tehran, and Colin Powell, military assistant to US Defense Secretary Caspar Weinberger.[1]

Although Colin Powell was not directly involved in the arms transfer negotiations, which had been entrusted to Coronel Oliver North, he was, according to press reports, among "at least five men within the Pentagon who knew arms were being transferred to the CIA".[2]

Lieutenant General Powell was directly instrumental in giving the "green light" to lower-level officials in blatant violation of congressional procedures. According to the *New York Times*, Colin Powell took the decision (at the level of military procurement), to allow the delivery of weapons to Iran:

> Hurriedly, one of the men closest to Secretary of Defense Weinberger, Maj. Gen. Colin Powell, bypassed the written "focal point system" procedures and ordered the Defense Logistics Agency [responsible for procurement] to turn over the first of 2,008 TOW missiles to the CIA, which acted as cutout for delivery to Iran.[3]

Richard Armitage, who was Deputy Secretary of State during George W. Bush's first term (2001-2004) played a key role in launching the "war on terrorism" in the immediate wake of 9/11, leading to the invasion of Afghanistan in October 2001. (See Chapter 4.)

During the Reagan Administration, Armitage held the position of Assistant Secretary of Defense. He was in charge of coordinating covert military operations including the Iran-Contra operation. He was in close liaison with Coronel Oliver North. His deputy and chief anti-terrorist official Noel Koch was part of the team set up by Oliver North. Following the delivery of the TOW anti-tank missiles to Iran, the proceeds of these sales were deposited in numbered bank accounts and the money was used to finance the Nicaraguan Contra.[4]

A classified Israeli report provided to the Iran-Contra panels of the Congressional inquiry confirmed that Armitage "was in the picture on the Iranian issue."[5]

> With a Pentagon position that placed him over the military's covert operations branch, Armitage was a party to the secret arms dealing from the outset. He also was associated with former national security aide Oliver L. North in a White House counterterrorism group, another area that would also have been a likely focus of congressional inquiry.[6]

Financing the Islamic Brigades

The Iran-Contra procedure was similar to that used in Afghanistan, where covert financial assistance had been channeled to the militant "Islamic brigades". Barely mentioned by the press reports, part of the proceeds of the weapons sales to Iran had been channeled to finance the Mujahideen:

> The Washington Post reported that profits from the Iran arms sales were deposited in one CIA-managed account into which the US and Saudi Arabia had placed $250 million apiece. That money was disbursed not only to the Contras in Central America but to the rebels fighting Soviet troops in Afghanistan.[7]

The Irangate Cover-up

In the wake of the Iran-Contra disclosure, Reagan's National Security Adviser Rear Admiral John Pointdexter, later indicted on conspiracy charges and for lying to Congress, was replaced by Frank Carlucci. Major General Colin Powell was appointed deputy to Frank Carlucci, occupying a senior position on Reagan's National Security team:

> Both [Carlucci and Powell] came to the White House after the Iran-Contra revelations and the NSC [National Security Council] housecleaning that followed [the Irangate scandal].[8]

This "housecleaning" operation was a cover-up, as Colin Powell was fully aware of the Iran-Contra affair.

While several Irangate officials including John Pointdexter and Oliver North were accused of criminal wrongdoing, several of the main actors in the CIA and the Pentagon, namely Armitage and Casey, were never indicted, neither was Lieutenant General Colin Powell who had authorized the procurement of TOW missiles from the Defense Logistics Agency and their delivery to Iran.

Moreover, while weapons were being sold covertly to Iran, Washington was also supplying weapons through official channels to Baghdad. In other words, Washington was arming both sides in the Iran-Iraq war. And Donald Rumsfeld, as Special Envoy to the Middle East under President Reagan, was put in charge of negotiating US weapons sales to Baghdad.

Notes

1. *The Guardian*, 10 December 1986.

2. *The Record*, 29 December 1986.

3. *The New York Times*, 16 February 1987.

4. UPI, 27 November 1987.

5. *The New York Times*, 26 May 1989:

6. *Washington Post*, 26 May 1989. See also *US News and World Report*, 15 December 1986.

7. *US News & World Report*, 15 December 1986.

8. The MacNeil/Lehrer NewsHour, 16 June 1987.

CHAPTER XIII
Providing a Face to the Enemy: Who is Abu Musab Al-Zarqawi?

The "war on terrorism" requires a humanitarian mandate. It is presented as a "Just War" to be fought on moral grounds "to redress a wrong suffered".

The Just War theory defines "good" and "evil". It concretely portrays and personifies the terrorist leaders as "evil individuals".

Several prominent American intellectuals and antiwar activists, who stand firmly opposed to the Bush administration, are nonetheless supporters of the Just War theory: "We are against war in all its forms but we support the campaign against international terrorism."

To reach its foreign policy objectives, the images of terrorism must remain vivid in the minds of the citizens, who are constantly reminded of the terrorist threat.

The propaganda campaign presents the portraits of the leaders behind the terror network. In other words, at the level of what constitutes an "advertising" campaign, "it gives a face to terror".

The "war on terrorism" rests on the creation of one or more evil bogeymen, the terror leaders, Osama bin Laden, Abu Musab Al-Zarqawi, et al., whose names and photos are presented ad nauseam in daily news reports.

Abu Musab Al-Zarqawi: New Terrorist Mastermind

Since the war on Iraq, Abu Musab Al-Zarqawi has been presented to World public opinion as the new terrorist mastermind, overshadowing "Enemy Number One", Osama bin Laden.

The US State Department has increased the reward for his arrest from $10 million to $25 million, which puts his "market value" at par with that of Osama. Ironically, Al-Zarqawi is not on the FBI most wanted fugitives' list.[1]

Al-Zarqawi is often described in official government statements as well as in media reports as an "Osama associate", allegedly responsible for numerous terrorist attacks in several countries. In other reports, often emanating from the same sources, he is said to have no links to Al Qaeda and to operate quite independently. He is often presented as an individual who is challenging the leadership of bin Laden.

Osama belongs to the powerful bin Laden family, which has business ties to the Bushes and prominent members of the Texas oil establishment. Osama bin Laden was recruited by the CIA during the Soviet-Afghan war and fought as a Mujahideen. In other words, there is a longstanding documented history of bin Laden-CIA and bin Laden-Bush family links, which are an obvious source of embarrassment to the US Government. (See Chapter II)

In contrast to bin Laden, Al-Zarqawi has no family history. He comes from an impoverished Palestinian family in Jordan. His parents are dead. He emerges out of the blue.

"Lone Wolf"

Al-Zarqawi is described by CNN as "a lone wolf" who is said to act quite independently of the Al Qaeda network. Yet surprisingly, this "lone wolf" is present in several countries, in Iraq, which is now his base, but also in Western Europe. He is also suspected of preparing a terrorist attack on American soil.

The media reports suggest that he is in several places at the same time. He is described as "the chief US enemy", "a master of disguise and bogus identification papers". We are led to believe that this "lone wolf" manages to outwit the most astute US intelligence operatives.

According to the *Weekly Standard*—which is known to have a close relationship to the Neocons in the Bush administration:

> Abu Musab Al-Zarqawi is hot right now. He masterminded not only [Nicholas] Berg's murder [in 2004] but also the Madrid carnage on March 11 [2004], the bombardment of Shia worshippers in Iraq the same month, and the April 24 [2004] suicide attack on the port of Basra. But he is far from a newcomer to slaughter. Well before 9/11, he had already concocted a plot to kill Israeli and American tourists in Jordan. His label is on terrorist groups and attacks on four continents.[2]

Al-Zarqawi's profile "is mounting a challenge to bin Laden's leadership of the global jihad."

In Iraq, according to press reports, he is preparing to "ignite a civil war between Sunnis and Shiites". But is that not precisely what US intelligence is aiming at ("divide and rule") as confirmed by several analysts of the US led war? Pitting one group against the other with a view to weakening the resistance movement.[3]

The CIA, with its $40 billion plus budget, pleads ignorance: they say they know nothing about him, they have a photograph, but, according to the *Weekly Standard*, they apparently do not know his weight or height.

The aura of mystery surrounding this individual is part of the propaganda ploy. Zarqawi is described as "so secretive even some operatives who work with him do not know his identity."[4]

Consistent Media Pattern

What is the role of this new terrorist mastermind in the Pentagon's disinformation campaign?

In previous war propaganda ploys, the CIA hired Public Relations firms to organize core disinformation campaigns. In 1990, the British PR firm Hill and Knowlton launched the 1990 Kuwaiti incubator media scam, where Kuwaiti babies were allegedly removed from incubators in a totally fabricated news story, which was then used to get Congressional approval for the 1991 Gulf War.

Almost immediately in the wake of a terrorist event or warning, US network television announces (in substance) that, they think this mysterious individual Abu Musab Al-Zarqawi is possibly behind it, invariably without presenting supporting evidence, and prior to the conduct of an investigation by the relevant police and intelligence authorities.

In some cases, upon the immediate occurrence of the terrorist event, there is an initial report which mentions Al-Zarqawi as the possible mastermind. The report will often say (in substance) that they think he did it, but it is not yet confirmed and there is some doubt on the identity of those behind the attack. One or two days later, the reports will be confirmed, at which time CNN may come up with a more definitive statement, quoting official police, military and/or intelligence sources.

Often the CNN report is based on information published on an Islamic website, or a mysterious video or audio tape. The authenticity of the website and/or the tapes is not the object of discussion or detailed investigation.

The news reports never mention that Al-Zarqawi was recruited by the CIA to fight in the Soviet-Afghan war, as acknowledged by Secretary Colin Powell in his presentation to the UN Security Council on 5 February 2003. (See Chapter XI.) Moreover, the press usually presents the terrorist warnings emanating from the CIA as genuine, without acknowledging the fact that US intelligence has provided covert support to the Islamic militant network consistently for more than 20 years. (See Chapters I and III.)

History of Abu Musab Al-Zarqawi

Abu Musab Al-Zarqawi's name was first mentioned in relation to the thwarted attack on the Radisson SAS Hotel in Amman, Jordan, during the December 1999 millennium celebrations. According to press reports, he had previously gone under another name: Ahmed Fadil Al-Khalayleh, among several other aliases.

An Al-Zarqawi legend was in the making. According to *The New York Times*, Al-Zarqawi is said to have fled Afghanistan to Iran in late 2001, following the entry of US troops. According to news reports, he had been "collaborating with hard-liners" in the Iranian military and intelligence apparatus:

> United States intelligence officials say they are increasingly concerned by the mounting evidence of Tehran's renewed interest in terrorism [and support to Al-Zarqawi], including covert surveillance by Iranian agents of possible American targets abroad. American officials said Iran appeared to view terrorism as [a] deterrent against [a] possible attack by the United States.
>
> Since the surprise election of reformer Mohammad Khatami as president of Iran in 1997 and his wide public support, Washington has been counting on a new moderate political majority to emerge. But the hard-line faction has maintained its grip on Iran's security apparatus, frustrating American efforts to ease tensions with Tehran.
>
> Now, Iranian actions to destabilize the new interim government in Afghanistan, its willingness to assist Al Qaeda members and its fuelling of the Palestinian uprising are prompting a reassessment in Washington, officials say.[5]

Presenting the Tehran government as having links to Al Qaeda was part of an evolving disinformation campaign, consisting in portraying Iran as a sponsor of the "Islamic terror network".

Turning Point in the Disinformation Campaign

In the months leading up to the invasion of Iraq in March 2003, Al-Zarqawi's name reemerges, this time almost on a daily basis, with reports focusing on his "sinister relationship to Saddam Hussein".

A major turning point in the propaganda campaign occurs on February 5, 2003 at the United Nations Security Council, following Colin Powell's historic address to the UN body.

Focussing on the central role of Al-Zarqawi, Secretary Colin Powell presented detailed "documentation" on the ties between Saddam Hussein and Al Qaeda, and linked this "sinister nexus" to Iraq's alleged possession of weapons of mass destruction:

Our concern is not just about these illicit weapons; it's the way that these illicit weapons can be connected to terrorists and terrorist organizations. ...

But what I want to bring to your attention today is the potentially much more *sinister nexus between Iraq and the Al Qaeda terrorist network, a nexus that combines classic terrorist organizations and modern methods of murder. Iraq today harbors a deadly terrorist network, headed by Abu Musaab al-Zarqawi, an associate and collaborator of Osama bin Laden and his Al Qaeda lieutenants.*

Zarqawi, a Palestinian born in Jordan, fought in the Afghan War more than a decade ago [as a Mujahideen recruited by the CIA]. Returning to Afghanistan in 2000, he oversaw a terrorist training camp. One of his specialities and one of the specialities of this camp is poisons. ...

We know these affiliates are connected to Zarqawi because they remain, even today, in regular contact with his direct subordinates, including the poison cell plotters. And they are involved in moving more than money and materiel. Last year, two suspected Al Qaeda operatives were arrested crossing from Iraq into Saudi Arabia. They were linked to associates of the Baghdad cell, and one of them received training in Afghanistan on how to use cyanide.

From his terrorist network in Iraq, Zarqawi can direct his network in the Middle East and beyond. [Al-Zarqawi is presented here as being active in several countries at the same time.] ...

According to detainees, Abu Atiya, who graduated from Zarqawi's terrorist camp in Afghanistan, tasked at least nine North African extremists in 2001 to travel to Europe to conduct poison and explosive attacks. Since last year, members of this network have been apprehended in France, Britain, Spain and Italy. By our last count, 116 operatives connected to this global web have been arrested. The chart you are seeing shows the network in Europe.

We know about this European network, and we know about its links to Zarqawi, because the detainee who provided the information about the targets also provided the names of members of the network. ...

We also know that Zarqawi's colleagues have been active in the Pankisi Gorge, Georgia, and in Chechnya, Russia. The plotting to which they are linked is not mere chatter. Members of Zarqawi's network say their goal was to kill Russians with toxins.

We are not surprised that Iraq is harboring Zarqawi and his subordinates. This understanding builds on decades-long experience with respect to ties between Iraq and al Qaeda. ...

As I said at the outset, none of this should come as a surprise to any of us. *Terrorism has been a tool used by Saddam for decades. Saddam was a supporter of terrorism long before these terrorist networks had a name, and this support continues.* The nexus of poisons and terror is new; the nexus of Iraq and terror is old. The combination is lethal.

With this track record, Iraqi denials of supporting terrorism take their place alongside the other Iraqi denials of weapons of mass destruction. It is all a web of lies. When we confront a regime that harbors ambitions for regional domination, hides weapons of mass destruction, and provides haven and active support for terrorists, we are not confronting the past, we are confronting the present. And unless we act, we are confronting an even more frightening future.[6]

Following Powell's February 2003 UN Security Council presentation, Al-Zarqawi immediately gained in public notoriety as a terrorist mastermind involved in planning chemical and biological weapons attacks.

The Ansar Al-Islam Connection

Based on fake intelligence, Secretary Powell's presentation to the UN Security Council consisted in linking the secular Baathist regime to the "Islamic terror network", with a view to justifying the invasion and occupation of Iraq.

According to Powell, Al-Zarqawi had been working hand in glove with Ansar Al-Islam, an obscure Islamist group, based in Northern Iraq.

In the wake of 9/11, Ansar had allegedly been responsible for plotting terror attacks in a number of countries including France, Britain, and Germany. US officials had also pointed to the sinister role of Iraq's embassy in Islamabad, which was allegedly used as a liaison between Ansar Al-Islam operatives and representatives of the Iraqi government of Saddam Hussein.

Ironically, Ansar was allowed to develop in a region which had been under US military control since the 1991 Gulf War, namely Kurdish held Northern Iraq. This region—which was in "the no fly zone"—was not under the control of the Saddam government. It became a de facto US protectorate in the wake of the 1991 Gulf War.

There was no evidence of Saddam Hussein's support to Ansar Al-Islam. In fact, quite the opposite. The US military authorities stationed in the region had turned a blind eye to the presence of alleged Islamic terrorists. With virtually no interference from the US military, "Al Qaida affiliates [had] been operating freely in the [regional] capital, … coordinating the movement of people, money and supplies for Ansar al-Islam".[7]

The spiritual founder of Ansar Al-Islam, Mullah Krekar confirmed that "like most militant Islamists, [he] hates Saddam." At the time of the US invasion of Iraq, Mullah Krekar was living in Norway, where he had refugee status. "The US has not requested his arrest. If Iraq is guilty of occasional meetings with second-level Al Qaeda operatives, then what is the Norwegian government guilty of?"[8]

Ansar Al-Islam was largely involved in terrorist attacks directed against the secular institutions of the Kurdish regional governments. It was also involved in assassinations of members of the Kurdish Patriotic Union of Kurdistan (PUK).

In fact in the days following Colin Powell's February 5, 2003 presentation to the United Nations Security Council, a senior military leader of PUK forces General Shawkat Haj Mushir was assassinated allegedly by Ansar Al-Islam.[9] Surrounded in mystery, the assassination of Shawkat was barely mentioned in the US press.

In the days following Colin Powell's February 5, 2003 UN address, the Iraqi foreign ministry clarified in an official statement that:

> the Iraqi government [of Saddam Hussein] helped the [PUK] Kurdish leader Jalal Talabani against the Ansar al-Islam group. He [the spokesman] accused Ansar al-Islam of carrying out acts of sabotage inside Iraq … [and] that the United States had turned down an Iraqi offer to cooperate on the issue of terrorism.[10]

While accusing Baghdad of links to the terror network, the presence and activities of Islamic fundamentalist groups in Northern Iraq was largely serving US interests.

These groups were committed to the establishment of a Muslim theocracy. They had contributed to triggering political instability while at the same time weakening the institutions of the two dominant secular Kurdish parties, both of which had been on occasion been involved in negotiations with the government of Saddam Hussein.

Quoting a "top secret British document", the BBC revealed on the very same day Colin Powell made his presentation to the UN Security Council (5 February 2003): "that there is nothing but enmity between Iraq and Al Qaeda. The BBC said the leak came from [British] intelligence officials upset that their work was being used to justify war."[11]

Moreover, the powerful Council on Foreign Relations (CFR) which plays a behind the scenes role in US military planning also refuted the substance of Colin Powell's statement to the UN Security Council concerning the links between the Iraqi government and the Islamic terror network. (This refutation is all the more serious, in view of the fact that these alleged links were used as a justification for the invasion of Iraq.):

> The question of Iraqi links to Al Qaeda remains murky, although senior Bush administration officials insist such ties exist. ... [M]any experts and State Department officials note that any Al Qaeda presence in Iraq probably lies in northern regions beyond Saddam's control. Many experts say there is scant evidence of ties between Al Qaeda and Iraq, noting that Al Qaeda's loathing for "impious" Arab governments makes it an unlikely bedfellow for Saddam's secular regime.[12]

Mysterious Chemical-Biological Weapons Plant in Northern Iraq

The substance of Powell's UN statement with regard to Al-Zarqawi rested on the existence of an Ansar al-Islam chemical-biological weapons plant in Northern Iraq which was producing ricin, sarin and other biological weapons, to be used in terror attacks on the US and Western Europe:

> When our coalition ousted the Taliban, *the Zarqawi network helped establish another poison and explosive training center camp, and this camp is located in North-Eastern Iraq.*
>
> The network is teaching its operative how to produce ricin and other poisons. Let me remind you how ricin works. Less than a pinch—imagine a pinch of salt—less than a pinch of ricin, eating just this amount in your food would cause shock, followed by circulatory failure. Death comes within 72 hours and there is no antidote. There is no cure. It is fatal.
>
> Those helping to run this camp are Zarqawi lieutenants operating in northern Kurdish areas outside Saddam Hussein's controlled Iraq, but Baghdad has an agent in the most senior levels of the radical organization Ansar al-Islam, that controls this corner of Iraq. In 2000, this agent offered Al Qaeda safe haven in the region. After we swept Al Qaeda from Afghanistan, some of its members accepted this safe haven. They remain there today.

The above statement by Colin Powell, concerning the North Iraqi facility where the ricin was being produced, *was refuted by several media reports, prior to the US-led invasion*:

> *There is no sign of chemical weapons anywhere—only the smell of paraffin and vegetable butter used for cooking.* In the kitchen, I discovered some chopped up tomatoes but not much else. The cook had left his Kalashnikov propped neatly against the wall. Ansar al-Islam—the Islamic group that uses the compound identified as a military HQ by Powell—yesterday invited me and several other foreign journalists into their territory for the first time. "We are just a group of Muslims trying to do our duty," Mohammad Hasan, spokesman for Ansar al-Islam, explained. "We don't have any drugs for our fighters. We don't even have any aspirin. How can we produce any chemicals or weapons of mass destruction?"[13]

The intelligence contained in Colin Powell's UN statement had been fabricated. At the height of the military invasion of Iraq, a few weeks later, US Special Forces, together with their "embedded" journalists, entered the alleged chemical-biological weapons facility in Northern Iraq. Their report also refutes Colin Powell's statements to the UN body:

> What they [US Special Forces] found was a camp devastated by cruise missile strikes during the first days of the war. A specialized biochemical team scoured the rubble for samples. They wore protective masks as they entered a building they suspected was a weapons lab. Inside they found mortar shells, medical supplies, and grim prison cells, but no immediate proof of chemical or biological agents. For this unit, such evidence would have been a so-called smoking gun, proof that it has banned weapons. But instead, this was a disappointing day for these troops on the front line of the hunt for weapons of mass destruction here. Jim Sciutto, ABC News, with US Special Forces in Northern Iraq.[14]

The Alleged Ricin Threat in the US

On February 8, 2003, three days after Colin Powell's UN speech, the ricin threat reemerged, this time in the US. Al-Zarqawi was said to be responsible for "the suspicious white powder found in a letter sent to Senate Majority Leader Bill Frist which contained the [same] deadly poison ricin."[15]

In a CIA report which was supposedly "leaked" to *Newsweek*, a group of CIA analysts predicted authoritatively that:

> "[There was] a 59 percent probability that an attack on the US homeland involving WMD would occur before 31 March 2003." ... It all seems so precise and frightening: a better than 90 percent chance that Saddam will succeed in hitting America with a weapon spewing radiation, germs or poison. But it is important to remember that the odds are determined by averaging a bunch of guesses, informed perhaps, but from experts whose careers can only be ruined by underestimating the threat.[16]

The picture of "terrorist mastermind" Al-Zarqawi was featured prominently in *Newsweek*'s cover story article.

In the *National Review* (February 18, 2003), one month before the onslaught of the invasion of Iraq, Al-Zarqawi was described as Al Qaeda's "chief biochemical engineer":

It is widely known that Zarqawi, Al Qaeda's chief biochemical engineer, was at the safe house in Afghanistan where traces of ricin and other poisons were originally found. What is not widely known-but was briefly alluded to in Sec. Powell's UN address-is that starting in the mid-1990s, Iraq's embassy in Islamabad routinely played host to Saddam's biochemical scientists, some of whom interacted with al Qaeda operatives, including Zarqawi and his lab technicians, under the diplomatic cover of the Taliban embassy nearby to teach them the art of mixing poisons from home grown and readily available raw materials.[17]

Radioactive Dirty Bombs

In the immediate aftermath of Powell's speech, there was a code orange alert. Reality had been turned upside down. The US was not attacking Iraq. Iraq was preparing to attack America with the support of "Islamic terrorists". Official statements also pointed to the dangers of a dirty radioactive bomb attack in the US. Again Al-Zarqawi was identified as the number one suspect.[18]

Meanwhile, Al-Zarqawi had been identified as the terror mastermind behind the (thwarted) ricin attacks in several European countries including Britain and Spain, in the months leading up to the invasion of Iraq.

Britain's Ricin Threat

In January 2003, there was a ricin terror alert, which supposedly had also been ordered by Al-Zarqawi. The ricin had allegedly been discovered in a London apartment. It was to be used in a terror attack in the London subway. British press reports, quoting official statements claimed that the terrorists had learnt to produce the ricin at the Ansar al-Islam camp in Northern Iraq.

Two years later, the police investigation revealed that the ricin threats in Britain had been fabricated, and Britain's system of justice had been "tailored to a time of terror":

> There was no ricin and no Al Qaeda recipe, only a formula apparently confected by a white American Christian survivalist and downloaded from the Internet. Even if Bourgass, a nasty and deluded

loner, had managed to create his poison and smear it on car-door handles, it would not have worked. Had Bourgass the poisoner devoted himself to creating the perfect Nigella chickpea couscous, he could hardly have been a less likely mass exterminator ...

In the absence of chemical poison, a war against Iraq, a fake link between Al Qaeda and Saddam and a double helping of contempt of court were brewed up on Kamel Bourgass's hob. Tony Blair, David Blunkett, Colin Powell and senior police officers all used the arrests to illustrate the existence of a new breed of Islamist super-terrorist. A criminal prosecution was exploited to fit a political agenda. A war was justified and civil liberties imperiled by the ricin stash that never was.

Lawyers for the eight cleared men are outraged at the way their clients have been portrayed by the media and politicians, and there is so little acknowledgment of a just result, from the Home Office and elsewhere, that one wonders if dodgy convictions would have left some politicians more satisfied. Meanwhile, a new terror law, more draconian than expected, is in the Labour manifesto, pushing criminal trials for those who "glorify or condone acts of terror".

The affair of the sham ricin casts a long shadow over the police, the Crown Prosecution Service, the credulous sensationalists of the media and, most of all, over politicians. ...

Eight innocent men were presumed guilty. Ten others held for two years without charge reportedly had non-existent links to the ricin plot cited on their government control orders.[19]

It is worth mentioning that "authoritative" news stories on the ricin threat as well as the (nonexistent) chemical weapons plants in Northern Iraq, continued to be churned out in the wake of the invasion, despite the fact that official reports confirmed that they did not exist. In a June 2004 report in the *Washington Times*:

> Zarqawi stands as stark evidence of a link between Saddam Hussein's autocratic regime and bin Laden's al Qaeda terror network. Zarqawi, 38, operated a terrorist camp in northern Iraq that specialized in developing poisons and chemical weapons.

The Spanish Connection

In the months leading up to the invasion of Iraq, fabricated threats of chemical weapons attacks had emerged in several countries at the same time. Was the disinformation campaign being coordinated by intelligence officials in several countries?

In Spain, in the months prior to the March 2003 invasion, Bush's indefectible coalition partner, Prime Minister Jose Maria Aznar had initiated his own disinformation campaign, no doubt in liaison with the office of the US Secretary of State.

The timing seemed perfect: on the very same day Colin Powell was presenting the Al-Zarqawi dossier to the UN (focussing on the sinister chemical weapons facility in Northern Iraq), Prime Minister Jose Maria Aznar was busy briefing the Spanish parliament on an alleged chemical terror attack in Spain, in which Al-Zarqawi was supposedly also involved.

According to Prime Minister Aznar, Al-Zarqawi had established links to a number of European Islamic "collaborators" including Merouane Ben Ahmed, "an expert in chemistry and explosives who visited Barcelona".[20]

Prime Minister Aznar confirmed in his speech to the Chamber of Deputies (Camera de diputados) on the 5th of February 2001 that the sixteen Al Qaeda suspects, allegedly in possession of explosives and lethal chemicals, had been working hand in glove with "terrorist mastermind" Al-Zarqawi.

Prime Minister Aznar's statements concerning these "lethal chemical weapons in the hands of terrorists" was also based on fabricated intelligence. An official report of the Spanish Ministry of Defense confirmed that "the tests on chemicals seized from 16 suspected Al Qaeda men in Spain ... have revealed that they are harmless and some were household detergent."[21]

> A defense ministry lab outside Madrid tested the substances—a bag containing more than half a pound of powder and several bottles or containers with liquids or residues—for the easy-to-make biological poison ricin .... The Spanish defense ministry, which carried out the tests, and the lab itself declined to comment.[22]

3/11: The Madrid 11 March 2004 Train Bombing

In the wake of the US led invasion of Iraq, Al-Zarqawi's name was being routinely associated, without supporting evidence, with numerous terror threats and incidents in Western Europe and the US.

While the press reports regarding the March 11, 2004 Madrid train bombing did not generally point to Al-Zarqawi's involvement, they nonetheless hinted that the Moroccan group which allegedly "supervised the bombings in Madrid, [was] acting [according to the CIA] as a link between Al-Zarqawi and a cell of mostly Moroccan Al Qaeda members."[23]

This type of reporting, which broadly replicates the sinister relationship described by Prime Minister Aznar in his February 5, 2003 statement to the Spanish Parliament, provides a face to the outside enemy.

Two days after the 3/11 Madrid bombing, CNN reported, quoting US intelligence sources, that Al-Zarqawi, described as "a lone wolf", might be planning attacks on "soft targets" in Western Europe:

> LISOVICZ: And Jonathan, specifically, Abu Musaab Al-Zarqawi is someone you have described as Al Qaeda 2.0, which is pretty scary.
>
> SCHANZER: *Yes. Abu Musab Al-Zarqawi is the man we caught; we intercepted his memo last month. US intelligence officials found this memo. It indicated that he was trying to continue to carry out attacks against the United States.*
>
> CAFFERTY: Where do we stand in your opinion on this war on terrorism? *We have got this terrible situation in Madrid. We've got this fellow, Zarqawi, you are talking about, the lone Wolf that is active, some think inside Iraq. We have got terrorist attacks happening there. There is discussion all over Western Europe of fear of terrorism, possibly being about to increase there. Are we winning this war or are we losing it? What is your read?*
>
> SCHANZER: I think we're winning it. We've certainly—I mean counterterrorism at its core is just restricting the terrorist environment. So we've cut down on the amount of finances moving around in the terrorist world. We have arrested a number of key figures. So we are doing a good job.[24]

"Are we winning or loosing" the war on terrorism. "We are doing a good job." These catch phrases are part of the disinformation campaign. While they acknowledge "weaknesses" in US counter-errorism, their function is to justify enhanced military-intelligence operations against this illusive individual, who is confronting US military might, all over the World.

The April 2004 Osama Tape

Meanwhile, another mysterious Osama tape (April 2004) had emerged in which bin Laden acknowledged his responsibility for the 9/11 attacks on the World Trade Center and the 3/11 train bombing in Madrid in March 2004:

> "I [Osama] am offering a truce to European countries, and its core is our commitment to cease operations against any country which does not carry out an onslaught against Muslims or interfere in their affairs as part of the big American conspiracy against the Islamic world. ... The truce will begin when the last soldier leaves our countries. ... Whoever wants reconciliation and the right (way), then we are the ones who initiated it, so stop spilling our blood so we can stop spilling your blood. ... What happened on September 11 and March 11 was your goods delivered back to you.[25]

In other words, Osama bin Laden offers "a truce" if the various European countries involved in Iraq accept to withdraw their troops. In return, Al Qaeda will declare a moratorium on terrorist attacks in Europe.

Without further investigation, the Western media described the controversial April 2004 Osama tape as an attempt by "Enemy Number One" to create a rift between America and its European allies.

The tape in all likelihood was a hoax of US intelligence. The propaganda ploy consists not only in upholding the US-led occupation of Iraq as part of the broader "war on terrorism", it also provides a pretext to European governments, pressured by citizens movements, to turn a blind eye to the US-UK sponsored war crimes in Iraq. In the words of France's President Jacques Chirac, "nothing can justify terrorism and, on that basis, nothing can allow any discussion with terrorists."

Underlying the Osama tape is the presumption that the "extremists" in Iraq are the same people responsible for the 9/11 and 3/11 terrorist attacks. It follows, according to one US press report, that the "anti-war zealots", by opposing the US led occupation, are in fact providing ammunition to Osama bin Laden's Al Qaeda:

> Bin Laden's deranged fantasies are frighteningly similar to those many anti-war zealots harbor both here and abroad. ... He also apparently tries to justify the attacks of 9/11 as retaliation for US support for Jews in Palestine, and US invasions in the Gulf War and Somalia. "Our actions are reactions to your actions," he said.
>
> This is gibberish, but it is typical of a megalomaniacal mind. Even Hitler, after all, insisted his attack on Poland was in self-defense. Evil often comes cloaked in the counterfeit robes of virtue.
>
> But it's also easy to see how such arguments can gain traction among impoverished Arabs who long have been repressed by their own governments and are searching for answers.
>
> The United States should be grateful for this latest tape. It puts a lot of things in perspective. Europe and the United States are at war together, and the enemy is someone of flesh and blood who can be frightened—enough so that he feels it necessary to propose a truce.[26]

Al-Zarqawi and the Abu Ghraib Prison Scandal

The Abu Ghraib torture scandal, including the release of the photographs of tortured POWs, reached its climax with the broadcast of CBS's "60 Minutes" hosted by Dan Rather on the 28th of April 2004.[27]

Within days of an impending scandal involving the upper echelons of the Pentagon, which directly implicated Defense Secretary Donald Rumsfeld, Al-Zarqawi was reported to be planning simultaneous large scale terrorist attacks in several countries, including a major terrorist operation in Jordan.

With Al-Zarqawi featured prominently on network television, these reports served to usefully distract public attention from the Abu Ghraib torture scandal.

A mysterious videotape was released, describing in minute detail how "terrorist mastermind" Al-Zarqawi was planning to wage a major attack inside Jordan. The alleged attack consisted in using "a combination of 71 lethal chemicals, including blistering agents to cause third-degree burns, nerve gas and choking agents, which would have formed a lethal toxic cloud over a square mile of the capital, Amman".[28]

According to the news reports, "the alleged terrorist plot was just days away from execution". The targets were the Jordanian intelligence headquarters, the prime minister's office and the US Embassy. According to CNN, which broadcast excerpts of the mysterious videotape, "the Jordanian government fears the death toll could have run into the thousands, *more deadly even than 9/11*".[29]

> [In CNN's coverage], Jordanian special forces [are] raiding an apartment house in Amman in the hunt for an al Qaeda cell. Some of the suspects are killed, others arrested, ending what Jordanian intelligence says was a bold plan to use chemical weapons and truck bombs in their capital. … The Jordanian government fears the death toll could have run into the thousands, more deadly even than 9/11.
>
> For the first time the alleged plotters were interviewed on videotape, aired on Jordanian TV. CNN obtained copies of the tapes from the Jordanians. This man revealing his orders came from a man named Azme Jayoussi, the cell's alleged ringleader.
>
> HUSSEIN SHARIF (through translator): The aim of this operation was to strike Jordan and the Hashemite royal family, a war against the crusaders and infidels. Azme told me that this would be the first chemical suicide attack that al Qaeda would execute.
>
> VAUSE: Also appearing on the tape, *Azme Jayoussi, who says his orders came from this man, Abu Musab al-Zarqawi, the same man the US says is behind many of the violent attacks in Iraq.*
>
> AZME JAYOUSSI, ACCUSED PLOTTER (through translator): I took advanced explosives course, poisons, high level, then I pledged allegiance to Abu Musab al-Zarqawi, to obey him without any questioning, to be on his side. After this Afghanistan fell. I met Abu Musab al-Zarqawi in Iraq.[30]

Al-Zarqawi 's "Attack on America"

Two days later on the 29 April 2004, immediately following the reports on the terrorist threat in Jordan, the State Department announced that Al-Zarqawi was now planning a similar chemical weapons attack on America.[31]

The " freelancer" and "lone wolf, … acting alone in the name of Al Qaeda" had been crossing international borders unnoticed. One day, he's in Jordan, the next day in the US, and back again a few days later in Iraq.

According to the US State Department *Annual Report on Terrorism,* quoted by CNN:

> [T]he number of terrorist attacks around the world declined last year, but the government's annual report on terrorism includes a chilling warning about the year ahead. … The State Department says terrorists are planning an attack on US soil. High on their anxiety list, terrorist Abu Musab Al-Zarqawi.
>
> [According to the State Department's Coordinator for Counterterrorism, Cofer Black] "He [Al-Zarqawi] is representative of a very real and credible threat. His operatives are planning and attempting now to attack American targets, and we are after them with a vengeance.[32]

The State Department report was released on the same day as the CBS's "60 Minutes" program on the Abu Ghraib prison scandal.

The Nicholas Berg Execution

Barely a couple of weeks later, Al-Zarqawi is named as the mastermind behind the execution in Iraq of Nicholas Berg on May 11, 2004. Media coverage of Berg's terrible death was based on a mysterious report (and video) on an Islamic website, which according to CNN provided evidence that Al-Zarqawi might be involved:

> ENSOR: The Web site claims that the killing was done by Abu Musab al-Zarqawi, a Jordanian terrorist whose al Qaeda affiliated group is held responsible by US intelligence for a string of bombings in Iraq and for the killing of an American diplomat in Amman. CNN Arab linguists say, however, that the voice on the tape has the wrong accent.

They do not believe it is Zarqawi. US officials said the killers tried to take advantage of the prison abuse controversy to gain attention. ...

BROWN: So, the administration said today we'll track these people down. We will get them beyond, I guess, this belief that Zarqawi somehow was involved. Are there any clues out there that we heard about?

ENSOR: This is going to be very, very difficult. They've been looking for Abu Musab al-Zarqawi for several years now. There's a large price on his head. He's been blowing up a lot of things in Iraq according to him and according to US intelligence. They don't know where he is, so it's—I don't think they have any clues right now, at least none that I know of—Aaron.[33]

While initially expressing doubts on the identity of the masked individual, a subsequent and more definitive report, based on "authoritative intelligence", was aired two days later by CNN on 13 May 2004:

> *The CIA confirms that Nicholas Berg's killer was Abu Musab Al-Zarqawi; The CIA acknowledges sticking to strict rules in tough interrogations of top al Qaeda prisoners.*
>
> BLITZER Because originally our own linguists here at CNN suspected that—they listened to this audiotape and they didn't think that it sounded like Abu Musab al-Zarqawi. *But now definitively, the experts at the CIA say it almost certainly is Abu Musab al-Zarqawi?*
>
> ENSOR: They say it almost certainly is. There's just a disagreement between the CNN linguists and the CIA linguists. *The US Government now believes that the person speaking on that tape and killing Nick Berg on that tape is the actual man, Abu Musab al-Zarqawi.*[34]

The report on the Nicholas Berg assassination, coincided with calls by US senators for the resignation of Defense Secretary Donald Rumsfeld over the Abu Ghraib prison scandal. It occurred a few days after President Bush's "apology" for the Abu Ghraib prison "abuses". It served once again to distract public attention from the war crimes ordered by key members of the Bush Administration.

Authenticity of the Video

The video footage published on the website was called "Abu Musab Al-Zarqawi shows killing of an American".

While CIA experts released a statement saying that Abu Musab
Al-Zarqawi "was the man in the mask who beheaded the US citizen Nick Berg in front of a camera," several reports question the
authenticity of the video.[35]

Al-Zarqawi is Jordanian. Yet the man in the video "posing as
Jordanian native Zarqawi does not speak the Jordanian dialect.
Zarqawi has an artificial leg, but none of these murderers did. The
man presented as Zarqawi had a yellow ring, presumably a golden
one, which Muslim men are banned from wearing, especially so-
called fundamentalists."[36]

When the issue of his artificial leg was mentioned in relation
to the video, US officials immediately revised their story, stating
they were not quite sure whether he had actually lost a leg: "US
intelligence officials, who used to believe that Zarqawi had lost a leg
in Afghanistan, recently revised that assessment, concluding that he
still has both legs."[37]

Nicholas Berg was assassinated. The identity of the killers was
not firmly established. Moreover, there were a number of other
aspects pertaining to the video, which suggested that it was a fake.

Another report stated that Zarqawi was dead.

The audio was not in synchrony with the video, indicating that
the video footage might have been manipulated.

The Iraqi Resistance Movement

In the wake of the invasion of Iraq, the disinformation campaign
consisted in presenting the Iraqi resistance movement as "terrorists".

The image of "terrorists" fighting US peacekeepers is presented
on television screens across the globe.

Portrayed as an evil enemy, Al-Zarqawi was used profusely in
Bush's press conferences and speeches, in an obvious public relations ploy:

> You know, I hate to predict violence, but I just understand the nature
> of the killers. This guy, Zarqawi, an al Qaeda associate—who was in
> Baghdad, by the way, prior to the removal of Saddam Hussein—is still
> at large in Iraq. And as you might remember, part of his operational
> plan was to sow violence and discord amongst the various groups in

Iraq by cold-blooded killing. And we need to help find Zarqawi so that the people of Iraq can have a more bright—bright future.[38]

The portrait of terror mastermind Al-Zarqawi was used to personify the Iraqi resistance.

In an almost routine and repetitive fashion, his name is linked to the numerous "terrorist attacks" in Iraq against the US led-occupation.

> While the Western media highlights these various occurrences including the kidnappings of paid mercenaries, on contract to Western security firms, there is a deafening silence on the massacre of more than one hundred thousand Iraqi civilians by coalition forces, since the beginning of the US-led occupation in April 2003.[39]

The 2004-2005 operation in Fallujah, which resulted in several thousand civilian deaths, was casually described by the Bush administration as "a crackdown" against extremists working under the leadership of Al-Zarqawi. According to official statements, Al Qaeda mastermind Abu Musab al-Zarqawi was in Fallujah, which had become a so-called "hotbed for foreign fighters". In the words of *Newsweek*: "Saddam may not have had direct ties to Al Qaeda, but the Jihadists are eager to fill his shoes."[40]

In other words, the Bush administration needs Al-Zarqawi and the "war on terrorism" as a justification for the killing of civilians in Iraq, which it continues to describe as "collateral damage".

Consistently, a barrage of media reports had surfaced on Al Qaeda links to the Iraqi resistance movement. The insurgents are described as Islamic extremists and fundamentalists: "hard-line Sunnis, foreign extremists, and, now, Sadr and his disenfranchised Shiite followers".[41]

The secular character of the resistance movement is denied. In a completely twisted logic, Al Qaeda is said to constitute a significant force behind the Iraqi insurgents.

The disinformation campaign ultimately consists in convincing the US public that the "Defense of the Homeland" and the occupation of Iraq are part of the same process and involving the same enemy. In the words of former CIA Director James Woolsey in a CNN interview:

> Iraqi intelligence, trained al Qaeda in poison gases and conventional explosives. And had senior-level contacts going back a decade. And the Islamists from the Sunni side, from the al Qaeda, work with people like Hezbollah. They're perfectly happy to work together against us. It's sort of like three Mafia families, but they insult each other, but can still cooperate.... I think it's Islamist totalitarians masquerading as part of a religion. Certainly if anybody in the intelligence community is surprised by this, the really surprising thing would be that they are really surprised. Some of them have had an idea fix for a long time, that al Qaeda would never work with the Ba'athist and the Shiite Islamist would never work with the Sunni. It's just nuts. They work together on important things. It's not that one necessarily controls the other. It's not sort of like state sponsorship, but cooperation, support here and there against us, sure, they've been doing it for years and years and years.[42]

New Propaganda Ploy

As the resistance movement in Iraq unfolds and challenges the US military occupation, Al-Zarqawi is increasingly portrayed by the media as the main obstacle to the holding of "free and fair elections" in Iraq.

Barely a week prior to the January 2005 Iraqi elections sponsored and organized by the Bush administration, with the support of the "international community," another mysterious Al-Zarqawi audiotape surfaced on the Internet.

While the news reports initially stated that "the authenticity of the tape could not be determined", they later confirmed, quoting "authoritative intelligence" that "the voice in the tape appeared to be that of Al-Zarqawi". In his own words, Al-Zarqawi had now declared "a fierce war on this evil principle of democracy and those who follow this wrong ideology".[43]

The Al-Zarqawi pre-election audiotape usefully served the disinformation campaign, by underscoring the evil and insidious links between Al-Zarqawi and former Saddam regime loyalists.

Secular Sunni Baathists and jihadists are said to have joined hands. In the Zarqawi audiotape, the Shiite majority is presented as "evil", serving to create divisions within Iraqi society:

> The leader of Al Qaeda in Iraq, Abu Musab al-Zarqawi, whose "young lions" are attacking polling stations and killing candidates, has described Shias as "the most evil of mankind ... the lurking snakes and the crafty scorpions, the spying enemy and the penetrating venom". Understanding that elections favor the majority, he said that the US had engineered the poll to get a Shia government into power.[44]

Again, reality is turned upside down. The existence of an Iraqi resistance movement to the US-led occupation is denied. The "insurgents" are "terrorists" opposed to democracy. Al-Zarqawi is pinpointed as attempting to sabotage what both the American and European media have described in chorus as "the first democratic elections in half a century". Meanwhile, the US-UK military mandate in Iraq is upheld by the "international community" and Washington's European allies.

"Clash of Civilizations"

With Iraq under continued US military occupation, the propaganda ploy now consists in focussing on the "clash of civilizations": the great divide between the societies of the Islamic Middle East and the Judeo-Christian West. Whereas the latter is recognized as "a moral system" closely associated with modern forms of Western democracy, the former is said to be entrenched in theocratic and authoritarian forms of government, dominated directly or indirectly by the tenets of Islamic fundamentalism.

It is on the premises of this "clash of civilizations" that America has formulated its messianic mission "to spread liberty in the world". In the words of President George W. Bush, there is "no neutral ground in the fight between civilisation and terror"

"The clash of civilizations," as described by Samuel Huntington, had become an integral part of the propaganda campaign.

Islam is not only heralded as being broadly "un-democratic" and incompatible with a (Western) system of representative government, the jihadists—including bin Laden and Al-Zarqawi are ushered in as the sole spokesmen for an Iraqi "insurgency" described in press reports and on network television, as being composed of "terrorists" and "criminal gangs":

> The questions Zarqawi raises go way beyond the elections in Iraq to the whole issue of modernization of the Arab world. Is democracy un-Islamic? Is there a fundamental clash between the principles of representative government and the principles of Islam?[45]

Meanwhile, the illegality of the US occupation under international law and the Nuremberg charter goes unmentioned.

Under the disguise of "peace-keeping", the United Nations is actively collaborating with the occupying forces. The deaths of thousands of civilians, the torture chambers and the concentration camps, the destruction of an entire country's infrastructure—not to mention the issue of the missing "weapons of mass destruction"—have been overshadowed by the fabricated image of an American commitment to democracy and post-war reconstruction.

Notes

1. Federal Bureau of Investigation (FBI), "FBI Most Wanted" at http://www.fbi.gov/mostwant/topten/fugitives/fugitives.htm.

2. *Weekly Standard*, 24 May 2004.

3. See Michel Collon, "Washington has Found the Solution 'Let's Divide Iraq as We Did in Yugoslavia!'", Centre for Research on Globalization, 23 December 2003, http://globalresearch.ca/articles/COL312A.html. See also Vladimir Radyuhin, "From Kosovo to Iraq", *The Hindu*, 18 August 2003,

4. *Washington Times*, 8 June 2004.

5. *New York Times*, 24 March 2002.

6. US Secretary of State Colin Powell's address to the UN Security Council, 5 February 2003.

7 *Midland Independent*, 6 February 2003.

8. Glen Rangwala, "Claims in Secretary of State Colin Powell's UN Presentation concerning Iraq, 5th February 2003", http://www.traprockpeace.org/firstresponse.html On Mullah Krekar, see *Daily News*, New York, 6 February 2003.

9. *The Australian*, 11 February 2003.

10. News Conference by Lieutenant-General Amir al-Sa'di, adviser at the Iraqi Presidency; Dr Sa'id al-Musawi, head of the Organizations' Department at the Iraqi Foreign Ministry; and Major-General Husam Muhammad Amin, head of the Iraqi National Monitoring Directorate, BBC Monitoring Service, 6 February 2003.

11. Quoted in *Daily News*, New York, 6 February 2003.

12. Council on Foreign Relations (CFR) website at http://www.cfrterrorism.org/groups/alqaeda3.html.

13. *The Observer*, London, 9 February 2003.

14. ABC News, 29 March 2003.

15. *Pittsburgh Post Gazette*, 8 February 2004.

16. *Newsweek*, 24 February 2003.

17. *National Review*, 18 February 2003.

18. ABC News, 13 February 2003.

19. Mary Riddell, "With poison in their souls: The demonisation of the ricin suspects by politicians and the media smacks of Salem", *The Observer*, 17 April 2005

20. Reported *in El País*, Madrid, 6 February 2003.

21. Europe Intelligence Wire, 27 February 2003.

22. Irish News, 27 February 2003.

23. *The Australian*, 27 May 2004.

24. CNN, 13 March 2004, emphasis added, For details on the Madrid bombing see, "Madrid 'blueprint': a dodgy document" by Brendan O'Neill, Centre for Research on Globalization, 1 April 2004, http://www.globalresearch.ca/articles/ONE404A.html

Ibid., See also the report by Al Jazeera, Centre for Research on Globalization, 17 April 2004, http://globalresearch.ca/articles/ALJ404A.html

26. *Deseret Morning News*, Salt Lake City, 15 April 2004.

27. Torture of Iraqi POWs in Baghdad's Abu Ghraib Prison, CBS Transcript: "60 Minutes", 28 April 2004.

28. *Charleston Post Courier*, 28 April 2004.

29. CNN, 27 April 2004, emphasis added.

30. *Ibid*, emphasis added.

31. CNN, 29 April 2003.

32. *Ibid.*

33. CNN, 11 May 2004.

34. CNN, 13 May 2004.

35. Sirajin Sattayev, "Was Nick Berg killed by US intelligence?", Centre for Research on Globalization, 23 May 2004, http://www.globalresearch.ca/articles/ SAT405A.html.

36. *Ibid.*

37. *US News and World Report*, 24 May 2004.

38. President George W. Bush, Press Conference, 1 June 2004, emphasis added.

39. See Les Roberts, Riyadh Lafta, Richard Garfield, Jamal Khudhairi, Gilbert Burnham, "Mortality before and after the 2003 invasion of Iraq", *Lancet*, 29 October 2004.

40. *Newsweek*, 19 April 2004.

41. *US News and World Report*, 19 April 2004.

42. Quoted from CNN, Lou Dobbs, Tonight, 15 April 2004.

43. Associated Press Report, 23 January 2005.

44. Quoted in *The New Statesman*, 31 January 2005.

45. *The Washington Post*, 30 January 2004.

CHAPTER XIV
Protecting Al Qaeda Fighters
in the War Theater

In late November 2001, the Northern Alliance, supported by US bombing raids, took the hill town of Kunduz in Northern Afghanistan. Eight thousand or more men "had been trapped inside the city in the last days of the siege, roughly half of whom were Pakistanis. Afghans, Uzbeks, Chechens, and various Arab mercenaries accounted for the rest."[1]

Also among these fighters, were several senior Pakistani military and intelligence officers, who had been dispatched to the war theater by the Pakistani military.

The presence of high-ranking Pakistani military and intelligence advisers in the ranks of the Taliban/Al Qaeda forces was known and approved by Washington. Pakistan's military intelligence, the ISI, which was indirectly involved in the 9/11 attacks, was overseeing the operation. (For details on the links of ISI to the CIA, see chapters II, IV and X.)

In a statement in the Rose Garden of the White House, President Bush confirmed America's resolve to going after the terrorists:

> I said a long time ago, one of our objectives is to smoke them out and
> get them running and bring them to justice. … I also said we'll use
> whatever means necessary to achieve that objective—and that's
> exactly what we're going to do.[2]

Most of the foreign fighters, however, were never brought to
justice, nor were they detained or interrogated. In fact, quite the
opposite occurred. As confirmed by Seymour Hersh, they were
flown to safety on the orders of Defense Secretary Donald Rumsfeld:

> The Administration ordered the US Central Command to set up a
> special air corridor to help insure the safety of the Pakistani rescue
> flights from Kunduz to the northwest corner of Pakistan. …
>
> [Pakistan President] Musharraf won American support for the
> airlift by warning that the humiliation of losing hundreds—and per-
> haps thousands—of Pakistani Army men and intelligence opera-
> tives would jeopardize his political survival. "Clearly, there is a great
> willingness to help Musharraf," an American intelligence official told
> me [Seymour Hersh]. A CIA analyst said that it was his under-
> standing that the decision to permit the airlift was made by the White
> House and was indeed driven by a desire to protect the Pakistani
> leader. The airlift "made sense at the time," the CIA analyst said.
> "Many of the people they spirited away were the Taliban leader-
> ship"—who Pakistan hoped could play a role in a postwar Afghan
> government. According to this person, "Musharraf wanted to have
> these people to put another card on the table" in future political
> negotiations. "We were supposed to have access to them," he said,
> but "it didn't happen," and the rescued Taliban remain unavailable
> to American intelligence.
>
> According to a former high-level American defense official, the air-
> lift was approved because of representations by the Pakistanis that
> "there were guys—intelligence agents and underground guys—who
> needed to get out.[3]

Out of some 8000 or more men, 3300 surrendered to the
Northern Alliance, leaving between 4000 and 5000 men "unaccounted for". Indeed, according to Indian intelligence sources
(quoted by Seymour Hersh), at least 4000 men including two
Pakistani Army generals had been evacuated. The operation was

casually described as a big mistake, leading to "unintended consequences". According to US officials:

> What was supposed to be a limited evacuation, apparently slipped out
> of control, and, as an unintended consequence, an unknown num-
> ber of Taliban and Al Qaeda fighters managed to join in the exo-
> dus.[4]

An Indian Press report confirmed that those evacuated by the
US were not the moderate elements of the Taliban, but rather "hard-
core Taliban" and Al Qaeda fighters.[5]

"Terrorists" or "Intelligence Assets"?
The foreign and Pakistani Al Qaeda fighters were evacuated to
North Pakistan as part of a military-intelligence operation led by
officials of Pakistan's Inter-Services Intelligence (ISI) in consultation with their CIA counterparts.

Many of these "foreign fighters" were subsequently incorporated into the two main Kashmiri terrorist rebel groups, Lashkar-
e-Taiba (Army of the Pure) and Jaish-e-Muhammad (Army of
Mohammed). (See Chapter II.) In other words, one of the main
consequences of the US sponsored evacuation was to reinforce
these Kashmiri terrorist organizations:

> Even today [March 2002], over 70 per cent of those involved in ter-
> rorism in Jammu and Kashmir are not Kashmiri youths but ISI
> trained Pakistani nationals. There are also a few thousand such
> Jehadis in Pakistan Occupied Kashmir prepared to cross the [Line of
> Control] LOC. It is also a matter of time before hundreds from
> amongst those the Bush Administration so generously allowed to
> be airlifted and escape from Kunduz in Afghanistan join these ter-
> rorists in Jammu and Kashmir.[6]

A few months following the November 2001 "Getaway", the
Indian Parliament in Delhi was attacked by Lashkar-e-Taiba and
Jaish-e-Muhammad. (See Chapter II.)

Saving Al Qaeda Fighters, Kidnapping Civilians

Why were several thousand Al Qaeda fighters airlifted and flown to safety? Why were they not arrested and sent to the Pentagon's concentration camp in Guantanamo?

What is the relationship between the evacuation of "foreign fighters" on the one hand and the detention (on trumped up charges) and imprisonment of so-called "enemy combatants" at the Guantanamo concentration camp.

The plight of the Guantanamo "terrorist suspects" has come to light with the release of a number of prisoners from Camp Delta in Guantanamo, after several years of captivity.

While Defense Secretary Rumsfeld claims that the Guantanamo detainees, are "vicious killers", the evidence suggests that most of those arrested and sent to Guantanamo were in fact civilians:

> The Northern Alliance has received millions of dollars from the US Government, and motivated the arrest of thousands of innocent civilians in Afghanistan on the pretext they were terrorists, to help the US Government justify the "war on terror". Some Guantanamo prisoners "were grabbed by Pakistani soldiers patrolling the Afghan border who collected bounties for prisoners." Other prisoners were caught by Afghan warlords and sold for bounty offered by the US for Al Qaeda and Taliban fighters. Many of the prisoners are described in classified intelligence reports as "farmers, taxi drivers, cobblers, and laborers". (Testimony provided by the Lawyer of Sageer, see Appendix to this chapter by Leuren Moret.)

Whereas Al Qaeda fighters and their senior Pakistani advisers were "saved" on the orders of Donald Rumsfeld, innocent civilians, who had no relationship whatsoever to the war theater, were routinely categorized as "enemy combatants", kidnapped, interrogated, tortured and sent to Guantanamo. Compare, in this regard, Seymour Hersh's account in the "Getaway" with the testimonies pertaining to the deportation of innocent civilians to Guantanamo. (See Appendix to this chapter.)

This leads us to the following question. Did the Bush administration need to "recruit detainees" amidst the civilian population and pass them off as "terrorists" with a view to justifying its com-

mitment to the "war on terrorism"? In other words, are these detentions part of the Pentagon's propaganda campaign?

Did they need to boost up the numbers "to fill the gap" resulting from the several thousand Al Qaeda fighters, who had been
secretly evacuated, on the orders of Donald Rumsfeld and flown to
safety?

Were these "terrorists" needed in the Kashmiri Islamic militant
groups in the context of an ISI-CIA covert operation?

At least 660 people from 42 countries, were sent to the Camp
Delta concentration camp in Guantanamo. While US officials continue to claim that they are "enemy combatants" arrested in
Afghanistan, a large number of those detained had never set foot in
Afghanistan until they were taken there by US forces. They were
kidnapped as part of a Pentagon Special-access program (SAP) in
several foreign countries including Pakistan, Bosnia and The Gambia
on the West Coast of Africa, and taken to the US military base in
Bagram, Afghanistan, before being transported to Guantanamo.

Moreover, two years later, in October 2003, the Bush administration decided to expand the facilities of the Guantanamo camp.
Kellogg, Brown & Root (KBR), the British subsidiary of Vice
President Dick Cheney's company Halliburton was granted a mul-
timillion dollar contract to expand the facilities of the Guantanamo
concentration camp including the construction of prisoner cells,
guard barracks and interrogation rooms. The objective was to bring
"detainee capacity to 1,000".[7]

Several children were held at Guantanamo, aged between 13
and 15 years old. Indeed, according to Pentagon officials, "the boys
were brought to Guantanamo Bay because they were considered a
threat and they had 'high value' intelligence that US authorities
wanted".[8] According to Britain's Muslim News, "out of the window
has gone any regard for the norms of international law and order
… with Muslims liable to be kidnapped in any part of the world to
be transported to Guantanamo Bay and face summary justice".[9]

Going after Al Qaeda in Northern Pakistan

Also in October 2003, the Pentagon decided to boost its counter-terrorism operations in Northern Pakistan with the support of the Pakistani military. These operations were launched in the tribal areas of northern Pakistan, following the visit to Islamabad of Deputy Secretary of State Richard Armitage and Assistant Secretary of State Christina Rocca.

The operation was aired live on network TV in the months leading up to the November 2004 US presidential elections. The targets were bin Laden and his deputy Ayman al-Zawahri, who were said to be hiding in these border regions of Northern Pakistan.

Both the Pentagon and the media described the strategy of "going after" bin Laden as a "hammer and anvil" approach, "with Pakistani troops moving into semiautonomous tribal areas on their side of the border, and Afghans and American forces sweeping the forbidding terrain on the other".[10]

In March 2004, Britain's *Sunday Express,* quoting "a US intelligence source" reported that:

> Bin Laden and about 50 supporters had been boxed in among the Toba Kakar mountainous north of the Pakistani city of Quetta and were being watched by satellite. … Pakistan then sent several thousand extra troops to the tribal area of South Waziristan, just to the North.[11]

In a bitter irony, it was to this Northern region of Pakistan that an estimated 4,000 Al Qaeda fighters had been airlifted in the first place, back in November 2001, on the explicit orders of Secretary Donald Rumsfeld. And these Al Qaeda units were also being supplied by Pakistan's ISI.[12]

In other words, the same units of Pakistan's military intelligence, the ISI—which coordinated the November 2001 evacuation of foreign fighters on behalf of the US—were also involved in the "hammer and anvil" search for Al Qaeda in northern Pakistan, with the support of Pakistani regular forces and US Special Forces.

From a military standpoint, it does not make sense. Evacuate the enemy to a safe-haven, and then two years later (in the months leading up to the 2004 presidential elections), "go after them" in the tribal hills of Northern Pakistan.

Why did they not arrest these Al Qaeda fighters in November 2001?

Was it incompetence or poor military planning? Or was a covert operation to safeguard and sustain "Enemy Number One"? Because without this "outside enemy" personified by Osama bin Laden, Musab Al-Zarqawi and Ayman al-Zawahri, there would be no justification for the "war on terrorism".

The terrorists are there, we put them there. And then "we go after them" and show the World in a vast media disinformation campaign that we are committed to weeding out the terrorists.

The timing of this operation in Northern Pakistan was crucial. "The war on terrorism" had become the cornerstone of Bush's 2004 presidential election campaign. The Bush campaign needed more than the rhetoric of the "war on terrorism". It needed a "real" war on terrorism, within the chosen theater of the tribal areas of Northern Pakistan, broadcast on network TV in the US and around the World.

Notes

1. Seymour M. Hersh, "The Getaway", *The New Yorker*, 21 January 2002,

2. The White House, November 26, 2001.

3. Seymour Hersh, *op cit.*

4. Quoted in *Hersh, op cit.*

5. *The Times of India*, 24 January 2002.

6. Business Line, 4 March 2002.

7. *Vanity Fair*, January 2004.

8. *The Washington Post*, 23 August 2003.

9. *Muslim News*, 11 March 2004. http://www.muslimnews.co.uk/index/press.php?pr=177

10. *The Record*, Kitchener, 13 March 2004.

11. Quoted in *The South China Morning Post*, 7 March 2004.

12. United Press International, 1 November 2001.

APPENDIX TO CHAPTER XIV
The Deportation of Civilians to the Guantanamo Concentration Camp

by Leuren Moret

In November 2001, during the Holy Month of Ramadan, a contingent of ten missionary members from Pakistan made a Tableegh Dora, routine preaching visit to the Northern Afghanistan Province of Kunduz. Among them was Mr. Sagheer, 54, a religious man from Phattan, a town in Pakistan near the border of Afghanistan, who had traveled as a preacher on other Tableegh (preaching missions). During this visit he was swept up and arrested with thousands of others by Uzbek warlord Abdul Rashid Dostum, the area Northern Alliance commander, "on the instructions and orders of the US Government/Army ... in a hunt against Al Qaeda, Osama bin-Laden, the Taliban and [Taliban leader] Mullah Umer".[1]

Mr. Sagheer was transported from Kunduz by truck with other prisoners in containers where many died, some who were injured were buried alive, others held in jails in Afghanistan, and finally he was transported by the US military to Guantanamo Bay.[2] There he was held like other prisoners in small cages, subjected to torture, humiliation, violation of religious prohibitions, denied legal rights, beaten and interrogated at Camp Delta.

After ten months, he was told by a senior US military officer at Camp Delta that he was found to be innocent and would be released. He was transported from Guantanamo back to Pakistan on a US military plane and released with a compensation of $100 from the US Government for his ordeal of nearly one year.

Mr. Sagheer, was arrested by the Northern Alliance. More than 30,000 detainees were also swept up in an indiscriminate arrest of civilians, but many died in Kunduz due to ground fire or bombardment by the US Air Force.

Mr. Sagheer witnessed wounded and injured men buried alive with the dead. He was in a group of 250 who were blindfolded, handcuffed, chained and put into trucks and taken to Mazar-e-Sharif by the Dostum Forces. At Mazar-e-Sharif they were held as prisoners and guarded for nearly six weeks by fifteen to twenty armed US military, assisted by local Northern Alliance commanders.

Later at Mazar-e-Sharif, they were crowded into airtight containers by US Forces and local soldiers for transport to the Shabargan Jail 75 miles west of Mazar-e-Sharif. Sagheer was one of about 250 crowded into one airtight container, which had a capacity of 50-60 people. Mr. Sagheer said that more than 50 died in the container from suffocation, lack of food, water and medical aid. In other containers, people died or were wounded when soldiers were ordered by US commanders to shoot holes for air into containers full of prisoners.[3]

Thousands more died in containers and were dumped in the desert by Afghan drivers hired by the US military forces.[4] In this regard, *Massacre in Mazar*, a disturbing documentary film by Irish director Jamie Doran, documents the torture and mass killings of POWs and civilians in Mazar-e-Sharif by US forces.[5]

At Shabargan Jail in Kandahar where they were detained two weeks, there were more than 3000 prisoners including Mr. Sagheer, accused of being Taliban. The FBI, with the US military, participated in the torture of prisoners there. Prisoners were thrashed, deprived of water, made to lie down on the dirt at midnight and not allowed to sleep.

Inside Guantanamo: Concentration Camp

At Guantanamo, Mohammed Sagheer was identified with an ID bracelet labeled "Delta" for Guantanamo which he still retains. The prisoners were put like animals in chain-link cages with roofs on cement pads out in the open—6ft. X 6 ft. X 7 ft.—where they were fully chained and locked inside the cages. They were subjected to physical and mental torture, starved, forced to drink urine, and not allowed to speak.

Prisoners were detained on "suspicion of terrorism" without charges and provided with no legal mechanism for appeal, condemning them to long-term imprisonment.[6]

Notes

1. Mohammad Sagheer vs. Government of USA, complaint filed November 3, 2003, District Court, Islamabad, by Muhammad Ikram Chaudhry, Ikram Law Associates.

2, "Cuba calls Guantanamo 'concentration camp'", *USA Today,* 27 December 2003

3 S. Steinberg, "Massacre in Mazar-I-Sharif", World Socialist Website, December 2001, http://www.wsws.org.

4. *Ibid.*

5. *Ibid.*

6. J. Andrews, "Bush goes ahead with 'Enemy Combatant Detentions'", *Global Outlook* Issue 3, Winter 2003.

Leuren Moret is an independent scientist who works on radiation and public health issues. After leaving the Livermore nuclear weapons laboratory, she has dedicated her life to revealing and understanding the health effects of radiation exposure resulting from US led military operations.

The complete text of Leuren Moret's article entitled "Inside Guantanamo Concentration Camp: Former Detainee Sues Bush Administration", was published by the Centre for Research on Globalization at www.globalresearch.ca, 6 January 2004. The above excerpt was reprinted with the permission of Leuren Moret. © Leuren Moret, All Rights Reserved, 2004.

PART IV
The New World Order

CHAPTER XV
War Criminals in High Office

Under the Bush administration, torture has become an official US Government policy. The orders to torture POWs in Iraq and Guantanamo emanated from the highest governmental levels. Prison guards, interrogators in the US military and the CIA were responding to precise guidelines.

The President directly authorized the use of torture including "sleep deprivation, stress positions, the use of military dogs, and sensory deprivation through the use of hoods, etc."[1]

This authorization was confirmed in a secret FBI email dated May 22, 2004. The latter indicated that president Bush had "personally signed off on certain interrogation techniques in an executive order."[2]

Another FBI email dated December 2003, described how military interrogators at Guantanamo had impersonated FBI agents, "to avoid possible blame in subsequent inquiries", and that this interrogation method had the approval of (former) Deputy Defense Secretary Paul Wolfowitz:

[The email] describes an incident in which Defense Department interrogators at Guantánamo Bay impersonated FBI agents while using "torture techniques" against a detainee. The e-mail concludes: "If this detainee is ever released or his story made public in any way, DOD interrogators will not be held accountable because these torture techniques were done [sic] [by] the 'FBI' interrogators. The FBI will [be] [sic] left holding the bag before the public."[3]

The document also stated that no "intelligence of a threat neutralization nature" was garnered by the "FBI" interrogation, and that the FBI's Criminal Investigation Task Force (CITF) believes that the Defense Department's actions have destroyed any chance of prosecuting the detainee. The author of the e-mail writes that he or she is documenting the incident "in order to protect the FBI".[4]

A third incriminating FBI email dated June 25, 2003 entitled "Urgent Report",

showed that the Sacramento field office warned the FBI director that it had received testimony of "numerous physical abuse incidents of Iraqi civilian detainees", including "strangulation, beatings, and placement of lit cigarettes into the detainees' ear openings". Other documents reported incidents such as detainees being dropped onto barbed wire, having Israeli flags wrapped around them, spat on and knocked unconscious, and shackled until they defecated on themselves.[5]

The evidence also confirmed that the US military was also involved in "mock executions" and the application of burning and electric shocks to detainees.[6]

Moreover, while several dozen detainees died in US custody, the records of these deaths were tampered with and the autopsy reports in many cases were not conducted, with a view to concealing the acts of torture.[7]

Abu Ghraib

The 2004 Abu Ghraib Taguba investigation (as well as two other reports) commissioned by the US military into "inhumane interrogation techniques" had exempted Donald Rumsfeld, Paul

Wolfowitz and of course, President Bush, of any wrongdoing or involvement.[8]

Despite the evidence, the reports placed the blame on lower rank servicemen and commanders in Iraq:

> Several US Army Soldiers have committed egregious acts and grave breaches of international law at Abu Ghraib/BCCF and Camp Bucca, Iraq. Furthermore, key senior leaders in both the 800th MP Brigade and the 205th MI Brigade failed to comply with established regulations, policies, and command directives in preventing detainee abuses at Abu Ghraib (BCCF) and at Camp Bucca.[9]

The conclusion of the report was that command directives to prevent the occurrence of torture were not followed.

In other words, the reports not only denied the existence of official US policy guidelines on torture (e.g.. the August 2002 and March 2003 memoranda), they stated that the directives were explicitly "not to torture POWs" and that command orders had been disregarded. Their conclusions should come as no surprise, since Defense Secretary Donald Rumsfeld had approved the conduct of these investigations.

Following the investigation, Brigadier General Janice Karpinksi in command of the military police unit at Abu Ghraib was suspended, whereas several lower rank servicemen and women were subjected to court martial procedures.

Court martial procedures were, therefore, initiated on the orders of Defense Secretary Donald Rumsfeld, when in fact it was Donald Rumsfeld and the President who had issued the Executive Order to torture the POWs.

War criminals in high office thus ordered the holding of these show trials, which essentially served to camouflage a systematic policy of torturing POWs, in violation of the Geneva convention, while also exempting these officials in high office from prosecution.

Torture is "Un-American"
President Bush "apologized" following the release of the Abu Ghraib photos in May 2004:

People in Iraq must understand that I view those practices as abhorrent. ... They must also understand that what took place in that prison does not represent the America that I know. ... There will be investigations, people will be brought to justice.[10]

Rumsfeld also apologized in a statement to the Senate Armed Services Committee:

We didn't, and that was wrong, ... So to those Iraqis who were mistreated by members of the US armed forces, I offer my deepest apology.[11]

The Legalization of Torture
Torture is permitted "under certain circumstances", according to an August 2002 Justice Department "legal opinion":

if a government employee were to torture a suspect in captivity, "he would be doing so in order to prevent further attacks on the United States by the Al Qaeda terrorist network," said the memo, from the Justice Department's office of legal counsel, written in response to a CIA request for legal guidance. It added that arguments centering on "necessity and self-defense could provide justifications that would eliminate any criminal liability" later.[12]

Even if an interrogation method might arguably cross the line drawn in Section and application of the stature was not held to be an unconstitutional infringement of the President's Commander in Chief authority, we believe that under current circumstances [since the "war on terrorism"] certain justification defenses might be available that would potentially eliminate criminal liability.[13]

A subsequent Department of Defense Memorandum dated March 2003 drafted by military lawyers, leaked to *The Wall Street Journal*, follows in the footsteps of the August 2002 "legal opinion":

Compliance with international treaties and US laws prohibiting torture could be overlooked because of legal technicalities and national security needs.[14]

These "legal opinions" are casually presented as a surrogate for bona fide legislation. They suggest, in an utterly twisted logic, that the Commander in Chief can quite legitimately authorize the use torture, because the victims of torture in this case are "terrorists", who are said to routinely apply the same methods against Americans.

New "Legal Opinion": Torture is no longer Un-American

Coinciding with the release of the incriminating FBI memos in mid December 2004, the Justice Department ordered the drafting of a new "legal opinion" on so-called "permissible US military interrogation techniques" to replace that of August 2002:

> [Attorney General] Gonzales "commissioned" the infamous Justice Department memo of 2002 that asserted President Bush's right to order torture, even redefining the meaning of torture not to include any pain short of organ failure, death or permanent psychological damage. This prompted other legal decisions approving such interrogation practices as "stress positions" and intimidation with dogs, leading then to the abyss of abuses at Abu Ghraib.[15]

The Criminalization of Justice

"Legal opinions" drafted on the behest of war criminals are being used to "legalize" torture and redefine Justice.

War criminals legitimately occupy positions of authority, which enable them to redefine the contours of the judicial system and the process of law enforcement.

It provides them with a mandate to decide "who are the criminals", when in fact they are the criminals.

In other words, what we are dealing with is the criminalization of the State and its various institutions including the criminalization of Justice.

The truth is twisted and turned upside down. State propaganda builds a consensus within the Executive, the US Congress and the Military. This consensus is then ratified by the Judicial, through a process of outright legal manipulation.

Media disinformation instills within the consciousness of Americans that somehow the use of torture, the existence of concentration camps, extra judicial assassinations of "rogue enemies"— all of which are happening—are, "under certain circumstances," "acceptable" and perfectly "legal" because the Justice Department's Office of Legal Counsel (OLC) says "it's legit".

The existence of an illusive outside enemy who is threatening the Homeland is the cornerstone of the propaganda campaign. The latter consists in galvanizing US citizens not only in favor of "the war on terrorism", but in support of a social order which upholds the legitimate use of torture, directed against "terrorists", as a justifiable means to preserving human rights, democracy, freedom, etc.

The Spanish Inquisition

In other words, we have reached a new threshold in US legal history. Torture is no longer a covert activity, removed from the public eye.

War criminals within the State and the Military are no longer trying to camouflage their crimes. Until recently, the logic was "We're sorry for the torture, we didn't do it. We're against torture. Those responsible will be punished."

The logic in the wake of 9/11 is entirely different and is reminiscent of the Spanish Inquisition.

Under the Inquisition, there was no need to conceal the acts of torture. In fact, quite the opposite. Torture is a public policy with a humanitarian mandate. "Democracy" and "freedom" are to be upheld by "going after the terrorists".

"The war on the terrorism" is said to be in the public interest. Moreover, anybody who questions its practices—which now includes torture, political assassination and concentration camps—is liable to be arrested under the antiterrorist legislation.

The Inquisition, which started in the 12th century and lasted for more than four hundred years was a consensus imposed by the ruling feudal social order. Its purpose was to maintain and sustain those in authority.

The Inquisition had a network of religious courts, which eventually evolved into a system of political and social control.

The great Inquisitor was similar to the Department of Homeland Security.

The underlying principles governing the courts were straightforward, and apart from the rhetoric, similar to today's procedures: "You find them and take 'em out":

> [H]eresy cannot be destroyed unless heretics are destroyed and ... their defenders and [supporters] are destroyed, and this is effected in two ways: ...they are converted to the true catholic faith, or ... burned [alive].[16]

Those who refused to recant and give up their heresy, were burned alive. Moreover, no lawyers were allowed, because it was considered heresy to defend a heretic:

> A bishop came out and shouted out the names of the condemned. Then the heretics were led out, wearing black robes decorated with red demons and flames. Officials of the government tied them to the stake.
>
> "Do you give up your heresy against the holy church?" a priest would challenge.
>
> Anyone who repented would be strangled to death before the fires were lit. Most, however, stood silent or defiant. The fires were lit, and the square echoed with the screams of the heretics and cheers from the crowd.[17]

The Road towards a Police State

Today's World is far more sophisticated. CIA torture manuals developed under successive US Administrations are more advanced. The anti-terrorist legislation (PATRIOT Acts I and II) and law enforcement apparatus, although built on the same logic, are better equipped to deal with large population groups.

In contrast to the Spanish Inquisition, the contemporary inquisitorial system has almost unlimited capabilities of spying on and categorizing individuals.

People are tagged and labeled, their emails, telephones and faxes are monitored. Detailed personal data is entered into giant Big Brother data banks. Once this cataloging has been completed, people are locked into watertight compartments. Their profiles are established and entered into a computerized system.

Law enforcement is systematic. The witch-hunt is not only directed against presumed "terrorists" through ethnic profiling, etc. The various human rights, affirmative action, antiwar cohorts are themselves the object of the anti-terrorist legislation and so on. Converting or recanting by antiwar heretics is not permitted.

Meanwhile, war criminals occupy positions of authority. The citizenry is galvanized into supporting rulers "committed to their safety and well-being" and "who are going after the bad guys."

Historically, the Inquisition was carried out in Spain, France and Italy, at the neighborhood level in communities across the land. Today in America, the mission of the Citizens Corps operating at the local level is to "make communities safer, stronger, and better prepared to respond to the threats of terrorism".

The Citizens Corps in liaison with Homeland Security are establishing "Neighborhood Watch Teams" as well as a "Volunteer Police Service" in partnership with local law enforcement.[18]

> When the inquisition came to a suspected area, the local bishop assembled the people to hear the inquisitor preach against heresy. He would announce a grace period of up to a month for heretics to confess their guilt, recant, and inform on others.
>
> If two witnesses under oath accused someone of heresy, the accused person would be summoned to appear. Opinions, prejudices, rumors, and gossip were all accepted as evidence. The accused was never told the names of the accusers, nor even the exact charges.
>
> The inquisition would collect accusations, where neighbors can be denounced.[19]

Under an inquisitorial system, the Executive Order personally signed by the president to torture becomes a public statement endorsed by the citizenry. It is no longer a secret FBI memorandum.

No need to conceal acts of torture.

The practice of torture against terrorists gains public acceptance, it becomes part of a broad bipartisan consensus.

It is no longer Un-American to torture "the bad guys".

Under the Inquisition, people firmly believed that torture and burning was a good thing and that torture served to purify society.

We have not quite reached that point. But we are nearly there.

With regard to the Executive order to torture, several media in the US including the *Washington Post*, condemned Secretary of Defense Donald Rumsfeld, calling for his resignation.

They have not, however, acknowledged the fact that torture has for some time been a routine practice of the Military and Intelligence apparatus, since the days of "Operation Condor" and the US sponsored Central American Death Squadrons. The latter were overseen at the time by John Negroponte, who now heads the Directorate of National Intelligence.

What comes next?

When the Justice Department emits a legal opinion stating that the Executive order to torture is "legit", that means that a legal and political consensus is being built.

In which case, the war criminals in high office, have "the right" to commit atrocities in the name of democracy and freedom. It is no longer necessary for them to lie, to hide their actions or to "say sorry" if and when these actions are brought to public attention.

Under this logic, torture is no longer seen as "Un-American", as stated by President Bush when the Abu Ghraib photos were first released in 2004.

In other words, under an inquisitorial system, the public does not question the wisdom of the rulers. Citizens are compelled into accepting the political consensus. They must endorse the acts of torture ordered by those who rule in their name. Moreover, political assassinations are no longer conducted as covert operations. The intent to assassinate is announced, debated in the US Congress, presented as a safeguard of democracy. In turn, the alleged terrorists are sent to concentration camps and this information is public.

Why is Camp X-Ray in Guantanamo, Cuba, public knowledge?

Precisely, to gradually develop, over several years, a broad public consensus that concentration camps and torture directed against "terrorists" are ultimately acceptable and in the public interest.

When we reach that point of acceptance, of broad consensus, there is no going back.

The lie becomes the truth. "Democracy and Freedom" are sustained through State terror. The police state and its ideological underpinnings become fully operational.

Unseat the Inquisitors

And that is why at this critical juncture in our history, it is crucial for people across the land, in the US, Canada, Europe and around the world, to take an articulate stance on President Bush's Executive Order to torture POWs.

But one does not reverse the tide by firing Rumsfeld and putting in a new Defense Secretary or by asking president Bush to please abide by the Geneva Convention.

How can one break the Inquisition?

Essentially by breaking the consensus which sustains the inquisitorial social order.

To shunt the American Inquisition and disable its propaganda machine, we must "unseat the Inquisitors" and prosecute the war criminals in high office, implying criminal procedures against those who ordered torture.

If the Judicial system supports torture, that means we have to dismantle the Judicial.

It is not sufficient, however, to remove the Inquisition's high priests: George W. Bush or Tony Blair, who are mere puppets.

Increasingly, the military-intelligence establishment (rather than the State Department, the White House and the US Congress) is calling the shots on US foreign policy. Meanwhile, the Anglo-American oil giants, Wall Street, the powerful media giants and the Washington think tanks are operating discretely behind the scenes, setting the next stage in this ongoing militarization of civilian institutions.

"Fear and Surprise"

To break the Inquisition, we must break the propaganda, fear and intimidation campaign, which galvanizes public opinion into accepting the "war on terrorism".

TEXT BOX 15.1

Break the Spanish Inquisition

by Monty Python

Nobody expects the Spanish Inquisition!

Our chief weapon is surprise ... surprise and fear ... fear and surprise ....

Our two weapons are fear and surprise ...and ruthless efficiency....

Our three weapons are fear, surprise, and ruthless efficiency ... and an almost fanatical devotion to the Pope ....

I didn't expect a kind of Spanish Inquisition.

... Nobody expects the ...um ... the Spanish ... um ... Inquisition.

I know, I know! Nobody expects the Spanish Inquisition.

Our chief weapons are ... ... um ... er ... Surprise ...

Okay, stop. Stop. Stop there—stop there. Stop. Phew! Ah! ...

Our chief weapons are surprise ...blah blah blah. Cardinal, read the charges.

You are hereby charged that you did on diverse dates commit heresy against the Holy Church.

Now, how do you plead? We're innocent.

Ha! Ha! Ha! Ha! Ha! [Diabolical Laughter].[20]

Osama bin Laden, Al-Zarqawi are names which are repeated ad nauseam, day after day, identified in official statements as enemies of America, commented on network TV and pasted on a daily basis across the news tabloids.

We must break the big lie.

Fear and Disinformation constitutes the cornerstone of Bush's propaganda campaign.

Without fear, there can be no inquisitorial social order.

"Code Orange Terror Alerts."

"The terrorists are preparing to attack America."

"A terrorist, massive, casualty-producing event [will occur] somewhere in the Western world—it may be in the United States of America—that causes our population to question our own Constitution and to begin to militarize our country in order to avoid a repeat of another mass, casualty-producing event." (Former CENTCOM Commander Tommy Franks)

"If we go to Red [code alert] … it basically shuts down the country", (Former Secretary for Homeland Security, Tom Ridge)

"You ask, 'Is it serious?' Yes, you bet your life. People don't do that unless it's a serious situation." (Vice President Dick Cheney)

Notes

1. See American Civil Liberties Union (ACLU), "FBI E-Mail Refers to Presidential Order Authorizing Inhumane Interrogation Techniques", 20 December 2004

2. Text of the original FBI Memo dated 15 December 2004, ACLU website

3. *Ibid.*

4. ACLU, *op cit.*

5. *The Boston Globe*, 23 December 2004.

6. *The Washington Post*, 23 December 2004.

7. *Ibid.*

8. See also Army Report, Department of Defense, August 2004.

9. Taguba Report, http://www.globalsecurity.org/intell/library/reports/2004/800-mp-bde.htm.

10. President Bush, 5 May 2004, interview for the US-funded al-Hurra network and the Al-Arabiya satellite channel, 5 May 2004.

11. Transcript of Donald Rumsfeld's Statement, Senate Armed Services Committee, 6 May 2004.

12. Dana Priest and R. Jeffrey Smith, "Memo Offered Justification for Use of Torture Justice Dept. Gave Advice in 2002", *Washington Post*, 6 June 2004

13. See complete August 1, 2002 Justice Department Memorandum: http://www.globalresearch.ca/articles/dojinterrogationmemo20020801.pdf.

14. See complete Department of Defense text leaked to the Wall Street Journal at http://news.findlaw.com/wp/docs/torture/30603wgrpt.html.

15. *Observer-Dispatch* (Utica, NY), 9 December 2004.

16. See Constitutional Rights Foundation, http://www.crf-usa.org/bria/bria9_1.htm

17. *Ibid.*

18. See Citizens Corps website at http://www.citizencorps.gov/pdf/council.pdf.

19. Constitutional Rights Foundation, http://www.crf-usa.org/bria/bria9_1.htm.

20. Excerpts from the BBC TV Show, Monty Python, The Spanish Inquisition by Monty Python, http://people.csail.mit.edu/paulfitz/spanish/index.html.

Chapter XVI
The Spoils of War: Afghanistan's Multibillion Dollar Heroin Trade

Since the US-led invasion of Afghanistan in October 2001, the Golden Crescent opium trade has soared.

According to the US media, this lucrative contraband is protected by Osama bin Laden and the Taliban, as well as, of course, the regional warlords, in defiance of the "international community". The heroin business is said to be "filling the coffers of the Taliban". In the words of the US State Department:

> Opium is a source of literally billions of dollars to extremist and criminal groups …. [C]utting down the opium supply is central to establishing a secure and stable democracy, as well as winning the global war on terrorism.[1]

"Operation Containment"
In the wake of the 2001 invasion, the Bush administration boosted its counter terrorism activities, in response to the post-Taliban surge in opium production, which was described as being protected by "terrorists". It also allocated substantial amounts of public money to the Drug Enforcement Administration's West Asia initiative, dubbed "Operation Containment."

Table 16.1

Opium Poppy Cultivation in Afghanistan

Year	Cultivation in hectares	Production in tons
1994	71,470	3,400
1995	53,759	2,300
1996	56,824	2,200
1997	58,416	2,800
1998	63,674	2,700
1999	90,983	4,600
2000	82,172	3,300
2001	7,606	185
2002	74,000	3,400
2003	80,000	3,600
2004	131,000	4,100

Source: United Nations Drug Control Programme (UNDCP), *Afghanistan, Opium Poppy Survey, 2001,* United Nations Office on Drugs ands Crime (UNOCD), *Afghanistan, Opium Poppy Survey, 2004,* Opium Poppy survey, 2002 and 2003. See the 2004 Survey at: http://www.unodc.org/pdf/afg/afghanistan_opium_survey_2004.pdf.

The various reports and official statements on the matter were accompanied by the usual "balanced" self critique that "the international community is not doing enough" to contain the drug trade, and that what is needed is "transparency".

The surge in opium production was also used as a pretext for the US-led military occupation of Afghanistan. The headlines were "Drugs, warlords and insecurity overshadow Afghanistan's path to democracy". In chorus, the US media accused the defunct "hard-line Islamic regime" of protecting the drug trade, without acknowledging that the Taliban—in collaboration with the United Nations—had imposed an impressive drug eradication program, leading to a complete ban on poppy cultivation. By 2001, prior the US led invasion, opium production had collapsed by more than 90 per cent.

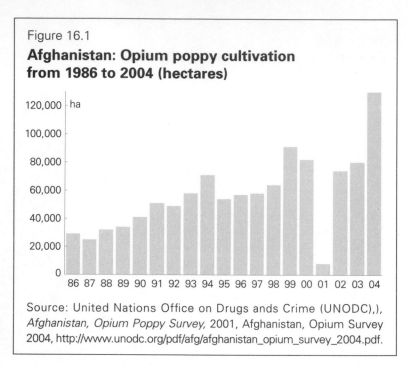

Figure 16.1

Afghanistan: Opium poppy cultivation from 1986 to 2004 (hectares)

Source: United Nations Office on Drugs ands Crime (UNODC),), *Afghanistan, Opium Poppy Survey,* 2001, Afghanistan, Opium Survey 2004, http://www.unodc.org/pdf/afg/afghanistan_opium_survey_2004.pdf.

According to the United Nations Office on Drugs and Crime (UNODC), opium production had increased from 185 tons in 2001 under the Taliban, to 4,100 tons in 2004, an impressive twenty-twofold increase. The renewed surge in opium cultivation coincided with the onslaught of the US-led military operation and the downfall of the Taliban regime. From October to December 2001, farmers started to replant poppy on an extensive basis. The areas under cultivation soared from 7,600 in 2001 (prior to invasion) to 130,000 hectares in 2004.[2]

The Taliban Drug Eradication Program

The success of Afghanistan's 2000 drug eradication program under the Taliban government was recognized by the United Nations. In the history of the Vienna based United Nations Office on Drugs and Crime (UNODC), no other country was able to implement a comparable program.

This achievement was casually acknowledged, without a word of praise, by the UNODC's Executive Director at the October 2001 session of the UN General Assembly which took place barely a few days after the beginning of the US bombing raids on Kabul:

> Turning first to drug control, I had expected to concentrate my remarks on the implications of the Taliban's ban on opium poppy cultivation in areas under their control. ... We now have the results of our annual ground survey of poppy cultivation in Afghanistan. This year's production [2001] is around 185 tons. This is down from the 3300 tons last year [2000], a decrease of over 94 per cent. Compared to the record harvest of 4700 tons two years ago, the decrease is well over 97 per cent. ...
>
> Any decrease in illicit cultivation is welcomed, especially in cases like this when no displacement, locally or in other countries, took place to weaken the achievement.[3]

United Nations Cover-up
In the wake of the 2001 US led-invasion of Afghanistan, a shift in rhetoric occurred. The United Nations body was acting as if the 2000 opium ban implemented by the Taliban government, had never happened:

> The battle against narcotics cultivation has been fought and won in other countries and it [is] possible to do so here [in Afghanistan], with strong, democratic governance, international assistance and improved security and integrity.[4]

Both Washington and the Vienna-based UN body, were now saying, in chorus that the objective of the Taliban government in 2000, was not really "drug eradication" but a devious scheme to trigger "an artificial shortfall in supply", which would drive up World prices of heroin.

Ironically, this twisted logic, which now forms part of a new "UN consensus", is refuted by a 2003 report by the UNODC office in Pakistan, which states that there was no evidence of stockpiling by the Taliban.[5]

Washington's Hidden Agenda: Restore the Drug Trade

In the wake of the 2001 invasion of Afghanistan, the British government of Tony Blair was entrusted by the G-8 Group of leading industrial nations to carry out a drug eradication program. In theory, this program was to allow Afghan farmers to switch out of poppy cultivation into alternative crops. The British were working out of Kabul in close liaison with the US Drug Enforcement Administration's (DEA) "Operation Containment".

The UK-sponsored crop eradication program was an obvious smokescreen. The presence of occupation forces in Afghanistan did not result in the eradication of poppy cultivation: quite the opposite.

Global Trade in Narcotics

Based on recent figures, drug trafficking constitutes "the third biggest global commodity in cash terms after oil and the arms trade".[6]

Supported by powerful interests, heroin is a multibillion-dollar business, which requires a steady and secure commodity flow. But, the Taliban prohibition caused "the beginning of a heroin shortage in Europe by the end of 2001", as acknowledged by the United Nations Office on Drugs ands Crime (UNODC).

One of the hidden objectives of the war was effectively to restore the CIA sponsored drug trade to its historical levels and exert direct control over the drug routes. Immediately following the October 2001 invasion, opium markets were restored. Opium prices spiraled. By early 2002, the domestic price of opium in Afghanistan (in dollars/kg) was almost 10 times higher than in 2000.

At the height of the opium trade during the Taliban regime, roughly 70 percent of the global supply of heroin originated from Afghanistan. In the wake of the US-led invasion, Afghanistan accounts for more than 85 percent of the global heroin market. In turn, the latter represents a sizeable fraction of the global narcotics market, estimated by the UN to be of the order of $400-500 billion a year.[7]

What distinguishes narcotics from legal commodity trade is that narcotics constitute a major source of wealth formation not only for organized crime but also for the US intelligence apparatus, which also represents a powerful actor in the spheres of finance and banking.

Intelligence agencies and powerful business syndicates, which are allied with organized crime, are competing for the strategic control over the heroin routes. The multi-billion dollar revenues of narcotics are deposited in the Western banking system. Most of the large international banks, together with their affiliates in the off-shore banking havens, launder large amounts of narco-dollars.

This trade can only prosper if the main actors involved in narcotics have "political friends in high places". Legal and illegal undertakings are increasingly intertwined; the dividing line between "business people" and criminals is blurred. In turn, the relationship among criminals, politicians and members of the intelligence establishment has tainted the structures of the State and the role of its institutions.

Behind the trade in narcotics, there are powerful business and financial interests. The productive system underlying the Golden Crescent heroin market is protected by a US-sponsored regime in Kabul. US foreign policy serves these interests. Geopolitical and military control over the multibillion dollar drug routes constitutes a (hidden) strategic objective, comparable, in some regards, to the militarization of oil pipeline routes out of Central Asia. (See Chapter VI.)

Multibillion Dollar Trade

Where does the money go? Who exactly benefits from the Afghan opium trade?

A complex web of intermediaries characterizes this trade. There are various stages of the drug trade, several interlocked markets, from the impoverished poppy farmer in Afghanistan to the wholesale and retail heroin markets in Western countries. In other words, there is a "hierarchy of prices" for opiates.

According to the US State Department, "Afghan heroin sells on the international narcotics market for 100 times the price farmers get for their opium right out of the field".[8]

The UNODC estimates that in 2003, opium production in Afghanistan generated "an income of one billion US dollars for farmers and US $ 1.3 billion for traffickers, equivalent to over half of its national income." Consistent with these UNODC estimates, the average price for fresh opium was $350 a kg. (2002); the production for that same year was 3400 tons, rising to 4100 tons in 2004.[9]

Wholesale Prices of Heroin in Western Countries

The total revenues generated by the Afghan narcotics trade are substantially higher than those estimated by the UNODC. One kilo of opium produces approximately 100 grams of (pure) heroin, which was selling wholesale in New York in the late 1990s for $85,000 to $190,000 a kilo, in contrast to $3500 per ten kilos of fresh opium paid locally in Afghanistan by traffickers.[10]

The Hierarchy of Prices

The narcotics trade is characterized by a hierarchy of prices, from the farmgate price in Afghanistan, upwards to the final retail price on the streets of London, Paris and New York. The street price is 80-100 times the price paid to the farmer.

Opiate products thus transit through several markets from the highlands of Afghanistan, by land and sea to the so-called "transshipment countries", where they are transported to their final destination in the "consuming countries". Here there are wide margins between "the landing price" demanded by the drug cartels at the point of entry and the wholesale and retail street prices, protected by Western organized crime.

The Global Proceeds of the Afghan Narcotics Trade

In Afghanistan, the reported 4100 tons of opium produced in 2004 allowed for the production of approximately 410,000 kg. of pure heroin. The gross revenues accruing to Afghan farmers (according

TEXT BOX 16.1
Heroin Retail Prices in Britain and the US

The New York Police Department (NYPD) notes that retail heroin prices are down and purity is relatively high. Heroin previously sold for about $90 per gram but now sells for $65 to $70 per gram or less. Anecdotal information from the NYPD indicates that purity for a bag of heroin commonly ranges from 50 to 80 percent but can be as low as 30 percent. Information as of June 2000 indicates that bundles (10 bags) purchased by Dominican buyers from Dominican sellers in larger quantities (about 150 bundles) sold for as little as $40 each, or $55 each in Central Park. DEA reports that an ounce of heroin usually sells for $2,500 to $5,000, a gram for $70 to $95, a bundle for $80 to $90, and a bag for $10. The DMP reports that the average heroin purity at the street level in 1999 was about 62 percent.[11]

The NYPD and DEA retail price figures are consistent. The DEA price of $70- $95, with a purity of 62 percent, translates into $112 to $153 per gram of pure heroin. The NYPD figures are roughly similar with perhaps lower estimates for purity.

It should be noted that when heroin is purchased in very small quantities, the retail price tends to be much higher. In the US, purchase is often by "the bag"; the typical bag according to Rocheleau and Boyum contains 25 milligrams of pure heroin.[12]

A $10 dollar bag in NYC (according to the DEA figure quoted above) would convert into a price of $400 per gram, each bag containing 0.025 gr. of pure heroin.[13] For very small purchases marketed by street pushers, the retail margin tends to be significantly higher. In the case of the $10 bag purchase, it is roughly 3 to 4 times the corresponding retail price per gram ($112- $153).

United Kingdom Drug Prices

The retail street price per gram of heroin in the United Kingdom, according to British police sources, "has fallen from £74 in 1997 to £61 [in 2004]." [i.e., from approximately $133 to $110, based on the 2004 rate of exchange].[14] In some cities it was as low as £30-40 per gram with a low level of purity.[15] According to Drugscope, the average price for a gram of heroin in Britain was between £40 and £90 ($72- $162 per gram). The report does not mention purity. According to the National Criminal Intelligence Service, the street price of heroin was £60 per gram in April 2002.

to the UNODC) were roughly of the order of $1.13 billion, with $1.5 billion accruing to local traffickers (UNODC's had estimated $1 billion to farmers and $1.3 billion to traffickers for 2003, corresponding to 3600 tons of raw opium. The corresponding figures for 2004 are based on an extrapolation of these figures, assuming no changes in farmgate prices).

When sold in Western markets at a heroin wholesale price of the order of $100,000 a kg (with a 70 percent purity ratio), the wholesale proceeds (corresponding to 4100 tons of Afghan raw opium) would be of the order of 58.6 billion dollars. The latter constitutes a conservative estimate based on the various figures for wholesale prices mentioned above.

But this amount of $58.6 billion does not include the highly lucrative retail trade in Afghan heroin on the streets of major Western cities. In other words, the final retail value is the ultimate yardstick for measuring the contribution of the multibillion-heroin trade to the formation of wealth in the Western countries.

A meaningful estimate of the retail value, however, is almost impossible to ascertain. Retail street prices vary considerably within urban areas, from one city to another and between consuming countries, not to mention variations in purity and quality.

There is a significant markup between the wholesale and the retail price of heroin. More generally, the lion's share of the proceeds of this lucrative contraband accrues to criminal and business syndicates in Western countries involved in the local wholesale and retail narcotics markets. Moreover, "corporate" crime syndicates invariably protect the various criminal gangs involved in retail trade.

More than 90 percent of heroin consumed in the UK is from Afghanistan. Using the British retail price figure from UK police sources of $110 a gram (with an assumed 50 percent purity level), the total retail value of the Afghan narcotics trade in 2004 (4100 tons of opium) would be the order of 90.2 billion dollars. The latter figure should be considered as a simulation rather than an estimate.

In other words, slightly more than a billion dollars gross revenue to farmers in Afghanistan (2004) would generate global narcotics earnings—accruing at various stages and in various mar-kets—of the order of 90 billion dollars. This 1-90 ratio is consistent with the DEA's assessment that one dollar of opium production in Afghanistan generates $100 dollars in terms of retail value.

These global proceeds accrue to business syndicates, intelligence agencies, organized crime, financial institutions, wholesalers, retail-ers, etc., involved directly or indirectly in the drug trade. In turn, the proceeds are deposited in Western banks, which constitute an essential mechanism in the laundering of dirty money.

What these figures suggest is that the bulk of the revenues asso-ciated with the global trade in heroin are not appropriated by "ter-rorist groups" and "warlords". In fact, a very small percentage of the total turnover of the drug trade accrues to farmers and traders in the producing country. Bear in mind that the net income accru-ing to Afghan farmers is but a fraction of the estimated $1.13 bil-lion. The latter amount are the gross proceeds accruing to the farmer, according to UNODC, which do not take into account the payments of farm inputs, interest on loans to money lenders, polit-ical protection, etc.[16]

The Laundering of Drug Money

A large share of global money laundering is directly linked to the trade in narcotics. Money laundering, according to IMF estimates for the 1990s, was between 590 billion and 1.5 trillion dollars a year, representing 2-5 percent of global GDP.[17]

The proceeds of the drug trade are deposited in the banking system. Drug money is laundered in the numerous offshore bank-ing havens in Switzerland, Luxembourg, the British Channel Islands, the Cayman Islands and some 50 other locations around the globe. It is here that criminal syndicates involved in the drug trade and the representatives of the world's largest commercial banks interact. Dirty money is deposited in these offshore havens, which are con-trolled by major Western banks and financial institutions. The lat-ter, therefore, have a vested interest in maintaining and sustaining the drug trade.[18]

Once the money has been laundered, it can be recycled into bona fide investments not only in real estate, hotels, etc, but also in other areas such as the services economy and manufacturing. Dirty and covert money is also funneled into various financial instruments including speculative stock exchange transactions (derivatives), primary commodities, stocks and government bonds.

Narcotics and the "War on Terrorism"

US foreign policy and the "war on terrorism" support the workings of a thriving criminal economy in which the demarcation between organized capital and organized crime has become increasingly blurred.

The heroin business is not "filling the coffers of the Taliban" as claimed by the US Government and the international community.

Rather, the proceeds of this illegal trade are the source of wealth formation outside Afghanistan, largely reaped by powerful financial and business/criminal interests within Western countries. This process of wealth accumulation resulting from the drug trade is sustained and supported by the US "War on Terrorism". Decision-making in the US State Department, the CIA and the Pentagon is instrumental in supporting this highly profitable multibillion dollar trade, third in commodity value after oil and the arms trade.

Notes

1. Statement of Assistant Secretary of State Robert Charles. US House of Representatives Congressional Hearing, 1 April 2004.

2. United Nations Office on Drugs ands Crime (UNODC) at http://www.unodc.org/unodc/index.html.

3. Remarks on behalf of the United Nations Office on Drugs ands Crime (UNODC) Executive Director at the UN General Assembly, Oct 2001, http://www.unodc.org/unodc/en/speech_2001-10-12_1.htm.

4. Statement of the UNODC Representative in Afghanistan at the February 2004 International Counter Narcotics Conference, http://www.unodc.org/pdf/afg/afg_intl_counter_narcotics_conf_2004.pdf, p. 5.

5. *Deseret News*, Salt Lake City, Utah, 5 October 2003.

6. *The Independent,* 29 February 2004. At the time these UN figures were first brought out (1994), the (estimated) global trade in drugs was of the same order of magnitude as the global trade in oil.

7. Douglas Keh, "Drug Money in a Changing World", Technical Document No. 4, Vienna UNDCP, 1998, p. 4. See also United Nations Drug Control Program, Report of the International Narcotics Control Board for 1999, E/INCB/1999/1 United Nations, Vienna, 1999, p. 49-51, and Richard Lapper, "UN Fears Growth of Heroin Trade, *Financial Times,* 24 February 2000. There are no reliable estimates on the distribution of the global narcotics trade between the main categories: Cocaine, Opium/Heroin, Cannabis, Amphetamine Type Stimulants (ATS), Other Drugs.

8. US State Department, quoted by The Voice of America (VOA), 27 February 2004.

9. See http://www.poppies.org/news/104267739031389.shtml. The Afghan farmer receives a very small percentage of the global turnover of the trade in Afghan opiates, which the United Nations Office on Drugs ands Crime (UNODC) estimates at US $ 30 billion.

10. The US Drug Enforcement Administration (DEA) confirms that SWA [South West Asia meaning Afghanistan] heroin in New York City was selling in the late 1990s for $85,000 to $190,000 per kilogram wholesale with a 75 percent purity ratio. See National Drug Intelligence Center, http://www.usdoj.gov/ndic/pubs/648/ny_econ.htm.

According to the US Drug Enforcement Administration (DEA) "the price of SEA [South East Asian] heroin ranges from $70,000 to $100,000 per unit (700 grams) and the purity of SEA heroin ranges from 85 to 90 percent". The SEA unit of 700 grams (gr.) (85-90% purity) translates into a wholesale price per kg. for pure heroin ranging between $115,000 and $163,000. Whereas there was competition between different sources of heroin supply, the US heroin market, at the time these figures were collected, was largely being supplied out of Colombia.

In Britain, where more than 90 percent of the heroin originates from Afghanistan, the wholesale price of (pure) heroin in London, was of the order of 50,000 pounds sterling, approximately $80,000 a kilo (2002). See *The Guardian,* 11 August 2002.

11. National Drug Intelligence Center, http://www.usdoj.gov/ndic/pubs/648/ny_econ.htm.

12. See Office of National; Drug Control Policy, The White House, http://www.whitehousedrugpolicy.gov/publications/drugfact/american_users_spend/appc.html.

13. National Drug Intelligence Center, *op cit.*

14. *The Independent,* 3 March 2004.

15. AAP News, 3 March 2004. See Drugscope (UK): http://www.drugscope.org.uk.

16. See also UNODC, "The Opium Economy in Afghanistan", Vienna, 2003, http://www.unodc.org/pdf/publications/afg_opium_economy_www.pdf, p. 7-8.

17. *Asian Banker,* 15 August 2003.

18. For further details, see Michel Chossudovsky, "The Crimes of Business and the Business of Crimes", *Covert Action Quarterly,* Fall 1996.

CHAPTER XVII
Foreknowledge of 9/11

Simulations of a plane crashing into a building in a mock terrorist attack were conducted in the year leading up to 9/11.

Conducted by the CIA and the Pentagon, pre-9/11 "scenarios" of terror attacks were documented by official statements and press reports.

Since 9/11, the Bush administration has conducted several anti-terrorist exercises to prepare America in the case of a second 9/11 attack. (See Chapter XX.)

This chapter outlines two pre-9/11 simulations of a plane being used by terrorists to crash into a building, which suggest that US military and intelligence authorities had indeed contemplated the possibility of "a 9/11 type attack":

1. The Pentagon exercise, conducted eleven months before 9/11 in October 2000, consisted in establishing the scenario of a simulated passenger plane crashing into the Pentagon.
2. The CIA exercise held at CIA's Chantilly Virginia Reconnaissance Office on the morning of September 11, 2001.

In the second part of this chapter, the role of these anti-terror exercises in the disinformation campaign is examined, focussing on the broader issue of foreknowledge of 9/11.

The Pentagon Scenario of an Actual Terrorist Attack

In October 2000, a military exercise was conducted which consisted in establishing the scenario of a simulated passenger plane crashing into the Pentagon. The exercise was coordinated by the Defense Protective Services Police and the Pentagon's Command Emergency Response Team.

According to a detailed report by Dennis Ryan of Fort Myer Military Community's Pentagram, "the Pentagon Mass Casualty Exercise, as the crash was called, was just one of several scenarios that emergency response teams were exposed to on Oct. 24-26 [2000]":

> The fire and smoke from the downed passenger aircraft billows from the Pentagon courtyard. Defense Protective Services Police seal the crash sight. Army medics, nurses and doctors scramble to organize aid. … Don Abbott, of Command Emergency Response Training, walks over to the Pentagon and extinguishes the flames. The Pentagon was a model and the "plane crash" was a simulated one.
>
> On Oct. 24, there was a mock terrorist incident at the Pentagon Metro stop and a construction accident to name just some of the scenarios that were practiced to better prepare local agencies for real incidents.
>
> To conduct the exercise, emergency personnel hold radios that are used to rush help to the proper places, while toy trucks representing rescue equipment are pushed around the exercise table.
>
> Cards are then passed out to the various players designating the number of casualties and where they should be sent in a given scenario.
>
> To conduct the exercise, a medic reports to Army nurse Maj. Lorie Brown a list of 28 casualties so far. Brown then contacts her superior on the radio, Col. James Geiling, a doctor in the command room across the hall.

Geiling approves Brown's request for helicopters to evacuate the wounded. A policeman in the room recommends not moving bodies and Abbott, playing the role of referee, nods his head in agreement. ...

An Army medic found the practice realistic.

"You get to see the people that we'll be dealing with and to think about the scenarios and what you would do," Sgt. Kelly Brown said. "It's a real good scenario and one that could happen easily." ...

Abbott, in his after action critique, reminded the participants that the actual disaster is only one-fifth of the incident and that the whole emergency would run for seven to 20 days and might involve as many as 17 agencies.

"The emergency to a certain extent is the easiest part," Abbott said. He reminded the group of the personal side of a disaster. "Families wanting to come to the crash site for closure. ... In this particular crash there would have been 341 victims."[1]

The report refutes the claims of the Bush Administration that they could not have predicted the use of an aeroplane in a terrorist attack. In the words of Condoleezza Rice at her 16 May 2002 Press Conference:

> I don't think anybody could have predicted that these people would take an aeroplane and slam it into the World Trade Center, take another one and slam it into the Pentagon, that they would try to use an aeroplane as a missile, a hijacked aeroplane as a missile.

"The Pentagon Mass Casualty Exercise" had been ordered by senior Pentagon officials and Sec Donald Rumsfeld, whose office is on the third floor of the outer ring of the Pentagon, stated "I didn't know". Below is an excerpt of Rumsfeld's testimony at the 9/11 Commission in March 2004 (in response to Commissioner Ben-Veniste):

> BEN-VENISTE: So it seems to me when you make the statement, sir, that we didn't know that planes might be used as weapons in the summer of 2001, I just have to take issue with that.
>
> RUMSFELD: Well, I didn't say we didn't know. I said I didn't know. And if I just was handed a civil aviation circular that people did know. And they sent it out on June 22nd, 2001.[2]

The objective of the exercise, in the words of its Pentagon organizers, consisted in a "preparation for any potential disasters. ... 'This is important so that we're better prepared,' Brown said. 'This is to work out the bugs. Hopefully it will never happen, but this way we're prepared.'"[3]

Were they prepared ten months later on September 11, 2001, when the actual disaster occurred? What was the purpose of conducting this exercise?

The CIA's "Pre-Planned Simulation" of a Plane Crashing into a Building

On the morning of September 11, 2001, the CIA had been running "a pre-planned simulation to explore the emergency response issues that would be created if a plane were to strike a building". The simulation was held at the CIA Chantilly Virginia Reconnaissance Office.

The Bush administration described the event as "a bizarre coincidence".[4] The simulation consisted in a "scheduled exercise" held on the morning of September 11, 2001, where "a small corporate jet crashed into one of the four towers at the agency's headquarters building after experiencing a mechanical failure.[5]

> "Agency chiefs came up with the scenario to test employees' ability to respond to a disaster", said spokesman Art Haubold. ... "It was just an incredible coincidence that this happened to involve an aircraft crashing into our facility. ... As soon as the real world events began, we canceled the exercise."[6]

The news concerning the 9/11 Chantilly aircraft crashing simulation was hushed up. It was not made public at the time. It was revealed almost a year later, in the form of an innocuous announcement of a Homeland Security Conference. The latter entitled "Homeland Security: America's Leadership Challenge" was held in Chicago on September 6, 2002, barely a few days before the commemoration of the tragic events of 9/11.

The promotional literature for the conference under the auspices of the National Law Enforcement and Security Institute

(NLESI) stated what nobody in America knew about. On the morning of 9/11, the CIA was conducting a pre-planned simulation of a plane striking a building.

One of the key speakers at the National Law Enforcement and Security Institute conference was CIA's John Fulton, Chief of the Strategic War Gaming Division of the National Reconnaissance Office, a specialist in risk and threat response analysis, scenario gaming, and strategic planning:

> On the morning of September 11th 2001, Mr. Fulton and his team at the CIA were running a pre-planned simulation to explore the emergency response issues that would be created if a plane were to strike a building. Little did they know that the scenario would come true in a dramatic way that day. Information is the most powerful tool available in the homeland security effort. At the core of every initiative currently underway to protect our country and its citizens is the challenge of getting the right information to the right people at the right time. How can so much information from around the world be captured and processed in meaningful and timely ways? Mr. Fulton shares his insights into the intelligence community, and shares a vision of how today's information systems will be developed into even better counter-terrorism tools of tomorrow.[7]

The Role of Foreknowledge in the Disinformation Campaign

The Pentagon and CIA pre-9/11 "scenarios" of an actual terror attack refute the statements of US officials including those of Donald Rumsfeld and Condoleezza Rice.

While the pre-9/11 scenarios cast serious doubt on the official 9/11 narrative as conveyed in the 9/11 Commission Report, they contribute to sustaining the Al Qaeda legend. The conduct of these anti-terrorist drills in anticipation of a terror attack are part of a disinformation campaign. They convey the impression that the threat of Islamic terrorists is real.

Attorney General John Ashcroft had apparently been warned in August 2001 by the FBI to avoid commercial airlines, but this information was not made public.[8]

More generally, the holding of anti-terrorist drills both prior and in the wake of 9/11 has contributed to creating within the military, intelligence and law enforcement communities a broad consensus, that Al Qaeda is an enemy of the Homeland and that the threat is real.

The Bush administration had numerous "intelligence warnings". We also know that senior Bush officials lied under oath to the 9/11 Commission, when they stated that they had no information or forewarning of impending terrorist attacks.

But we also know from carefully documented research that:
– There were stand-down orders on 9/11. The US Air force did not intervene.[9]
– There was a cover-up of the WTC and Pentagon investigations. The WTC rubble was removed before it could be examined.[10] The plane debris at the Pentagon are unaccounted for.[11]
– There were reports of significant financial gains made as a result of 9/11, from insider trading in the days prior to 9/11.[12]
– Mystery surrounds WTC Building 7, which collapsed or was "pulled" down in the afternoon of September 11, 2001.[13]

The White House is being accused by its critics of "criminal negligence", for having casually disregarded the intelligence presented to president Bush and his national security team, and for not having acted to prevent the 9/11 terrorist attack.

The unfolding consensus among the critics is that "they knew but failed to act".

This line of reasoning is appealing to many 9/11 writers because it clearly places the blame on the Bush administration.

Yet in a bitter irony, the very process of *revealing the lies* of US officials regarding foreknowledge and expressing public outrage, has contributed to reinforcing the 9/11 cover-up.

The foreknowledge issue thus becomes part of the disinformation campaign, which serves to present Al Qaeda as a threat to the security of America, when in fact Al Qaeda is a creation of the US intelligence apparatus.

The presumption is that these forewarnings and intelligence briefs emanating from the intelligence establishment—not to mention the "scenarios" of actual terror attacks conducted by the Pentagon and the CIA—constitute a true and unbiased representation of the terrorist threat.

Meanwhile, the history of Al Qaeda and the CIA has been pushed to the background, not to mention its links to Pakistan's military intelligence. (See chapter IV.)

The central proposition that Islamic terrorists were responsible for 9/11 serves to justify everything else including the PATRIOT Acts, the wars on Afghanistan and Iraq, the spiraling defense and homeland security budgets, the detention of thousands of people of Muslim faith on trumped up charges, the arrest and deportation to Guantanamo of alleged "enemy combatants", etc.

The focus on foreknowledge has served to usefully distract attention from the US Government's longstanding relationship to the terror network since the Soviet-Afghan war, which inevitably raises the broader issue of treason and war crimes.

The foreknowledge issue in a sense erases the historical record because it denies the role of Al Qaeda as a US intelligence asset.

The anti-terror drills fit into the broader campaign of disinformation. The Bush administration is accused of not acting upon these terrorist warnings. In the words of Bush's adviser on counter-terrorism Richard Clarke:

> We must try to achieve a level of public discourse on these issues that is simultaneously energetic and mutually respectful. ... We all want to defeat the jihadists. [This is the consensus.] To do that, we need to encourage an active, critical and analytical debate in America about how that will best be done. And if there is another major terrorist attack in this country, we must not panic or stifle debate as we did for too long after 9/11.[14]

Bush and the White House intelligence team are said to have ignored these warnings.

Richard Clarke, who was in charge of counter terrorism on the National Security Council until February 2003, "apologized" to the American people and the families of the victims.

Bear in mind that Richard Clarke was part of the intelligence team which at the time was providing support to Al Qaeda in the Balkans. (See Chapter III.) He was also part of the Bush team when the US invaded Afghanistan, using 9/11 as a pretext for waging a "Just War".

This new anti-Bush consensus concerning the 9/11 attacks has engulfed part of the 9/11 truth movement. The outright lies in sworn testimony to the 9/11 Commission have been denounced in chorus; the families of the victims have expressed their indignation.

The debate centers on whether the Administration is responsible for an "intelligence failure" or whether it was the result of "incompetence". In both cases, the Al Qaeda legend remains unscathed. Bin Laden is the culprit. Al Qaeda sponsored Arab hijackers were responsible for 9/11.

Source of the Terrorist Warnings

Beneath the rhetoric, few people seem to have questioned the source of the "warnings" emanating from the intelligence apparatus, which is known to have supported Al Qaeda throughout the entire post Cold War era.

Are the terrorist "warnings" emanating out of the CIA based on solid intelligence. Do they constitute a true representation of the terrorist threat or are they part of the process of disinformation which seeks to uphold the figure of Osama bin Laden as an "Enemy of the Homeland"?

Meanwhile, the issue of "cover-up and complicity" at the highest levels of the Bush administration, which was raised in the immediate wake of the 9/11 attacks is no longer an object of serious debate. (See Chapters III, IV and X.) The role of Bush officials, their documented links to the terror network, the business ties between the Bushes and bin Laden families, the role of Pakistan's Military Intelligence (ISI), the fact that several Bush officials were the architects of Al Qaeda during the Reagan administration, as revealed by the Iran-Contra investigation: all of this, which is carefully documented, is no longer considered relevant.

"The Saudis Did It"

What the media, as well as some of the key 9/11 investigators are pushing is that "the Saudis did it". The outside enemy Al Qaeda is said to be supported by the Saudis.

This line of analysis, which characterizes the controversial trillion dollar law suit by the families of the victims directed against the financiers of 9/11, is in many regards contradictory. While it highlights the role of the Saudi financial elites, it fails to address the links between the Saudi financiers and their US sponsors.

"The Saudis did it" is also part of the US foreign policy agenda, to be eventually used to discredit the Saudi monarchy and destabilize the Saudi financiers, who oversee 25 percent of the World's oil reserves, almost ten times those of the US. In fact, this process has already begun with the Saudi privatization program, which seeks to transfer Saudi wealth and assets into foreign (Anglo-American) hands.

The Saudi financiers were never prime movers. In fact they were proxies who played a subordinate role. They worked closely with US intelligence and their American financial counterparts. They were involved in the laundering of drug money working closely with the CIA. The Wahabbi sects from Saudi Arabia were sent to Afghanistan to set up the madrassas. The Saudis channeled covert financing to the various Islamic insurgencies on behalf of the CIA. (See Chapter II).

"The Saudis did it" consensus essentially contributes to whitewashing the Bush administration, while also providing a foreign policy pretext to destabilize Saudi Arabia.

The Central Role of Al Qaeda
in Bush's National Security Doctrine

Spelled out in the National Security Strategy (NSS), the preemptive "defensive war" doctrine and the "war on terrorism" against Al Qaeda constitute the two essential building blocks of the Pentagon's propaganda campaign, (See Chapter XIX.)

No Al Qaeda, no war on terrorism.

No "rogue states" which sponsor Al Qaeda, no pretext for waging war.

No justification for invading and occupying Afghanistan and Iraq.

No justification for sending in US Special Forces into numerous countries around the World.

And no justification for developing tactical nuclear weapons to be used in conventional war theaters against Islamic terrorists, who according to official statements constitute a nuclear threat.

"The Bush Lied" Consensus upholds "The Big Lie"

The 1993 WTC bombing is heralded as one of the earlier Al Qaeda attacks on the Homeland.

The 1993 WTC bombing, the 1998 African US embassy bombings, the 2000 attack on USS Cole have become part of an evolving legend which describes Al Qaeda as "an outside enemy" involved in numerous terror attacks. In the words of National Security Adviser Condoleeza Rice in sworn testimony to the 9/11 Commission:

> The terrorist threat to our Nation did not emerge on September 11th, 2001. Long before that day, radical, freedom-hating terrorists declared war on America and on the civilized world. The attack on the Marine barracks in Lebanon in 1983, the hijacking of the Achille Lauro in 1985, the rise of Al Qaeda and the bombing of the World Trade Center in 1993, the attacks on American installations in Saudi Arabia in 1995 and 1996, the East Africa embassy bombings of 1998, the attack on the USS Cole in 2000, these and other atrocities were part of a sustained, systematic campaign to spread devastation and chaos and to murder innocent Americans.[14]

The legend of the "outside enemy" is making its way into American history books. The underlying consensus points to "intelligence failures", possible negligence on the part of US officials as well as the undercover role of the Saudis in supporting the "outside enemy".

It was incompetence and negligence but it was not treason. The wars in Afghanistan and Iraq were "Just Wars". They were carried out in accordance with the National Security doctrine, which upholds Al Qaeda as the outside enemy.

The 9/11 Commission Report had indeed revealed that Bush officials had lied under oath regarding the pre-9/11 terrorist warnings, emanating from US intelligence. Yet nobody had begged the key question: What is the significance of these "warnings" emanating from the intelligence apparatus, knowing that the CIA is the creator of Al Qaeda and that Al Qaeda is an "intelligence asset"?

The CIA is the sponsor of Al Qaeda and at the same time controls the warnings on impending terrorist attacks by Al Qaeda, not to mention the conduct of anti-terrorist drills conducted both prior as well as in the wake of 9/11. (On the post 9/11 anti-terrorist drills, see Chapter XXI.)

In other words, were Bush administration officials lying—in sworn testimony to the 9/11 Commission—on something which is true, or were they lying on something which is an even bigger lie?

While the Bush administration may take the blame for lying, the "war on terrorism" and its humanitarian mandate remain functionally intact.

Notes

1. Dennis Ryan, "Contingency planning, Pentagon MASCAL exercise simulates scenarios in preparing for emergencies", MDW NEWS 3 Nov 2000. http://www.mdw.army.mil/

2. See complete transcript of Rumfeld's testimony at the 9/11 Commission website archives at http://www.9-11commission.gov/

3. Ryan, *op. cit.*

4. Quoted in Associated Press, 22 August 2002.

5 *Ibid.*

6 *Ibid.*

7. The National Law Enforcement and Security Institute website is: http://www.nlsi.net/ See also The Memory Hole at http://www.thememory-hole.org/911/cia-simulation.htm.

8. "The White House had (at least) 28 Advanced Intelligence Warnings Prior to 9/11", compiled by Eric Smith, Centre for Research on Globalization, 11 February 2004, http://globalresearch.ca/articles/SMI402A.html.

9. See George Szamuely, "Scrambled Messages on 9/11", *New York Press*, 14 December 2001. See also by the same author, "Nothing Urgent", *New York Press*, Vol. 15, No. 2, See also David Ray Griffin, *The New Pearl Harbor: Disturbing Questions about the Bush Administration and 9/11*, Interlink Publishing, 2004. Michael Ruppert, *Crossing the Rubicon*, New Society Books, Vancouver, 2004. Mark Elsis, "9/11 Stand Down", Centre for Research on Globalization, May 2003, http://www.globalresearch.ca/articles/ELS305B.html, Eric Hufschmid, *Painful Questions*, 2003.

10. See Bill Manning, "Selling Out the Investigation", *Fire Engineering Magazine*, January 2002.

11. There is a vast literature on this subject. See Thierry Meyssan's earlier text: "Who was behind the September eleventh attacks?" transcript of a speech at the Zayed Center in Abu Dhabi (United Arab Emirates), 8 April 2002, Centre for Research on Globalization, http://www.globalresearch.ca/articles/MEY204C.html, Thierry Meyssan, *Pentagate*, Carnot USA Books, August 2002.

12. The issue of inside trade has been object of extensive research. Michael Ruppert was among the first writers to focus on this issue in the immediate wake of 9/11. See Michael Ruppert, "Suppressed Details of Criminal Insider Trading lead directly into the CIA's Highest Ranks", From the Wilderness Publications, 9 October 2001. See also Michael Ruppert, *Crossing the Rubicon*, New Society Books, Vancouver, 2004.

13. Several authors have written on this subject. See for instance, Scott Loughrey, "WTC-7: The Improbable Collapse", Centre for Research on Globalization, 10 August 2003, at http://www.globalresearch.ca/articles/LOU308A.html, Jeremy Baker, "The Demolition of WTC 7 Revisited", *Global Outlook*, No. 7, Spring 2004.

14. See complete transcript of Condoleeza Rice's testimony at the 9/11 Commission website archives at http://www.9-11commission.gov/. Also available at Federal Documents Clearing House Archive, 8 April 2004.

Chapter XVIII

On the Morning of 9/11:
What Happened on the Planes?

"We Have Some Planes"

The 9/11 Commission's Report provides an almost visual description of the Arab hijackers. It gives a face to the "terrorists". It depicts in minute detail events occurring inside the cabin of the four hijacked planes.[1]

In the absence of surviving passengers, this "corroborating evidence" was based on passengers' cell and air phone conversations with their loved ones. According to the Report, the cockpit voice recorder (CVR) was only recovered in the case of one of the flights (UAL 93). Focusing on the personal drama of the passengers, the Commission has built much of its narrative around the phone conversations. The Arabs are portrayed with their knives and box cutters, scheming in the name of Allah, to bring down the planes and turn them "into large guided missiles". (Report, Chapter 1.)

Wireless Transmission Technology

The Report conveys the impression that ground-to-air cell phone communication from high altitude was of reasonably good quality, and that there was no major impediment or obstruction in wireless transmission.

Some of the conversations reported by the Commission were with onboard air phones, which, contrary to the cell phones, provide for good quality transmission. The report does not draw a clear demarcation between the two types of calls.

More significantly, what the Commission fails to mention is that, given the prevailing technology in September 2001, it was extremely difficult, if not impossible, to place a wireless cell call from an aircraft travelling at high speed above 8000 feet:

> Wireless communications networks weren't designed for ground-to-air communication. Cellular experts privately admit that they're surprised the calls [on September 11, 2001] were able to be placed from the hijacked planes, and that they lasted as long as they did. They speculate that the only reason that the calls went through in the first place is that the aircraft were flying so close to the ground.[2]

Expert opinion within the wireless telecom industry casts serious doubt on the findings of the 9/11 Commission. According to Alexa Graf, AT&T spokesman, commenting in the immediate wake of the 9/11 attacks:

> It was almost a fluke that the [9/11] calls reached their destinations. ... From high altitudes, the call quality is not very good, and most callers will experience drops. Although calls are not reliable, callers can pick up and hold calls for a little while below a certain altitude.[3]

New Wireless Technology

Within days of the release of the 9/11 Commission Report in July 2004, American Airlines and Qualcomm, proudly announced the development of a new wireless technology—which would *at some future date* allow airline passengers using their cell phones to contact family and friends from a commercial aircraft.[4]

> Travelers could be talking on their personal cellphones as early as 2006. Earlier this month [July 2004], American Airlines conducted a trial run on a modified aircraft that permitted cell phone calls.[5]

While serious doubts had been expressed with regard to the cell phone conversations in the immediate aftermath of 9/11, this announcement of a new landmark in the wireless telecom industry had contributed to upsetting the Commission's credibility. *Aviation Week* described this new technology in an authoritative report published within a couple of weeks of the release of the 9/11 Commission Report:

> Qualcomm and American Airlines are exploring [July 2004] ways for passengers to use commercial cell phones inflight for air-to-ground communication. In a recent 2-hr. proof-of-concept flight, representatives from government and the media used commercial Code Division Multiple Access (CDMA) third-generation cell phones to place and receive calls and text messages from friends on the ground.
>
> For the test flight from Dallas-Fort Worth, the aircraft was equipped with an antenna in the front and rear of the cabin to transmit cell phone calls to a small in-cabin CDMA cellular base station. This "pico cell" transmitted cell phone calls from the aircraft via a Globalstar satellite to the worldwide terrestrial phone network.[6]

Neither the service, nor the "third generation" hardware, nor the "Picco cell" CDMA base station inside the cabin (which so to speak mimics a cell phone communication tower inside the plane) were available on the morning of September 11, 2001.[7]

The 9/11 Commission points to the clarity and detail of these telephone conversations.

In substance, the *Aviation Week* report had created yet another embarrassing hitch in the official story.

The untimely July 2004 American Airlines/Qualcomm announcement acted as a cold shower. Barely acknowledged in press reports, it confirmed that the Bush administration had embroidered the cell phone narrative and that the 9/11 Commission's account was either flawed or grossly exaggerated.

Altitude and Cellphone Transmission

According to industry experts, the crucial link in wireless cell phone transmission from an aircraft is altitude. Beyond a certain altitude, which is usually reached within a few minutes after takeoff, cell phone calls are no longer possible.

In other words, given the wireless technology available on September 11, 2001, these cell phone calls could not have been placed from high altitude.

The only way passengers could have communicated with family and friends using their cell phones, is if the planes were flying below 8000 feet. Yet even at low altitude, below 8000 feet, cell phone communication is of poor quality.

The crucial question: at what altitude were the planes travelling, when the calls were placed?

While the information provided by the Commission is scanty, the Report's timeline suggests that the planes were not consistently travelling at low altitude. In fact the Report confirms that a fair number of the cell phone calls were placed while the plane was travelling at altitudes above 8000 feet, which is considered as the cutoff altitude for cell phone transmission.

Let us review the timeline of these calls in relation to the information provided by the Report on flight paths and altitude. (Italics are added to highlight key events in the timeline.)

United Airlines Flight 175
United Airlines Flight 175 departed for Los Angeles at 8:00:

> "It pushed back from its gate at 7:58 and departed Logan Airport at 8:14."

The Report confirms that *by 8:33, "it had reached its assigned cruising altitude of 31,000 feet." According to the Report, it maintained this cruising altitude until 8:51, when it "deviated from its assigned altitude"*:

> The first operational evidence that something was abnormal on United 175 came at 8:47, when the aircraft changed beacon codes twice within a minute. At 8:51, the flight deviated from its assigned altitude, and a minute later New York air traffic controllers began repeatedly and unsuccessfully trying to contact it.

And one minute later at 8.52, Lee Hanson receives a call from his son Peter.

> At 8:52, in Easton, Connecticut, a man named Lee Hanson received a phone call from his son Peter, a passenger on United 175. His son told him: "I think they've taken over the cockpit—An attendant has been stabbed—and someone else up front may have been killed. The plane is making strange moves. Call United Airlines—Tell them it's Flight 175, Boston to LA."

Press reports confirm that Peter Hanson was using his cell (i.e., it was not an air phone). *Unless the plane had suddenly nose-dived, the plane was still at high altitude at 8:52.*

Another call was received at 8:52 (one minute after it deviated from its assigned altitude of 31,000 feet). The Report does not say whether this was an air phone or a cell phone call:

> Also at 8:52, a male flight attendant called a United office in San Francisco, reaching Marc Policastro. The flight attendant reported that the flight had been hijacked, both pilots had been killed, a flight attendant had been stabbed, and the hijackers were probably flying the plane. The call lasted about two minutes, after which Policastro and a colleague tried unsuccessfully to contact the flight.

It is not clear whether this was a call to Policastro's cell phone or to the UAL switchboard.

> At 8:58, UAL 175 "took a heading toward New York City."

> At 8:59, Flight 175 passenger Brian David Sweeney tried to call his wife, Julie. He left a message on their home answering machine that the plane had been hijacked. He then called his mother, Louise Sweeney, told her the flight had been hijacked, and added that the passengers were thinking about storming the cockpit to take control of the plane away from the hijackers.

At 9:00, Lee Hanson received a second call from his son Peter:

> It's getting bad, Dad—A stewardess was stabbed—They seem to have knives and Mace—They said they have a bomb—It's getting very bad on the plane—Passengers are throwing up and getting sick—

The plane is making jerky movements—I don't think the pilot is flying the plane—I think we are going down—I think they intend to go
to Chicago or someplace and fly into a building—Don't worry, Dad—
If it happens, it'll be very fast—My God, my God.

The call ended abruptly. Lee Hanson had heard a woman scream
just before it cut off. He turned on a television, and in her home so
did Louise Sweeney. Both then saw the second aircraft hit the World
Trade Center. At 9:03:11, United Airlines Flight 175 struck the South
Tower of the World Trade Center. All on board, along with an
unknown number of people in the tower, were killed instantly.

American Airlines Flight 77
American Airlines Flight 77 was scheduled to depart from
Washington Dulles Airport for Los Angeles at 8:10. *"At 8:46, the
flight reached its assigned cruising altitude of 35,000 feet."*

> At 8:51, American 77 transmitted its last routine radio communi-
> cation. The hijacking began between 8:51 and 8:54. As on American
> 11 and United 175, the hijackers used knives (reported by one pas-
> senger) and moved all the passengers (and possibly crew) to the rear
> of the aircraft (reported by one flight attendant and one passenger).
> Unlike the earlier flights, the Flight 77 hijackers were reported by a
> passenger to have box cutters. Finally, a passenger reported that an
> announcement had been made by the "pilot" that the plane had been
> hijacked.

On flight AA 77, which allegedly crashed into the Pentagon, the
transponder was turned off at 8:56am; the recorded altitude at the
time the transponder was turned off was not mentioned. According
to the Commission's Report, cell calls started 16 minutes later, at
9:12am, twenty minutes before it allegedly crashed into the
Pentagon at 9:32am:

> [at 9:12] Renée May called her mother, Nancy May, in Las Vegas. She
> said her flight was being hijacked by six individuals who had moved
> them to the rear of the plane.

According to the Report, *when the autopilot was disengaged at 9:29am, the aircraft was at 7,000 feet* and some 38 miles west of the Pentagon. This happened two minutes before the crash.

Most of the calls on Flight 77 were placed between 9:12am and 9:26am, prior to the disengagement of automatic piloting at 9:29am. The plane could indeed have been traveling at either a higher or a lower altitude to that reached at 9:29am. Yet, at the same time there was no indication in the Report that the plane had been traveling below the 7000 feet level, which it reached at 9:29am.

At some point between 9:16 and 9:26, Barbara Olson called her husband, Ted Olson, the solicitor general of the United States. [using an airphone] (Report p.7.)

United Airlines Flight 93
UAL flight 93 was the only one of the four planes that, according to the official story, did not crash into a building. *Flight 93 passengers, apparently: "alerted through phone calls, attempted to subdue the hijackers. And the hijackers crashed the plane [in Pennsylvania] to prevent the passengers gaining control."* Another version of events, was that UAL 93 was shot down.[8]

According to the Commission's account:

> [T]he first 46 minutes of Flight 93's cross-country trip proceeded routinely. Radio communications from the plane were normal. Heading, speed, and altitude ran according to plan. At 9:24, Ballinger's warning to United 93 was received in the cockpit. Within two minutes, at 9:26, the pilot, Jason Dahl, responded with a note of puzzlement: "Ed, confirm latest mssg plz—Jason." The hijackers attacked at 9:28. *While traveling 35,000 feet above eastern Ohio, United 93 suddenly dropped 700 feet.* Eleven seconds into the descent, the FAA's air traffic control center in Cleveland received the first of two radio transmissions from the aircraft.

At least ten cell phone calls were reported to have taken place on flight 93.

The Report confirms that passengers started placing calls with cell and air phones shortly after 9:32am, four minutes after the Report's confirmation of the plane's attitude of 35,000 feet. In other words, the calls started some 9 minutes before the Cleveland Center lost UAL 93's transponder signal (9:41) and approximately 30 minutes before the crash in Pennsylvania (10:03):

> At 9:41, Cleveland Center lost United 93's transponder signal. The controller located it on primary radar, matched its position with visual sightings from other aircraft, and tracked the flight as it turned east, then south.

This suggests that the altitude was known to air traffic control up until the time when the transponder signal was lost by the Cleveland Center. (Radar and visual sightings provided information on its flight path from 9:41 to 10:03.)

Moreover, there was no indication from the Report that the aircraft had swooped down to a lower level of altitude, apart from the 700 feet drop recorded at 9:28. from a cruising altitude of 35,000 feet. The following excerpts describe in minute detail what happened inside the cabin. This description is based almost exclusively on the alleged cell phone conversations:

> At 9:32, a hijacker, probably Jarrah, made or attempted to make the following announcement to the passengers of Flight 93:"Ladies and Gentlemen: Here the captain, please sit down keep remaining sitting. ...
>
> We have a bomb on board. So, sit." The flight data recorder (also recovered) indicates that Jarrah then instructed the plane's autopilot to turn the aircraft around and head east. The cockpit voice recorder data indicate that a woman, most likely a flight attendant, was being held captive in the cockpit. She struggled with one of the hijackers who killed or otherwise silenced her.
>
> *Shortly thereafter, the passengers and flight crew began a series of calls from GTE airphones and cellular phones. These calls between family, friends, and colleagues took place until the end of the flight and provided those on the ground with firsthand accounts.* They enabled the passengers to gain critical information, including the news that two aircraft had slammed into the World Trade Center. ... At least two callers from the flight reported that the hijackers knew that passengers were making calls but did not seem to care.

The hijackers were wearing red bandanas, and they forced the passengers to the back of the aircraft. Callers reported that a passenger had been stabbed and that two people were lying on the floor of the cabin, injured or dead—possibly the captain and first officer. One caller reported that a flight attendant had been killed. One of the callers from United 93 also reported that he thought the hijackers might possess a gun. But none of the other callers reported the presence of a firearm. One recipient of a call from the aircraft recounted specifically asking her caller whether the hijackers had guns.

The passenger replied that he did not see one. No evidence of firearms or of their identifiable remains was found at the aircraft's crash site, and the cockpit voice recorder gives no indication of a gun being fired or mentioned at any time.

We believe that if the hijackers had possessed a gun, they would have used it in the flight's last minutes as the passengers fought back. Passengers on three flights reported the hijackers' claim of having a bomb. The FBI told us they found no trace of explosives at the crash sites. One of the passengers who mentioned a bomb expressed his belief that it was not real. Lacking any evidence that the hijackers attempted to smuggle such illegal items past the security screening checkpoints, we believe the bombs were probably fake. During at least five of the passengers' phone calls, information was shared about the attacks that had occurred earlier that morning at the World Trade Center. Five calls described the intent of passengers and surviving crew members to revolt against the hijackers. According to one call, they voted on whether to rush the terrorists in an attempt to retake the plane. They decided, and acted. At 9:57, the passenger assault began. Several passengers had terminated phone calls with loved ones in order to join the revolt. One of the callers ended her message as follows:

"Everyone's running up to first class. I've got to go. Bye." The cockpit voice recorder captured the sounds of the passenger assault muffled by the intervening cockpit door. Some family members who listened to the recording report that they can hear the voice of a loved one among the din.

We cannot identify whose voices can be heard. But the assault was sustained. In response, Jarrah immediately began to roll the airplane to the left and right, attempting to knock the passengers off balance. At 9:58:57, Jarrah told another hijacker in the cockpit to block the door. Jarrah continued to roll the airplane sharply left and right, but the assault continued. At 9:59, Jarrah changed tactics and pitched the nose of the airplane up and down to disrupt the assault. The recorder captured the sounds of loud thumps, crashes, shouts, and breaking glasses and plates.

At 10:00:03, Jarrah stabilized the airplane. Five seconds later, Jarrah asked, "Is that it? Shall we finish it off?" A hijacker responded, "No. Not yet. When they all come, we finish it off." The sounds of fighting continued outside the cockpit. Again, Jarrah pitched the nose of the aircraft up and down. At 10:00:26, a passenger in the background said, "In the cockpit. If we don't we'll die!" Sixteen seconds later, a passenger yelled, "Roll it!" Jarrah stopped the violent maneuvers at about 10:01:00 and said, "Allah is the greatest! Allah is the greatest!" He then asked another hijacker in the cockpit, "Is that it? I mean, shall we put it down?" to which the other replied, "Yes, put it in it, and pull it down." The passengers continued their assault and at 10:02:23, a hijacker said, "Pull it down! Pull it down!" The hijackers remained at the controls but must have judged that the passengers were only seconds from overcoming them. The airplane headed down; the control wheel was turned hard to the right.

The airplane rolled onto its back, and one of the hijackers began shouting "Allah is the greatest. Allah is the greatest." With the sounds of the passenger counterattack continuing, the aircraft plowed into an empty field in Shanksville, Pennsylvania, at 580 miles per hour, about 20 minutes' flying time from Washington D.C. Jarrah's objective was to crash his airliner into symbols of the American Republic, the Capitol or the White House. He was defeated by the alerted, unarmed passengers of United.

The Mysterious Call of Edward Felt from UAL 93

Early media coverage in the wake of 9/11 on the fate of UAL 93 had been based in part on a reported cell call from a passenger named Edward Felt, who supposedly managed to reach an emergency official in Pennsylvania. How he got the emergency supervisor's number and managed to reach him remains unclear.

The call was apparently received at 9.58 am, eight minutes before the reported time of the crash at 10.06 am in Pennsylvania:

Local emergency officials said they received a cell phone call at 9.58 am from a man who said he was a passenger aboard the flight. The man said he had locked himself in the bathroom and told emergency dispatchers that the plane had been hijacked. "We are being hijacked! We are being hijacked!" he was quoted as saying. A California man identified as Tom Burnett reportedly called his wife and told her that somebody on the plane had been stabbed. "We're all going to die, but three of us are going to do something," he told her. "I love you honey."

The alleged call by Edward Felt from the toilet of the aircraft of UAL 93 was answered by Glenn Cramer, the emergency supervisor in Pennsylvania who took the call.

It is worth noting that Glenn Cramer was subsequently gagged by the FBI.[9]

Ironically, this high profile cell call by Ed Felt, which would have provided crucial evidence to the 9/11 Commission was, for some reason, not mentioned in the Report.

American Airlines Flight 11

Flight 11 took off at 7:59. The Report outlines an airphone conversation of flight attendant Betty Ong just before 8:14. Much of the Report's narrative hinges upon this airphone conversation.

In contrast to the other plane flights, there is no explicit mention in the Report on the use of cell phones on Flight AA11. According to the Report, American Airlines AA11 crashed into the North Tower of the World Trade Center at 8.46.

Concluding Remarks

A large part of the description, regarding the 19 Arab hijackers relied on cell phone conversations with family and friends.

While a few of these calls (placed at low altitude) could have got through, the wireless technology was not available in September 2001 which would enable cell phone conversations to be placed at high altitude. On this issue, expert opinion within the wireless telecom industry is unequivocal.

Consequently, at least part of the Commission's script in Chapter I of the Report on the cell phone conversations, is subject to serious doubt.

According to the American Airline/Qualcomm announcement, the technology for cell phone transmission at high altitude will only be available aboard commercial aircraft in 2006.

In the eyes of public opinion, the cell phone conversations on the Arab hijackers is needed to sustain the illusion that America is under attack. Concretely, the script of what happened on the planes provides a face to the enemy. It is also an integral part of the disinformation campaign, which serves to dispel the historical role played by US intelligence in supporting the development of the terror network.

The "war on terrorism" underlying the National Security doctrine relies on real time "evidence" concerning the Arab hijackers. The latter personify, so to speak, this illusive "Outside Enemy" (Al Qaeda), which is threatening the Homeland.

Embodied into the Commission's script of 9/11, the narrative of what happened on the plane with the Arab hijackers is therefore crucial. It is an integral part of the Administration's propaganda program. It constitutes a justification for the anti-terror legislation under the PATRIOT Acts and the waging of America's preemptive wars against Afghanistan and Iraq.

Notes

1. National Commission on Terrorist Attacks upon the United States, Report, Washington DC, July 2004, Chapter 1, http://www.9-11commission.gov/report/911Report_Ch1.pdf.

2. http://www.elliott.org/technology/2001/cellpermit.htm

3. *Wireless Review*, 15 July 2004 http://wirelessreview.com/ar/wireless_final_contact/.

4. See Qualcomm Press Release at http://www.qualcomm.com/press/releases/2004/040715_aa_testflight.html.

5. *Washington Post*, 27 July 2004.

6. *Aviation Week*, 20 July 2004.

7. See Qualcomm on the Code Division Multiple Access (CDMA), http://www.qualcomm.com/technology/cdma101.html

8. Wikipedia at http://en.wikipedia.org/wiki/United_Airlines_flight_93. See also Richard Wallace, "What Happened to Flight 93", *Daily Mirror*, 12 September 2002

9. *Ibid.*

CHAPTER XIX
America's Pre-emptive War Doctrine

The Role of "Massive Casualty Producing Events" in Military Planning

Repeatedly since 9/11, the Bush administration has warned Americans of the danger of a "Second 9/11":

> [There are] "indications that [the] near-term attacks … will either rival or exceed the [9/11] attacks. … And it's pretty clear that the nation's capital and New York city would be on any list." (Tom Ridge, Christmas 2003)

> "You ask, 'Is it serious?' Yes, you bet your life. People don't do that unless it's a serious situation." (Donald Rumsfeld, Christmas 2003)

> "Credible reporting indicates that Al Qaeda is moving forward with its plans to carry out a large-scale attack in the United States in an effort to disrupt our democratic process…. This is sobering information about those who wish to do us harm…. But every day we strengthen the security of our nation." (George W. Bush, July 2004)

According to former US CentCom Commander, General Tommy Franks who led the invasion of Iraq in 2003, a terrorist attack on American soil of the size and nature of September 11, would lead the suspension of the Constitution and the installation of military rule in America:

> [A] terrorist, massive, casualty-producing event [will occur] some-where in the Western world—it may be in the United States of America—that causes our population to question our own Constitution and to begin to militarize our country in order to avoid a repeat of another mass, casualty-producing event.[1]

General Franks was alluding to a so-called "Pearl Harbor type event" which would be used to galvanize US public opinion in sup-port of a military government and police state.

The "terrorist massive casualty-producing event" was presented by General Franks as a crucial political turning point. The result-ing crisis and social turmoil is intended to facilitate a major shift in US political, social and institutional structures.

It is important to understand that General Franks was not giv-ing a personal opinion on this issue. His statement is consistent with the dominant viewpoint both in the Pentagon and the Homeland Security Department as to how events might unfold in the case of a national emergency.

The statement by General Franks comes from a man who has been actively involved in military and intelligence planning at the highest levels. The "militarization of our country" has become an ongoing operational assumption—a "talking point" within the mil-itary and intelligence establishment. It is part of the broader "Washington consensus". It identifies the Bush administration's "roadmap" of War and Homeland Defense.

The "war on terrorism" constitutes the cornerstone of Bush's National Security doctrine. It provides the required justification for repealing the Rule of Law, ultimately with a view to "preserv-ing civil liberties". In the words of David Rockefeller:

> We are on the verge of global transformation. All we need is the right major crisis and the nations will accept the New World Order.[2]

A similar statement, which no doubt reflects a consensus within the Council on Foreign Relations (CFR), was made by former

---

TEXT BOX 19.1
Operation Northwoods

"Operation Northwoods" was a Secret Plan of the Joint Chiefs of Staff entitled "Justification for US Military Intervention in Cuba". It was submitted by the Joint Chiefs of Staff to Secretary of Defense Robert McNamara on March 13, 1962.

The Top Secret memorandum describes US plans to trigger "massive casualty producing events" that would justify a US invasion of Cuba. These proposals—part of a secret anti-Castro program known as Operation Mongoose—included staging the assassinations of Cubans living in the United States, developing a fake "Communist Cuban terror campaign in the Miami area, in other Florida cities and even in Washington," including "sink[ing] a boatload of Cuban refugees (real or simulated)," faking a Cuban airforce attack on a civilian jetliner, and concocting a "Remember the Maine" incident by blowing up a US ship in Cuban waters and then blaming the incident on Cuban sabotage.

Author James Bamford wrote that Operation Northwoods "may be the most corrupt plan ever created by the US Government."

Source: James Bamford, *National Security Archive,* 30 April 2001. The Declassified document can be consulted at the National Security Archive website. URL of the original document: http://www.gwu.edu/~nsarchiv/news/20010430/doc1.pdf.

National Security adviser Zbigniew Brzezinski in his book, *The Grand Chessboard*:

> As America becomes an increasingly multicultural society, it may find it more difficult to fashion a consensus on foreign policy issues, except in the circumstances of a truly massive and widely perceived direct external threat.[3]

Similarly, the NeoCons' Project for the New American Century (PNAC), published in September 2000, had also pointed to the central role of what General Tommy Franks had entitled "a massive casualty producing event":

> The process of transformation, even if it brings revolutionary change,
> is likely to be a long one, absent some catastrophic and catalyzing
> event—like a new Pearl Harbor.[4]

The foregoing statement emanates from the architects of US foreign policy. In other words, America's leaders in Washington and Wall Street firmly believe in the righteousness of war and authoritarian forms of government as a means to "safeguarding democratic values".

The repeal of democracy is portrayed as a means to providing "domestic security" and upholding civil liberties. Truth is falsehood and falsehood is truth. Realities are turned upside down. Acts of war are heralded as "humanitarian interventions" geared towards upholding democracy. Military occupation and the killing of civilians are presented as "peace-keeping operations."

This dominant viewpoint is also shared by the mainstream media, which constitutes the cornerstone of the propaganda and disinformation campaign. Any attempt by antiwar critics to reveal the lies underlying these statements is defined as a "criminal act".

The "Criminalization of the State" occurs when war criminals, supported by Wall Street, the "big five" defense contractors and the Texas oil giants, legitimately occupy positions of authority, which enable them to decide "who are the criminals", when in fact they are the criminals.

The Project for a New American Century (PNAC)

In September 2000, a few months before the accession of George W. Bush to the White House, the Project for a New American Century (PNAC) published its blueprint for global domination under the title: *Rebuilding America's Defenses, Strategy, Forces and Resources for a New Century.*

The PNAC is a neo-conservative think tank linked to the Defense-Intelligence establishment, the Republican Party and the powerful Council on Foreign Relations (CFR) which plays a behind-the-scenes role in the formulation of US foreign policy.

The PNAC's declared objectives are to:

- Defend the American Homeland;
- Fight and decisively win multiple, simultaneous major theater wars;
- Perform the "constabulary" duties associated with shaping the security environment in critical regions";
- Transform US forces to exploit the "revolution in military affairs".[5]

Deputy Defense Secretary Paul Wolfowitz, Defense Secretary Donald Rumsfeld and Vice President Dick Cheney commissioned the PNAC blueprint prior to the 2000 presidential elections.

The PNAC outlines a roadmap of conquest.

It calls for "the direct imposition of US "forward bases" throughout Central Asia and the Middle East, with a view to ensuring economic domination of the world, while strangling any potential "rival" or any viable alternative to America's vision of a "free market" economy.

Distinct from theater wars, the so-called "constabulary functions" imply a form of global military policing using various instruments of military intervention including punitive bombings and the sending in of US Special Forces:

> The Pentagon must retain forces to preserve the current peace in ways that fall short of conduction major theater campaigns. ... These duties are today's most frequent missions, requiring forces configured for combat but capable of long-term, independent constabulary operations.[6]

The PNAC's "revolution in military affairs" also consists of the Strategic Defense Initiative, the weaponization of space and the development of a new generation of nuclear weapons.

The Strategic Defense Initiative (SDI) also known as Star Wars, not only includes the controversial "Missile Shield", but also a wide range of offensive laser-guided weapons with striking capabilities anywhere in the world.

The US military has also developed as part of its arsenal, so-called "environmental modification" (ENMOD) techniques. The most advanced instrument of environmental warfare has been developed under the US Air Force's High Altitude Auroral Research Program (HAARP). Recent scientific evidence suggests that HAARP is fully operational and has the ability of potentially triggering floods, droughts, hurricanes and earthquakes.[7]

From a military standpoint, HAARP is a weapon of mass destruction. Potentially, it constitutes an instrument of conquest capable of selectively destabilizing the agricultural and ecological systems of entire regions.

Also contemplated is the Pentagon's so-called FALCON program. FALCON is the ultimate New World Order weapons' system, to be used for global economic and political domination. It can strike from the continental US anywhere in the World. It is described as a "global reach" weapon to be used to "react promptly and decisively to destabilizing or threatening actions by hostile countries and terrorist organizations".[8]

This hypersonic cruise weapon system to be developed by Northrop Grumman "would allow the US to conduct effective, time-critical strike missions on a global basis without relying on overseas military bases." FALCON would allow the US to strike, either in support of conventional forces engaged in a war theater or in punitive bombings directed against countries that do not comply with US economic and political diktats.

The Preemptive War Doctrine

The preemptive "defensive war" doctrine and the "war on terrorism" against Al Qaeda constitute essential building blocks of the Pentagon's propaganda campaign.

To justify preemptive military actions, the National Security Strategy (NSS) requires the *fabrication* of a terrorist threat,—i.e., "an Outside Enemy". It also needs to link these terrorist threats to "State sponsorship" by so-called "rogue states."

The objective is to present "preemptive military action"—meaning war as an act of "self-defense" against two categories of enemies, "rogue States" and "Islamic terrorists", both of which are said to possess weapons of mass destruction:

The war against terrorists of global reach is a global enterprise of uncertain duration. … America will act against such emerging threats before they are fully formed. …

Rogue States and terrorists do not seek to attack us using conventional means. They know such attacks would fail. Instead, they rely on acts of terror and, potentially, the use of weapons of mass destruction …

The targets of these attacks are our military forces and our civilian population, in direct violation of one of the principal norms of the law of warfare. As was demonstrated by the losses on September 11, 2001, mass civilian casualties is the specific objective of terrorists and these losses would be exponentially more severe if terrorists acquired and used weapons of mass destruction.

The United States has long maintained the option of preemptive actions to counter a sufficient threat to our national security. The greater the threat, the greater is the risk of inaction—and the more compelling the case for taking anticipatory action to defend ourselves, …. To forestall or prevent such hostile acts by our adversaries, the United States will, if necessary, act preemptively.[9]

The "War on Terrorism" and the Nuclear Option

This "anticipatory action" under the NSS includes the use of tactical nuclear weapons, which are now classified as "in theater weapons" to be used in conventional war theaters alongside conventional weapons.

In the wake of September 11, 2001, the nuclear option, namely the pre-emptive use of nuclear weapons is intimately related to the "war on terrorism."

Nuclear weapons are now being presented as performing essentially defensive functions to be used against so-called "Rogue States" and terrorist organizations, including Al Qaeda, which are said to constitute a nuclear threat.

The propaganda emanating from the CIA and the Pentagon consists in presenting Al Qaeda as capable of developing a nuclear device, which could be used in an attack on the United States. According to a report of the CIA's Intelligence Directorate:

Al Qaeda's goal is the use of [chemical, biological, radiological or nuclear weapons] to cause mass casualties. …

[Islamist extremists] have a wide variety of potential agents and delivery means to choose from for chemical, biological and radiological or nuclear (CBRN) attacks.[10]

The alleged nuclear threat emanating from Al Qaeda is used in the National Security Strategy to justify the preemptive use of nuclear weapons to defend America against Al Qaeda.

While the media has its eyes riveted on Islamic terrorists and Al Qaeda, the threats to global security resulting from Washington's preemptive first strike use of nuclear weapons is barely mentioned.

The Privatization of Nuclear War

On August 6, 2003, the day the first atomic bomb was dropped on Hiroshima, 58 years ago, a secret meeting was held with senior executives from the nuclear industry and the military industrial complex at Central Command Headquarters at the Offutt Air Force Base in Nebraska.[11]

More than 150 military contractors, scientists from the weapons labs, and other government officials gathered at the headquarters of the US Strategic Command in Omaha, Nebraska to plot and plan for the possibility of "full-scale nuclear war" calling for the production of a new generation of nuclear weapons—more "usable" so-called "mini-nukes and earth penetrating "bunker busters" armed with atomic warheads.[12]

The new nuclear policy explicitly involves the large defense contractors in decision-making. It is tantamount to *the privatization of nuclear war*. The "war on terrorism" is its stated objective.

Corporations not only reap multibillion-dollar profits from the production of nuclear bombs, they also have a direct voice in setting the agenda regarding the use and deployment of nuclear weapons.

The nuclear weapons industry, which includes the production of nuclear devices as well as the missile delivery systems is controlled by a handful of defense contractors with Lockheed Martin, General Dynamics, Northrop, Raytheon and Boeing in the lead.

It is worth noting that barely a week prior to the historic August 6, 2003 meeting at the Offutt Air force base, the National Nuclear Security Administration (NNSA) disbanded its advisory committee which had a mandate to provide an "independent oversight" on the US nuclear arsenal, including the testing and/or use of new nuclear devices.[13]

Meanwhile, the Pentagon had unleashed a major propaganda and public relations campaign with a view to upholding the use of nuclear weapons for the "defense of the American Homeland" against "terrorists" and "rogue enemies".

Nuclear weapons are now presented as a means to building peace and preventing "collateral damage". The Pentagon had intimated, in this regard, that the "mini-nukes" are harmless to civilians because the explosions "take place under ground". Each of these "mini-nukes", nonetheless, constitutes—in terms of explosive capacity and potential radioactive fallout—a significant fraction of the atom bomb dropped on Hiroshima in 1945. The mini-nukes have an explosive capacity between one third to six times a Hiroshima bomb. In the case of "small" 5 and 10 kiloton bombs, the explosive capacity is respectively one third and two thirds of a Hiroshima bomb.

Formally endorsed by the US Congress in late 2003, the "mini-nukes" are thus considered to be "safe for civilians". Once this assumption—based on the "scientific assessments" conducted by the Pentagon—is built into military planning, it is no longer challenged. The technical specifications of the mini-nukes are entered into the various military manuals. Decisions pertaining to their use would be based on the specifications contained in these military manuals.

The disinformation campaign presents the mini-nukes as "harmless". It consists in building a consensus within the Military, while also convincing Congress that "the small nuclear bombs" are "safe for civilians". Based on this premise, the US Congress has given the "green light". This new generation of nuclear weapons is slated to be used in the next phase of the war, in "conventional war theaters" (e.g., in the Middle East and Central Asia) alongside conventional weapons, against "rogue enemies" and Islamic "terrorists". Meanwhile, the US Congress has allocated billions of dollars to further develop this new generation of "defensive" nuclear weapons.

National Defense Strategy:
From "Rogue States" to "Unstable Nations"

In March 2005, the Pentagon released a major document entitled, *The National Defense Strategy of the United States of America* (NDS), which broadly sketches Washington's agenda for global military domination.[14]

While the NDS follows in the footsteps of the Administration's "pre-emptive" war doctrine as outlined in the Project of the New American Century (PNAC), it goes much further in setting the contours of Washington's global military agenda.

Whereas the pre-emptive war doctrine envisages military action as a means of "self defense" against countries categorized as "hostile" to the US, the 2005 NSD goes one step further. It envisages the possibility of military intervention against countries, which do not visibly constitute a threat to the security of the American homeland.

It calls for a more "proactive" approach to warfare, beyond the weaker notion of "preemptive" and "defensive" actions, where military operations are launched against a "declared enemy" with a view to "preserving the peace" and "defending America".

The 2005 National Defense Strategy (NDS) consists in "enhancing US influence around the world", through increased troop deployments and a massive buildup of America's advanced weapons systems.

The new National Security doctrine outlines "four major threats to the United States":

- "Traditional challenges" are posed by well known and recognized military powers using "well-understood' forms of war.
- "Irregular threats" come from forces using so-called "unconventional" methods to counter stronger power.

- "The catastrophic challenge" pertains to the "use of weapons of mass destruction by an enemy.
- "Disruptive challenges" pertains to "potential adversaries utilizing new technologies to counter US advantages".[15]

The NDS document explicitly acknowledges America's global military mandate, beyond regional war theaters. This mandate also includes military operations directed against so-called "failed states" or "unstable nations".[16]

From a broad military and foreign policy perspective, the March 2005 Pentagon document constitutes an imperial design, which supports US corporate interests Worldwide.

> At its heart, the document is driven by the belief that the US is engaged in a continuous global struggle that extends far beyond specific battlegrounds, such as Iraq and Afghanistan. The vision is for a military that is far more proactive, focused on changing the world instead of just responding to conflicts such as a North Korean attack on South Korea, and assuming greater prominence in countries in which the US isn't at war.[17]

Countries on the Pentagon's Black List

Shortly after the release of the Pentagon's March 2005 NDS document, the newly formed *Office of Reconstruction and Stabilization* under the National Intelligence Council (NIC) of the State Department confirmed that "US intelligence experts are preparing a list of 25 countries deemed unstable and, thus, candidates for [military] intervention".[18]

The exercise consists in identifying countries of "greatest instability and risk", distinct from declared enemies or "Rogue States.

America's security is said to be threatened less by "conquering states than by the failed and failing ones":

> [C]onflict prevention and postwar reconstruction of failed and failing states had become a "mainstream foreign policy challenge" because of the dangers of terrorist groups and the availability of weapons of mass destruction. ...
>
> [The mandate of the Office of Reconstruction and Stabilization under the NIC is] to prevent conflict, but also to prepare to react

quickly when the US military had to intervene. Post-conflict work would focus on creating laws and institutions of a "market democracy". ... Planning would include forming a "reserve corps" of specialist civilian teams and devising reconstruction contracts in advance with private companies and NGOs.[19]

Whether these countries constitute a threat to National Security is not the issue. Military priorities will also be established in accordance with this list. Hostility to the US (e.g., by "rogue enemies" and/or "growing powers") is not the sole criterion for military intervention.

While the "watch-list" of 25 "unstable nations" remains a closely guarded secret, a number of countries have already been identified. These include *inter alia* Venezuela, Nepal (currently marked by a peasant-led insurrection), Haiti under military occupation, Algeria, Peru, Bolivia, Sudan, Nigeria, Sierra Leone, Liberia and Côte d'Ivoire.[20]

The justification for intervening militarily in these countries is based on America's mandate to "help them stabilize" and put them

---

TEXT BOX 19.1

The Office of the Coordinator for Reconstruction and Stabilization

The Office of the Coordinator for Reconstruction and Stabilization plans to bring together "civilian experts in such fields as political administration, law enforcement and economics and give them a seat at the table alongside the military during the planning of US intervention in troubled states. ... The office, relying in part on relationships with other federal agencies and private-sector groups, would accompany military troops in the field and lay the groundwork for rebuilding countries crumbling under conflict,

Official statement of the OCRS quoted in the *Washington Post,* 26 March 2005.

on "a sustainable path". One can expect that any national project which goes against Washington's conception of a "'free market democracy" will be a candidate for military possible intervention.

"Asymmetric Warfare"

In the words of its main architect Douglas Feith, the 2005 National Defense Strategy (NDS) implies the concept of "asymmetric warfare". The NDS categorizes "diplomatic and legal challenges" to US foreign policy by "non-State actors" as "asymmetric threats" to the security of America, namely as de facto aggressive acts. What is significant in this approach is that "civil society non-State actors" are now lumped together with the "terrorists".

Asymmetric warfare would include a "legal lines of attack" under the aupices of the International Criminal Court (ICC) or any initiative, legal or otherwise, which seeks "to criminalize [US] foreign policy and bring prosecutions where there is no proper basis for jurisdiction under international law as a way of trying to pressure American officials".[21]

> Our strength as a nation state will continue to be challenged by those who employ a strategy of the weak focusing on international forums, judicial processes and terrorism. …
>
> There are various actors around the world that are looking to either attack or constrain the United States, and they are going to find creative ways of doing that, that are not the obvious conventional military attacks. … We need to think broadly about diplomatic lines of attack, legal lines of attack, technological lines of attack, all kinds of asymmetric warfare that various actors can use to try to constrain, shape our behavior.[22]

The concept of "asymmetric warfare" suggests that challenges in the judicial and/or diplomatic arenas by State and non-State actors, including non-governmental organizations, would be the object of retaliatory actions on the part of the United States.

Global Military Deployment

US military involvement is not limited to the Middle East. Sending in Special Forces in military policing operations, under the disguise of peacekeeping and training, is contemplated in all major regions of the World.

To support these endeavors, the NDS points to the need for massive recruitment and training of troops. The latter would include new contingents of Special Forces, Green Berets and other specialized military personnel, involved in what the PNAC described in its September 2000 military blueprint as "constabulary functions":

> The classified guidance urges the military to come up with less doctrinaire solutions that include sending in smaller teams of culturally savvy soldiers to train and mentor indigenous forces.[23]

Moreover, the Pentagon has confirmed its intent "to shift to a more centralized 'global force management' model so it could quickly expand available troops anywhere in the world" in non-theater military operations:

> Under this concept, Combatant Commanders no longer "own" forces in their theaters, ... Forces are allocated to them as needed—sourced from anywhere in the world. This allows for greater flexibility to meet rapidly changing operational circumstances.[24]

Overshadowing Potential Military Rivals

America is spending more than 500 billion dollars a year on defense and military intelligence, an amount which is somewhat less than the GDP of the Russian Federation, estimated at $613 billion in 2004. In other words, the Cold war era super-power has been impoverished beyond bounds, dwarfed in terms of its defense capabilities. Even if it were to allocate a sizeable portion of its GDP to defense spending, it would not be able to rival the US.

According to the Stockholm International Peace Research Institute (SIPRI), global military expenditure is in excess of $950 billion of which approximately 50 percent is directly linked to the US military budget.[25]

> The US accounts for 40 to 50 per cent of global defense spending. In every sphere of warfare the US now has clear preponderance over other powers. No other power has the capacity to move large forces

around the globe and support its troops with precision firepower and unsurpassed amount of information and intelligence. Military resources as a result of the $400 billion military budget are formidable. The defense research establishment of the US receives more money than the entire defense budget of its largest European ally. No other power has B2 bombers, the satellite constellations, the aircraft carriers or the long range unmanned aircraft like that of the US Navy and Air Force.[26]

The underlying objective of the 2005 NDS consists in overshadowing, in terms of defense outlays, any other nation on earth including America's European allies:

> The United States military ... will be larger than the next 25 countries put together. ... If spending patterns hold, which is to say European defense spending is declining, American is rising, in about five years, the United States will be spending more money than the rest of the world put together on defense.[27]

In contrast, China, which is categorized in the Pentagon document as a "growing power", spent in 2004 less than 30 billion dollars on defense.

New Post Cold War Enemies

While the "war on terrorism" and the containment of "Rogue States" still constitute the official justification and driving force for military intervention, China and Russia are explicitly identified in the 2005 NDS as potential enemies:

> The US military ... is seeking to dissuade rising powers, such as China, from challenging US military dominance. Although weapons systems designed to fight guerrillas tend to be fairly cheap and low-tech, the review makes clear that to dissuade those countries from trying to compete, the US military must retain its dominance in key high-tech areas, such as stealth technology, precision weaponry and manned and unmanned surveillance systems.[28]

While the European Union is not mentioned, the stated objective is to shunt the development of all potential military rivals.

"Trying to Run with the Big Dog"

Washington intends to reach its goal of global military hegemony through the continued development of the US weapons industry, requiring a massive shift out of the production of civilian goods and services. In other words, spiraling defense spending feeds this new undeclared arms race, with vast amounts of public money channeled to America's major weapons producers.

The stated objective is to make the process of developing advanced weapons systems "so expensive", that no other power on earth will be able to compete or challenge "the Big Dog" without jeopardizing its civilian economy. According to a defense consultant hired to draft sections of the document:

> [A]t the core of this strategy is the belief that the US must maintain such a large lead in crucial technologies that growing powers will conclude that it is too expensive for these countries to even think about trying to run with the big dog. They will realize that it is not worth sacrificing their economic growth.[29]

Undeclared Arms Race between Europe and America

This new undeclared arms race is with the so-called "growing powers".

While China and Russia are mentioned as potential threats, America's (unofficial) rivals also include France, Germany and Japan. The recognized partners of the US—in the context of the Anglo-American axis—are Britain, Australia and Canada, not to mention Israel (unofficially).

In this context, there are at present two dominant Western military axes: the Anglo-American axis and the competing Franco-German alliance. The European military project, largely dominated by France and Germany, will attempt to undermine NATO, which remains dominated by the US. Moreover, Britain (through British Aerospace Systems Corporation) is firmly integrated into the US system of defense procurement in partnership with America's big five weapons producers. (See Chapter VII.)

This new arms race is firmly embedded in the proposed European Constitution, which envisages under EU auspices, a massive redirection of State financial resources towards military expenditure. Moreover, the EU monetary system—establishing the Euro as a global currency which challenges the hegemony of the US dollar—is intimately related to the development of an integrated EU defense force outside of NATO.

Under the European Constitution, there would be a unified European foreign policy position which would include a common defense component. It is understood, although never seriously debated in public, that the proposed European Defense Force is intended to challenge America's supremacy in military affairs: "under such a regime, trans-Atlantic relations will be dealt a fatal blow".[30]

This European military project, however, while encouraging an undeclared US-EU arms race, is not incompatible with continued US-EU cooperation in military affairs. The underlying objective for Europe is that EU corporate interests are protected and that European contractors are able to effectively cash in and "share the spoils" of the US-led wars in the Middle East and elsewhere.

In other words, by challenging "the Big Dog" from a position of strength, the EU seeks to retain its role as "a partner" of America in its various military ventures.

There is a presumption, particularly in France, that the only way to build good relations with Washington is to emulate the American Military Project, that is to adopt a similar strategy of beefing up Europe's advanced weapons systems.

What we are dealing with, therefore, is a fragile love-hate relationship between Old Europe and America, in defense systems, the oil industry as well as in the upper spheres of banking, finance and currency markets.

The important issue is how this fragile geopolitical relationship will evolve in terms of coalitions and alliances in the years to come. France and Germany have military cooperation agreements with both Russia and China. European Defense companies are supplying China with sophisticated weaponry. Ultimately, Europe is viewed as an encroachment by the US, and military conflict between competing Western superpowers cannot be ruled out.

Trans-Atlantic Consensus on the "War on Terrorism"

The new US-EU arms race has become the chosen avenue of the European Union, to foster "friendly relations" with the American superpower. Rather than opposing the US, Europe has embraced "the war on terrorism". It is actively collaborating with the US in the arrest of presumed terrorists. Several EU countries have established Big Brother anti-terrorist laws, which constitute a European "copy and paste" version of the US Homeland Security legislation.

European public opinion is now galvanized into supporting the "war on terrorism", which broadly benefits the European military industrial complex and the oil companies. In turn, the "war on terrorism" also provides a shaky legitimacy to the EU security agenda. The latter establishes a framework for implementing police-state measures, while also dismantling labor legislation and the European Welfare State.

In turn, the European media has also become a partner in the disinformation campaign. The "outside enemy" presented ad nauseam on network TV, on both sides of the Atlantic, is Osama bin Laden and Abu Musab Al-Zarqawi. The propaganda campaign serves to usefully camouflage the ongoing militarization of civilian institutions, which is occurring simultaneously in Europe and America.

Guns and Butter: The Demise of the Civilian Economy

The proposed EU Constitution—which was defeated in 2005 in country-level referenda—requires a massive expansion of military spending in all member countries to the obvious detriment of the civilian economy.

In effect, with the European Union's 3% limit on annual budget deficits, the expansion in military expenditure would result in a massive curtailment of all categories of civilian expenditure, including social services, public infrastructure, not to mention government support to agriculture and industry.

In this regard, "the war on terrorism" also serves—in the context of the EU's neoliberal reforms—as a pretext. It builds public acceptance for the imposition of austerity measures affecting civilian programs, on the grounds that money is needed to enhance national security and homeland defense.

The growth of military spending in Europe is directly related to the US military buildup. The more America spends on defense, the more Europe will want to spend on developing its own European Defense Force. "Keeping up with the Jones" in military affairs is presented for a good and worthy cause, namely fighting "Islamic terrorists" and defending the European Homeland.

EU enlargement is thus directly linked to the development and financing of the European weapons industry. The dominant European powers desperately need the contributions of the ten new EU members to finance the EU's military buildup. It is in this regard that the European Constitution requires "the adoption of a security strategy for Europe, accompanied by financial commitments on military spending".[31]

Ultimately, the backlash on employment and social programs is the inevitable byproduct of both the American and European military projects, which channel vast amounts of State financial resources towards the war economy, at the expense of the civilian sectors.

The results are plant closures and bankruptcies in the civilian economy, and a rising tide of poverty and unemployment throughout the Western World. Moreover, contrary to the 1930s, the dynamic development of the weapons industry creates very few jobs.

Meanwhile, as the Western war economy flourishes, the delocation of the production of manufactured goods to Third World countries has increased at a dramatic pace in recent years. China, which constitutes by far the largest producer of civilian manufactured goods, almost doubled its textile exports to the US in 2004, leading to a wave of plant closures and job losses.[32]

The global economy is characterized by a bipolar relationship. The rich Western countries produce weapons of mass destruction, whereas poor countries produce manufactured consumer goods.

America, in particular, has relied on this cheap supply of consumer goods to close down a large share of its manufacturing sector, while at the same time redirecting resources away from the civilian economy into the production of weapons of mass destruction. The latter are intended to to be used against the country which supplies America with a large share of its consumer goods, namely China.

The rich countries use their advanced weapons systems to threaten or wage war on the poor developing countries, which supply Western markets with large amounts of consumer goods produced in cheap labor assembly plants.

Notes

1. General Tommy Franks Interview, *Cigar Aficionado*, December 2003.

2. David Rockefeller, Statement to the United Nations Business Council, 1994.

3. Zbigniew Brzezinski, *The Grand Chessboard*, Basic Books, New York, 1997.

4. See Project for a New American Century, *Rebuilding America's Defenses*, www.newamericancentury.org/, 2000, p. 52.

5. *Ibid*, p. 18.

6. *Ibid.*

7 See Michel Chossudovsky, "Owning the Weather for Military Use", Centre for Research on Globalization, 27 September 2004, http://globalresearch.ca/articles/CHO409F.html.

8. "The Falcon Program", http://www.globalsecurity.org/space/systems/falcon-slv.htm.

9. National Security Strategy, White House, Washington, 2002, http://www.whitehouse.gov/nsc/nss.html.

10. Quoted in *The Washington Times*, 3 June 2003.

11. Reuven Pedatzur, "Blurring the Nuclear Boundaries", *Haaretz*, 14 August 2003.

12. Alice Slater, "Bush Nuclear Policy A Recipe for National Insecurity", Centre for Research on Globalization, August 2003, http://globalresearch.ca/articles/SLA308A.html.

13. *The Guardian*, 31 July 2003.

14. Department of Defense, *The National Defense Strategy of the United States of America*, Washington DC, March 2005, http://www.defenselink.mil/news/Mar2005/d20050318nds2.pdf.

15. *Ibid*, p. 2.

16. *Ibid.*

17. *Wall Street Journal,* 11 March 2005.

18. UPI, 29 March 2005.

19.*Financial Times,* 30 March 2005.

20 Author's review of US foreign policy statements reported by the Western media, April 2005.

21. Quoted in Associated Press, 18 March 2005.

22. *Ibid.*

23. *Wall Street Journal, op. cit.*

24. UPI, 18 March 2005.

25. See Stockholm International Peace Research Institute (SIPRI), http://www.sipri.org/.

26. *The Statesman,* India, 5 April 2005.

27. Council on Foreign Relations, Annual Corporate Conference, 10 March 2005.

28. *Wall Street Journal, op. cit.*

29. *Ibid.*

30. According to Martin Callanan, British Conservative member of the European Parliament, quoted in *The Washington Times,* 5 March 2005.

31. *European Report,* 3 July 2003.

32. *Asian Wall Street Journal,* 11 March 2005.

Chapter XX
The Post 9/11 Terror Alerts

The Bush Administration has put the country on "high risk" Code Orange terror alert on several occasions since September 11, 2001. Without exception, Osama bin Laden's Al Qaeda was identified as "a threat to the Homeland". The official announcement invariably points to "significant intelligence reports" or "credible sources" of a terrorist attack "from the international terrorist group Al Qaeda" or by "terrorist mastermind Al-Zarqawi". (See Chapter XIII.)

Since 9/11, most Americans have accepted these terrorist warnings at face value. The terror alerts have become part of a routine: people have become accustomed in their daily lives to the Code Orange terror alerts.

Moreover, they have also accepted the distinct possibility—stated time and again by the Department of Homeland Security—of a Code Red Alert, which would trigger an emergency situation. Supported by a barrage of media propaganda, these repeated terror alerts have created an environment of fear and intimidation, a wait and accept attitude, a false normality.

The disinformation campaign, which feeds the news chain on a daily basis, supports this process of shaping US public opinion. The hidden agenda ultimately consists in an environment of fear and intimidation, which mobilizes public support for an *actual* national emergency, leading to the declaration of martial law.

Terror Alerts based on Fabricated Intelligence

On 7 February 2003, two days after Colin Powell's flopped presentation on Iraq's alleged weapons of mass destruction to the UN Security Council, a Code Orange Alert was ordered. (See Chapter XIII.) Powell's intelligence dossier had been politely dismissed. The rebuttal came from UN Weapons Inspector Hans Blix, who showed that the intelligence presented by Colin Powell had been blatantly fabricated and was being used as pretext to wage war on Iraq.

The Bush administration declared a Code Orange terror alert as a "save face operation", which contributed to appeasing an impending scandal, while also upholding the Pentagon's planned invasion of Iraq.

Media attention was thus immediately shifted from Colin Powell's blunders at the UN Security Council to an imminent terrorist attack on America. Anti-aircraft missiles were immediately deployed around Washington. The media became inundated with stories on Iraqi support to an impending Al Qaeda attack on America.

The objective was to present Iraq as the aggressor:

> The nation is now on Orange Alert because intelligence intercepts and simple logic both suggest that our Islamic enemies know the best way to strike at us is through terrorism on US soil.[1]

Also planted in the news chain was a story—allegedly emanating from the CIA—on so-called "radioactive dirty bombs".[2] Secretary Powell had warned that "it would be easy for terrorists to cook up radioactive 'dirty' bombs to explode inside the US. ... 'How likely it is, I can't say. ... But I think it is wise for us to at least let the American people know of this possibility.'"[3] Meanwhile, network TV warned that "American hotels, shopping malls or apartment buildings could be Al Qaeda's targets as soon as next week."

In the weeks leading up to the March 2003 invasion of Iraq, the Administration's disinformation campaign consisted in linking

Baghdad to Al Qaeda. The objective was to muster unbending support for President Bush and weaken the anti-war protest movement.

Following the February 2003 announcement, tens of thousands of Americans rushed to purchase duct tape, plastic sheets and gas masks.

It later transpired that the terrorist alert was fabricated, in all likelihood in consultation with the upper echelons of the State Department.[4]

The FBI, for the first time had pointed its finger at the CIA.

> This piece of that puzzle turns out to be fabricated and therefore the reason for a lot of the alarm, particularly in Washington this week, has been dissipated after they found out that this information was not true," said Vince Cannistraro, former CIA counter-terrorism chief and ABCNEWS consultant. ...
>
> According to officials, the FBI and the CIA are pointing fingers at each other. An FBI spokesperson told ABCNEWS today he was "not familiar with the scenario," but did not think it was accurate.[5]

While tacitly acknowledging that the alert was a fake, Homeland Security Secretary Tom Ridge decided to maintain the Code Orange Alert:

> Despite the fabricated report, there are no plans to change the threat level. Officials said other intelligence has been validated and that the high level of precautions is fully warranted.[6]

A few days later, in another failed pre-invasion propaganda initiative, a mysterious Osama bin Laden audio-tape was presented by Sec. Colin Powell to the US Congress as "evidence" that the Islamic terrorists "are making common cause with a brutal dictator".[7] Curiously, the audio tape was in Colin Powell's possession prior to its broadcast by the Al Jazeera TV Network.[8]

Homeland Security's Fake Christmas Terror Alert
On December 21, 2003, four days before Christmas, the Homeland Security Department again raised the national threat level from "elevated" to "high risk".[9]

In his pre-Christmas Press Conference, Homeland Security Department Secretary Tom Ridge confirmed in much the same way as on February 7, 2003, that "the US intelligence community has received a substantial increase in the volume of threat-related intelligence reports". According to Tom Ridge, these "credible [intelligence] sources" raise "the possibility of attacks against the homeland, around the holiday season".[10]

While the circumstances and timing were different, Secretary Tom Ridge's December 21, 2003 statement had all the appearances of a "copy and paste" (*déjà vu*) version of his February 7, 2003 pre-invasion announcement, which the FBI identified as having been based on faulty intelligence.

The atmosphere of fear and confusion created across America contributed to breaking the spirit of Christmas. According to the media reports, the high-level terror alert was to "hang over the holidays and usher in the New Year". Defense Secretary Donald H. Rumsfeld warned that:

> Terrorists still threaten our country and we remain engaged in a dangerous—to be sure—difficult war and it will not be over soon. ... They can attack at any time and at any place." ... With America on high terror alert for the Christmas holiday season, intelligence officials fear Al Qaeda is eager to stage a spectacular attack—possibly hijacking a foreign airliner or cargo jet and crashing it into a high-profile target inside the United States.[11]

The official Christmas 2003 announcement by the Homeland Security Department dispelled any lingering doubts regarding the threat level:

> The risk [during the Christmas period] is perhaps greater now than at any point since September 11, 2001. ... Indications that [the] near-term attacks ... will either rival or exceed the [9/11] attacks. And it's pretty clear that the nation's capital and New York City would be on any list.[12]

Following Secretary Tom Ridge's announcement, anti-aircraft missile batteries were set up in Washington:

And the Pentagon said today, more combat air patrols will now be flying over select cities and facilities, with some airbases placed on higher alert.[13]

Defense Secretary Donald Rumsfeld commented: "You ask, 'Is it serious?' Yes, you bet your life. People don't do that unless it's a serious situation."[14]

According to an official statement: "intelligence indicate[d] that Al Qaeda-trained pilots may be working for overseas airlines and ready to carry out suicide attacks."[15]

More specifically, Al Qaeda and Taliban terrorists were, according to Homeland Security, planning to hijack an Air France plane and "crash it on US soil in a suicide terror strike similar to those carried out on September 11, 2001."

Air France Christmas flights out of Paris were grounded. F-16 fighters were patrolling the skies.

Yet once again, it turned out that the stand down orders on Air France's Christmas 2003 flights from Paris to Los Angeles, which had been used to justify the Code Orange Alert during the Christmas holiday, had been based on fabricated information.

According to the official version of events, Washington had identified six members of Al Qaeda and the Taliban on the Air France passenger list:

> US counter-terrorism officials said their investigation was focusing on the "informed belief" that about six men on Air France Flight 68, which arrives in Los Angeles daily at 4:05 p.m., may have been planning to hijack the jet and crash it near Los Angeles, or along the way.
>
> That belief, according to one senior US counter-terrorism official, was based on reliable and corroborated information from several sources. Some of the men had the same names as identified members of Al Qaeda and the Taliban, a senior US official said. One of the men is a trained pilot with a commercial license, according to a senior US official.
>
> US law-enforcement officials said the flights were canceled in response to the same intelligence that prompted ... Homeland Security ... to ratchet up the nation's terror-alert level to orange. ...

> With that information, US authorities contacted French intelli-
> gence. … They prevailed upon Air France to cancel [their flights],
> because the original intelligence information warned of more than
> one flight being commandeered.[16]

Other media confirmed that the reports gathered by American
agencies were "very, very precise". Meanwhile Fox News pointed to
the possibility that Al Qaeda was "trying to plant disinformation,
among other things to cost us money, to throw people into panic
and perhaps to probe our defenses to see how we respond."[17]

"Mistaken Identity"

Throughout the Christmas holiday, Los Angeles International airport was on "maximum deployment" with counter-terrorism and
FBI officials working around the clock.

Yet following the French investigation, it turned out that the
terror alert was a hoax. The information was not "very very precise"
as claimed by US intelligence.

The six Al Qaeda men turned out to be a five year old boy, an
elderly Chinese lady who used to run a restaurant in Paris, a Welsh
insurance salesman and three French nationals.[18]

On January 2, 2004, the French government finally released the
results of their investigation which indicated that the intelligence
was erroneous: There "was not a trace of Al Qaeda among the passengers".

The intelligence was fake. And this had already been uncovered
prior to the Christmas holiday, by France's antiterrorist services,
which had politely refuted the so-called "credible sources" emanating out of the US intelligence apparatus.

France's counter-terrorism experts were extremely "skeptical" of
their US counterparts:

> We [French police investigators] showed [on 23 December] that
> their arguments simply did not make sense, but despite the evidence,
> the flights were cancelled. … The main suspect [a Tunisian hijacker]
> turned out to be a child. … We really had the feeling of hostile and
> unfriendly treatment [by US officials] (*ils nous appliquent un traite-
> ment d'infamie*). The information was not transmitted through nor-

mal channels. It wasn't the FBI or the CIA which contacted us, everything went through diplomatic channels.[19]

The decision to cancel the six Air France flights was taken after two days of intense negotiations between French and American officials following the completion of the French investigation.

The flights were cancelled on the orders of the French Prime Minister following consultations with Secretary Colin Powell. Despite the fact that the information had been refuted, Homeland Security Secretary Tom Ridge insisted on maintaining the standdown order. If Air France had not complied, it would have been prevented from using US air space, namely banned from flying to the US.

It was after News Year's Day, once the holiday season was over, that the US authorities admitted that they were in error, claiming that it was an unavoidable case of "mistaken identity." While tacitly acknowledging their error, Homeland Security insisted that "the cancellations were based on solid information."

Emergency Planning

Had the flights not been cancelled, the Administration's justification for Code Orange Alert would have been put in jeopardy. Homeland Security needed to sustain the lie over the entire Christmas holiday. It also required an active Orange Alert to launch emergency planning procedures at the highest levels of the Bush Administration.

On December 22, 2003, the day following Secretary Ridge's Christmas announcement, President Bush was briefed by his "top anti-terror advisors" in closed door sessions at the White House. Later in the day, the Homeland Security Council (HSC) met, also at the White House. The executive body of the HSC, the so-called Principals Committee (HSC/PC), was headed by Secretary Tom Ridge. It included Donald Rumsfeld, CIA Director George Tenet, Attorney General John Ashcroft, FBI Director Robert Mueller and Michael D. Brown, Under Secretary, Emergency Preparedness and Response, who overseas the Federal Emergency Management Agency (FEMA).[20]

In the wake of the HSC meeting held on 22 December, Secretary Ridge confirmed that:

> we reviewed the specific plans and the specific action we have taken and will continue to take.[21]

In accordance with the official pre-Christmas statement, an "actual terrorist attack" in the near future on American soil would trigger a Code Red Alert, which in turn, would create conditions for the (temporary) suspension of the normal functions of civilian government. (See Chapter XXI) This scenario had in fact been envisaged by Secretary Tom Ridge in a CBS News Interview on December 22, 2003: "If we simply go to red ... it basically shuts down the country", meaning that civilian government bodies would be closed down and taken over by an Emergency Administration.[22]

Setting the Stage for a Pre-Election Terror Alert

Seven months later, at the height of the 2004 presidential election campaign, the Bush Administration launched yet another high profile terror alert. Based on so-called "credible" reports, Homeland Security Secretary Tom Ridge warned that Osama was "planning to disrupt the November [2004] elections". A large scale attack on American soil was supposedly being planned by Al Qaeda during the presidential election campaign:

> Credible reporting indicates that Al Qaeda is moving forward with its plans to carry out a large-scale attack in the United States in an effort to disrupt our democratic process. ... This is sobering information about those who wish to do us harm. ... But every day we strengthen the security of our nation.[23]

According to Secretary Ridge, "possible targets" included the Democratic National Convention scheduled for late July 2004 and the Republican Convention in New York in August 2004.

Barely a few days prior to Tom Ridge's somber announcement, a spokesman of Northern Command Headquarters at Peterson Air Force Base in Colorado, confirmed that NorthCom—which has a mandate to defend the Homeland—was "at a high level of readiness" and was proceeding with the (routine) deployment of jet fighters over major cities as well as the stationing of troops at key locations.[24]

This new terror warning by Homeland Security and the impending military deployment, served to create an aura of insecurity concerning the November presidential elections.

In other words, the Orange alert, triggered at the height of the presidential race, was an integral part of Bush's campaign. It consisted not only in galvanizing public opinion in support of his "war on terrorism" agenda, but also in creating an atmosphere of fear and intimidation in the months leading up to the November 2004 elections.

Homeland Security Department Secretary Tom Ridge did not elaborate on the nature of the intelligence: "we lack precise knowledge about time, place and method of attack. ... [T]he CIA, the FBI and other agencies, are actively working to gain that knowledge."[25]

These high profile statements had thus "set the stage". Barely a few days later, CIA Acting Director John McLaughlin confirmed that the threat was real:

> Their work is highly compartmented to a small group of people, probably living in a cave somewhere, and our country doesn't keep secrets very well. So we have to watch what we release about the details. But this is a serious threat period.[26]

The warning was based, according to CIA's Mc Laughlin, on "solid intelligence":

> I think the quality of the information we have is very good ...It is [however] necessary for us to hold back a lot of the specifics, because those are the things we need to stop this.[27]

The "Solid Intelligence" turns out to be Fake

Two weeks later, pursuant to McLauchlin's statement and the CIA's investigation, the administration triggered a Code Orange Alert in New York City, Washington DC and Northern New Jersey. This time it was Wall Street, the IMF and the World Bank which were supposedly being threatened by Al Qaeda.

Homeland Sec. Tom Ridge confirmed that the intelligence was "not the usual chatter. This is multiple sources that involve extraordinary detail":

> This afternoon we do have new and unusually specific information about where Al Qaida would like to attack. … The quality of this intelligence, based on multiple reporting streams in multiple locations, is rarely seen, and it is alarming in both the amount and specificity of the information. Now, while we are providing you with this immediate information, we will also continue to update you as the situation unfolds.
>
> As of now, this is what we know: Reports indicate that Al Qaeda is targeting several specific buildings, including the International Monetary Fund and World Bank in the District of Columbia, Prudential Financial in northern New Jersey and Citigroup buildings and the New York Stock Exchange in New York.
>
> Let me assure you—let me reassure you, actions to further strengthen security around these buildings are already under way. Additionally, we're concerned about targets beyond these and are working to get more information about them.
>
> Now, senior leadership across the Department of Homeland Security, in coordination with the White House, the CIA, the FBI, and other federal agencies, have been in constant contact with the governors, the mayors and the homeland security advisers of the affected locations I've just named.[28]

Yet barely two days later, US officials were obliged to admit that this high quality intelligence referred to by Secretary Tom Ridge was not so precise after all. In fact, it was even less "specific" than in previous terror alerts.

In an ABC interview, Deputy National Security Adviser Frances Townsend admitted that the August 1st 2004 alert was based on "outdated intelligence" going back to 2000/2001, i.e., prior to 9/11:

> What we have learned about the 9/11 attacks, is that they do them [plans for attacks], years in advance and then update them before they launch the attacks.[29]

According to Townsend, "the surveillance actions taken by the plotters were "originally done between 2000 and 2001, but were updated—some were updated—as recently as January of this year".[30]

Frances Townsend headed the White House counterterrorism program. She was Richard Clarke's successor on the National Security Council, holding the Number Two position after National Security Adviser Condoleezza Rice.

Her own statements on the nature of the intelligence blatantly contradicted DHS Sec Tom Ridge, who had referred to "the quality of this intelligence, based on multiple reporting streams in multiple locations".

The Mysterious Pakistani Computer Engineer

The hundreds of photos, sketches and written documents used to justify the "high risk" Code Orange terror alert, had emanated largely from one single source of information, following the highly publicized arrest in mid July of a 25 year old Pakistani computer engineer, Mohammad Naeem Noor Khan.[31]

Other than a *New York Times* report dated August 2, 2004 which had been quoted extensively by news agencies around the World, nothing was known about this mysterious individual. On his computer, Noor Khan, described as "a mid-ranking Al Qaeda operative", had information dating back to 2000 and this data, we were told, was the main source of the intelligence used by the CIA to document the threats to financial institutions in Washington DC, New York City and Newark, New Jersey.[32]

The Pakistani connection focusing on the 25-year-old engineer was presented by the media as the missing link.

The CIA Meeting at Langley on July 29

The CIA held a key counter-terrorism meeting on Thursday the 29th of July starting at 5 pm.[33] This meeting, which was described as routine, was attended by senior officials from the CIA, the Pentagon and the FBI.[34]

According to an unnamed senior intelligence official (who in all likelihood attended the meeting), the decision to launch the "high risk" (Code Orange) terror alert was taken on that same Thursday evening, within hours of Senator John Kerry's acceptance speech at the Democratic Convention:

> At the daily CIA's 5 p.m. counterterrorism meeting on Thursday [29 July 2004], the first information about the detailed al Qaeda surveillance of the five financial buildings was discussed among senior CIA, FBI and military officials. They decided to launch a number of worldwide operations, including the deployment of increased law enforcement around the five [financial] buildings [World Bank, IMF, NYSE, Citigroup, Prudential].[35]

On what solid intelligence was that far-reaching 29 July decision taken?

On that same Thursday at Langley, when the decision was taken to increase the threat level, the "precise" and "specific" information from the Pakistani engineer's computer, including "the trove of hundreds of photos and written documents", was not yet available.

> A senior intelligence official said translations of the computer documents and other intelligence started arriving on Friday [one day after the decision was taken to launch the operation].[36]

According to a White House aid, President Bush had been "informed of the potential threat Friday morning [July 30] aboard Air Force One".[37] The information from Mohammad Naeem Noor Khan's computer, however, was only made available ex post facto on the Friday. In other words, President Bush's approval to raising "the threat level" was granted in the absence of "specific" supporting intelligence:

> "We worked on it late, and through that night [Friday]" he [the intelligence official] said. "We had very specific, credible information, and when we laid it in on the threat environment we're in," officials decided they had to announce it.
>
> [At first], top administration officials had decided to wait until yesterday [Saturday] to announce the alert, but more intelligence information was coming in—both new translations of the documents, and analysis of other sources' statements—that deepened their concern about the information, and persuaded them to move ahead

swiftly. "There was a serious sense of urgency to get it out," the senior intelligence official said. ...

On Saturday, officials from the CIA, the FBI, the Homeland Security and Justice departments, the White House, and other agencies agreed with Ridge to recommend that the financial sectors in New York, Washington and North Jersey be placed on orange, or 'high,' alert. Ridge made the recommendation to Bush on Sunday morning, and Bush signed off on it at 10 am.[38]

Out of date Intelligence

Following the DHS's Sunday August 1st advisory that the Bretton Woods institutions were a potential target, the World Bank spokesman Dana Milverton retorted that the information obtained from the Pakistani engineer's computer was "largely out of date": "[A] lot of it was actually public information that anyone from outside the building could have gotten."[39]

> One federal law enforcement source said his understanding from reviewing the reports was that the material predated Sept. 11 and included photos that can be obtained from brochures and some actual snapshots. There also were some interior diagrams that appear to be publicly available.[40]

According to a *New York Times* report:

> The information, which officials said was indicative of preparations for a possible truck- or car-bomb attack, left significant gaps. It did not clearly describe the suspected plot, indicate when an attack was to take place nor did it describe the identities of people involved.[41]

Fabricated Intelligence for Political Gain

Not only was the "out of date intelligence" being used to justify a "high risk" threat level, the actual decision to launch the Code Orange alert was taken within hours of John Kerry's acceptance speech, prior to actually receiving the (out of date) supporting intelligence from Pakistan. No specific intelligence from the illusive Pakistan engineer's computer was reviewed at that Thursday evening meeting at CIA headquarters on 29 June 2004.[42]

TEXT BOX 20.1
Tom Ridge's Mea Culpa

Shortly after leaving his position at the HSD, Tom Ridge acknowledged that the terror alerts were indeed based on "flimsy evidence" and that he had been pressured by the CIA to raise the
threat level:

"The Bush administration periodically put the USA on high alert
for terrorist attacks even though then-Homeland Security chief
Tom Ridge argued there was only flimsy evidence to justify raising the threat level. … Ridge [said] he often disagreed with administration officials who wanted to elevate the threat level to orange,
or 'high' risk of terrorist attack, but was overruled.

"More often than not we were the least inclined to raise it.
… Sometimes we disagreed with the intelligence assessment.
Sometimes we thought even if the intelligence was good, you
don't necessarily put the country on [alert]. … There were times
when some people were really aggressive about raising it, and
we said, 'For that?'"[44]

Nothing indicated that the decision to increase the threat level
had a real foundation. When Tom Ridge was asked "what he would
say to skeptical people who see a political motive in the terror alert,
he replied: 'I wish I could give them all Top Secret clearances and
let them review the information that some of us have the responsibility to review. We don't do politics in the Department of
Homeland Security.'"[43]

The threat of an impending terror attack was fabricated. The
deployment around the five financial buildings was totally unnecessary. Public opinion was deliberately misled.

Notes

1. *The New York Post,* 11 February 2003.

2. ABC News, 13 February 2003

3. ABC News, 9 February. 2003.

4. ABC News, 13 February 2003,

5. *Ibid.*

6. *Ibid.*

7. US official quoted in *The Toronto Star,* 12 February. 2003.

8. *Ibid.*

9. See Department of Homeland Security at http://www.dhs.gov/dhspublic/index.jsp.

10. For complete statement of Secretary Tom Ridge, 21 December 2003, see http://www.dhs.gov/dhspublic/.

11. *Boston Globe,* 24 December 2003.

12. Tom Ridge's 21 December 2003 Statement, *op. cit.*

13. Associated Press, 23 December 2003.

14. Quoted by ABC News, 23 December 2003.

15. ABC News, 23 December 2003.

16. *Seattle Post Intelligencer,* 25 December 2003.

17. Fox News, 28 December 2003.

18. *Le Monde,* Paris and RTBF TV, Bruxelles, 2 January 2004.

19. *Ibid.*

20. White House Briefing, 22 December 2003. See also Stephanie Griffith, "Bush convenes anti-terror security meeting as US goes on higher alert", AFP, 22 December 2003.

21. *Ibid.*

22. *Ibid.*

23. Quoted in Associated Press, 8 July 2004.

24. *Atlantic Journal and Constitution,* 3 July 2004.

25. CNN, Tom Ridge interviewed by Wolf Blitzer, 11 July 2004.

26. CNN, John McLaughlin interviewed by Wolf Blitzer, 14 July 2004.

27. *Ibid.*

28. Tom Ridge's news conference, 31 July 2004, quoted in ABC Good Morning America, 3 August 2004.

29. *Ibid.*

30. NBC Today, 3 August 2004, quoted in *The Guardian,* 3 August 2004.

31. Associated Press, 3 August 2004.

32. *New York Times, 2* August 2004

33. *Washington Post,* 3 August 2004.

34. See The CIA website at http://www.cia.gov/terrorism/ctc.html.

35. *Washington Post,* 3 August 2004.

36. *Ibid.*

37. *Ibid.*

38. *Ibid.*

39. *The Guardian,* 3 August 2004.

40. *Ibid.*

41. *New York Times,* 3 August 2004.

42. W*ashington Post,* 3 August 2004.

43. *Washington Post,* 3 August 2004

44. *USA Today,* 10 May 2005.

Chapter XXI
Big Brother:
Towards the Homeland Security State

Defense of the Homeland is an integral part of the Adminstration's "preemptive war doctrine, presented to Americans as "one piece of a broader strategy [which] brings the battle to the enemy".[1]

Self-defense is the cornerstone of the National Security doctrine. The latter includes offensive military actions in foreign lands as well as anti-terrorist operations in the American Homeland directed against both "foreign" and "domestic" adversaries.

In the words of DHS Secretary Michael Chertoff:

> While one key to defense is offense, ... we also need a 'defense in depth' as part of the strategic whole. That means even as we pursue terrorists overseas, we work at home to prevent infiltration by terrorists and their weapons; to protect our people and places if infiltration occurs; and to respond and recover if an attack is carried out. This is embodied in our strategy of building multiple barriers to terrorist attacks.[2]

The "Universal Adversary"
The "enemy" is no longer limited to "foreign Islamic terrorists" and "Rogue States" as defined in earlier post 9/11 national secu-

rity statements, it also includes terrorist threats from within the US, emanating from so-called "domestic conspirators".

A July 2004 Report of the Homeland Security Council (HSC) entitled *Planning Scenarios* describes in minute detail, the Bush administration's "preparations" in the case of a terrorist attack by an enemy called the "Universal Adversary" (UA).[3] "The perpetrator" is identified in the "Planning Scenarios" as an abstract entity used for the purposes of simulation. Yet upon more careful examination, this Universal Adversary is by no means illusory. It includes the following categories of potential "conspirators":

- "foreign [Islamic] terrorists";
- "domestic radical groups", [antiwar and civil rights groups];
- "state sponsored adversaries" ["Rogue States", "unstable nations"];
- "disgruntled employees" [labor and union activists].

According to the *Planning Scenarios Report*:

> Because the attacks could be caused by foreign terrorists; domestic radical groups; state sponsored adversaries; or in some cases, disgruntled employees, the perpetrator has been named, the Universal Adversary (UA). The focus of the scenarios is on response capabilities and needs, not threat-based prevention activities.[4]

The "domestic radical groups" and labor activists, who question the legitimacy of the US-led war and civil rights agendas, are now conveniently lumped together with foreign Islamic terrorists, suggesting that the PATRIOT anti-terror laws together with the Big Brother law enforcement apparatus are eventually intended to be used against potential domestic "adversaries".

While the Universal Adversary is "make-believe", the simulations constitute a dress rehearsal of a real life emergency situation which is intended to curb all forms of political and social dissent in America: "The scenarios have been developed in a way that allows them to be adapted to local conditions throughout the country."[5]

Fifteen Distinct Scenarios

The scenarios cover the entire array of potential threats. Foreign terrorists are described as working hand in glove with domestic "conspirators". Fifteen distinct "threat scenarios" are contemplated, including, inter alia, a nuclear detonation (with a small 10-Kiloton improvised nuclear device, anthrax attacks, a biological disease outbreak including a pandemic influenza, not to mention a biological plague outbreak. Various forms of chemical weapons attacks are also envisaged including the use of toxic industrial chemicals, and nerve gas. Radiological attacks through the emission of a radioactive aerosol are also envisaged.[6]

What is revealing in these "doomsday scripts" is that they bear no resemblance to the weaponry used by clandestine "terrorists" operating in an urban area. In fact, in several cases, they correspond to weapons systems which are part of the US arsenal of WMD, used in US sponsored military operations. The description of the nuclear device bears a canny resemblance to America's tactical nuclear weapon ("mini nuke"), which also has a 10-kiloton yield, equivalent to two-thirds of a Hiroshima bomb.[7] That Homeland Security should actually envisage a make believe scenario of large scale nuclear attacks by "domestic radical groups'" and/or "foreign terrorists" borders on the absurd.

With regard to the nerve gas attack scenario, in a cruel irony, it is the same type of nerve gas (as well as mustard gas) used by the US military against civilians in Fallujah in 2004-2005.

TEXT BOX 21.1
Intelligence Disclaimer
[published at the Outset of the Report]

While the intelligence picture developed as part of each scenario generally reflects suspected terrorist capabilities and known tradecraft, the Federal Bureau of Investigation (FBI) is unaware of any credible intelligence that indicates that such an attack is being planned, or that the agents or devices in question are in possession of any known terrorist group.

Source: Homeland Security Council, *Planning Scenarios*, July 2004

Martial Law

The possibility of an emergency situation triggered by a Code Red Alert has been announced time and again since September 11 2001, with a view to preparing public opinion across America for martial law, if and when it occurs. (See Chapter XX.) What the US public, however, is not fully aware of, is that a Code Red Alert would create conditions for the ("temporary") suspension of the normal functions of civilian government. According to the Federal Emergency Management Agency (FEMA), Code Red would:

> Increase or redirect personnel to address critical emergency needs; Assign emergency response personnel and pre-position and mobilize specially trained teams or resources; Monitor, redirect, or constrain transportation systems; and Close public and government facilities not critical for continuity of essential operations, especially public safety.[8]

Northern Command (NorthCom) would intervene. Several functions of civilian administration would be suspended, others would be transferred to the jurisdiction of the Military. More generally, the procedure would disrupt government offices, businesses, schools, public services, transportation, etc.

Secret Shadow Government

On September 11, 2001, a secret "Shadow government" under the classified "Continuity of Operations Plan" (COOP) was installed.[9]

Known internally as "Continuity of Government" or COG, the secret Shadow government—initially set up during the Cold War—would become operational in the case of a Code Red Alert, leading to the redeployment of key staff to secret locations.

Federal agencies are required to establish "plans and procedures" as well as "alternate facilities" in the case of a national emergency. Moreover, the Continuity in Government Council (set up in Fall 2002) envisages concrete provisions relating to issues of "succession", in the case of a terrorist attack resulting in the death of the President or members of Congress.[10]

Code Red Alert would suspend civil liberties, including public gatherings and/or citizens' protests against the war or against the Administration's decision to declare martial law. Arrests could be directed against domestic "radical groups" and labor activists", as defined in the 2005 National Security Council Emergency Scenarios document.[11]

The emergency authorities would also have the authority to exert tight censorship over the media and would no doubt paralyze the alternative news media on the Internet.

Big Brother Citizens' Corps

In turn, Code Red Alert would trigger the "civilian" Homeland Emergency response system, which includes the DHS' Ready.Gov instructions, the Big Brother Citizen Corps, not to mention the USAonWatch and the Department of Justice Neighborhood Watch Program. The latter have a new post 9/11 mandate to "identify and report suspicious activity in neighborhoods" across America. Moreover, the DoJ Neighborhood Watch is involved in " Terrorism Awareness Education".[12]

Under the Citizen Corps, which is a component of the USA Freedom Corps, citizens are encouraged to participate in what could potentially develop into a civilian militia:

> Americans are responding to the evil and horror of the terrorist attacks of September 11 with a renewed commitment to doing good. … As part of that initiative, we created Citizen Corps to help coordinate volunteer activities that will make our communities safer, stronger, and better prepared to respond to any emergency situation. …
>
> We are asking cities and counties across the country to create Citizen Corps Councils of their own design, bringing together first responders, volunteer organizations, law enforcement agencies, and community-serving institutions, such as schools, hospitals, and houses of worship. Some Citizen Corps Councils will feature local activities that reflect new and existing national programs such as Neighborhood Watch, Community Emergency Response Teams, Volunteers in Police Service, and the Medical Reserve Corps. Some will include local programs that involve partnerships with law

enforcement agencies, hospitals, first responders, and schools. What all Citizen Corps Councils will have in common is that our local leaders will be working to expand opportunities for their community members to engage in volunteer service that will support emergency preparation, prevention, and response.[13]

The Conduct of Anti-Terrorist "Drills"

Preparations for Martial Law have been conducted in the form of large scale anti-terrorist exercises. Shortly after the invasion of Iraq, in May 2003, the Department of Homeland Security conducted a major "drill" entitled "Top Officials Exercise 2" (TOPOFF 2). Described as "the largest and most comprehensive terrorism response and homeland security exercise ever conducted in the US", TOPOFF 2 was based on Code Red assumptions involving a simulated terrorist attack.[14]

The "national response capability" in TOPOFF 2 was organized as a military style exercise by federal, State and local level

---

TEXT BOX 21.2

The Department of Homeland Security's "Ready.Gov Instructions"

Terrorists are working to obtain biological, chemical, nuclear and radiological weapons, and the threat of an attack is very real. Here at the Department of Homeland Security, throughout the federal government, and at organizations across America we are working hard to strengthen our Nation's security. Whenever possible, we want to stop terrorist attacks before they happen. All Americans should begin a process of learning about potential threats so we are better prepared to react during an attack. While there is no way to predict what will happen, or what your personal circumstances will be, there are simple things you can do now to prepare yourself and your loved ones.

Source: Ready.Gov America, Overview: http://www.ready.gov/overview.html

governments, including Canadian participants. Various attack scenarios by presumed "foreign terrorists" using "weapons of mass destruction were envisaged.[15]

TOPOFF 2 was conducted using the assumptions of a military exercise pertaining to a theater war:

> It assessed how responders, leaders, and other authorities would react to the simulated release of weapons of mass destruction (WMD) in two U. S. cities, Seattle, WA and Chicago, IL. The exercise scenario depicted a fictitious, foreign terrorist organization that detonated a simulated radiological dispersal device (RDD or dirty bomb) in Seattle and released the pneumonic plague in several Chicago metropolitan area locations. There was also significant pre-exercise intelligence play, a cyber-attack, and credible terrorism threats against other locations.[16]

Two years later, in April 2005, during Bush's second term, The Department of Homeland Security carried out larger and more comprehensive anti-terrorist exercise entitled TOPOFF 3, involving more than 10,000 "top officials" from 275 government and private sector organizations. Both Britain and Canada took part in the "drill", which was described as "a multilayered approach to improving North American security".[17]

The stated objective of the TOPOFF 3 "Full Scale Exercise" was to "prepare America" in the case of an actual bio-terrorism attack. The assumptions regarding the "Universal Adversary" (contained in the July 2004 Planned Scenarios document) and the roles of roles of both "foreign" and "domestic" conspirators, was embodied into the TOPOFF 3 exercises:

> We deliberately built the scenario as a very complex WMD bio-terrorism attack in New Jersey, as well as a kind of a dual-header in the state of Connecticut in terms of a vehicle-borne improvised explosive device, and then a simultaneous chemical attack.
>
> The system in TOPOFF 3 across the board was tested as never before, and this was deliberate. We wanted to test the full range of our incident management processes and protocols that spanned prevention, intelligence and information-sharing, and then the more classic or traditional response and recovery. But really for the first

time in a national-level exercise, we really got at a near simultaneous WMD attack which is, of course, very, very stressful for the federal folks, as well as our state, local and international partners.[18]

Building an Anti-Terrorist Consensus within the US State System

The objective of the anti-terrorist "drills" is not to "defend America" against Islamic terrorists. The drills contribute to building a broad consensus among "top officials", within federal, State and municipal bodies, as well as within the business community and civil society organizations (hospitals, schools, etc.) that the outside enemy exists and that "the threat is real". The exercises are applied to sensitize and "educate" key decision-makers. The simulated data, the various categories of "conspirators", the types of deadly weapons envisaged in the drills are part of a knowledge base.

The nature of the adversaries and the dangers of the attacks (ranging from nuclear detonations to nerve agents and anthrax) become "talking points" among key decision makers involved in the anti-terrorist drills. The conspirators including the "domestic radical groups" and "disgruntled employees" are described as being in possession of "weapons of mass destruction". In the drills, precise data sources are simulated and used to identify potential conspirators. The data sources "replicate actual terrorist networks down to names, photos, and drivers license numbers." The drills create a carefully designed "reality model" which shapes the behavior and understanding of key decision makers.

In this process, the "reality model" script of threats and conspirators replaces the real world.

> "We are moving forward in applying lessons learned to anticipate and address all possible attack scenarios," an FBI. spokeswoman said, asking not to be named because her department was not the lead author of the document. "With enhanced law enforcement and intelligence community partnerships, we are able to better detect terrorist plots and dismantle terrorist organizations."[19]

These fabricated realities penetrate the inner-consciousness of key decision makers. The reality model script molds the behavior of public officials; it builds a "knowledge" and "understanding", namely a shared ignorance regarding the war on terrorism and the "adversaries" who oppose the administration's war and homeland security agendas.

A world of fiction becomes reality. The drills "enable exercise players to simulate intelligence gathering and analysis", in preparation of an actual emergency situation which, according to the scenarios' assumptions, would lead to mass arrests of presumed terror suspects.

Fiction becomes fact.

Conversely fact becomes fiction. "Ignorance is strength". The "scenarios" require submission and conformity: for those key decision-makers at the federal, State and municipal levels, the US Government, namely the Bush Administration, is the unquestioned guardian of the truth.

We are not dealing with a propaganda ploy directed towards the broader American public. The TOPOFF anti-terror exercises as well as the "Planning Scenarios" were barely mentioned in the media. The propaganda in this case is targeted. It takes the form of "training" and emergency preparedness. The consensus building process is "internal": it does not consists in a mass campaign. It is largely addressed to key decision-makers within these various governmental and non-governmental bodies.

TOPOFF 3 included 10,000 top officials in important decision-making positions (federal and State officials, law enforcement, fire departments, hospitals, etc), who may be called to act in the case of an emergency situation. These individuals in turn have a mandate to spread the word within their respective organizations—i.e., to sensitize their coworkers and colleagues, as well as the people working under their direct supervision. This consensus building process thus reaches tens of thousands of people in positions of authority.

In turn, the holding of these antiterrorist exercises supports the National Security doctrine of "preemptive war",—i.e., that America has the legitimate right to self defense by intervening in foreign lands and that America must defend itself against terrorists. The TOPOFF exercises also sustain the myth of WMDs in the hands of terrorists, being used against America, when in fact the US is the largest producer of WMDs, with a defense budget of more than 400 billion dollars a year.

The objective is to sustain a consensus on the war and national security agenda—and to lay the path for martial law—within the governmental, nongovernmental and corporate business sectors.

Ultimately, the objective is to develop an acceptance for martial law across the land, by "top officials", their coworkers and subordinates, from the federal to the local level. This acceptance would necessarily entail, in the case of an emergency, the suspension of civil liberties and the rights of citizens.

> Officials will not give a specific figure, but they say the exercise involved several thousand fake deaths and thousands more injuries. This time, the sick and dying were only acting. But officials are aware that someday there could well be a real attack. They say the more they learn about how to coordinate prevention and response efforts, the better job they will be able to do to minimize casualties if and when that happens.[20]

The Anglo-American Homeland Defense Initiative

TOPOFF 3 involved the participation of Canada's Ministry of Public Safety and Emergency Preparedness as well as Britain's Home Office. The anti-terrorist exercise, involving simulations of attacks by Islamic terrorists were organized in terms of five separate "venues" in three countries: 1. Interagency exercise; 2. Connecticut; 3. New Jersey; 4. United Kingdom; 5. Canada.

> The FSE [Full Scale Exercise] offers agencies and jurisdictions a way to exercise a co-ordinated national and international response to a large scale, multipoint terrorist attack. It allows participants to test plans and skills in a real-time, realistic environment and gain the in-depth knowledge that only experience can provide.

The TOPOFF 3 scenario will depict a complex terrorist campaign and drive the exercise play through the homeland security system, beginning in Connecticut and New Jersey, and leading to national and international response.

Over the course of several days fire personnel will conduct search and rescue, hospitals will treat the injured (played by role players), subject-matter experts will analyze the effects of the attack on public health, and top officials will deploy resources and make the difficult decisions needed to save lives.

An internal Virtual News Network (VNN) and news website will provide real-time reporting of the story like an actual TV network would. The mock media will keep players up-to-date on unfolding events and enable decision makers to face the challenge of dealing with the real world media. Only participating agencies can view the VNN broadcast.[21]

The UK labeled its exercise "Atlantic Blue", whereas Canada designated its component of TOPOFF 3 as "Triple Play". While the media briefly acknowledged the Canadian attack scenarios, the details of Britain's "Atlantic Blue", held barely a month before the reelection of Prime Minister Tony Blair, were neither revealed, nor reviewed in the British press.

In the US based exercise, more than 200 federal, state, local, tribal, private sector, and international agencies and organizations including volunteer groups were involved.

Shaping the Behavior of Senior Officials

The "Top Officials exercises" (TOPOFF) prepare the Nation for an emergency under Code Red assumptions. More specifically, they set the stage within the various governmental bodies and organizations. The exercises shape the behavior of "top officials" and private sector decision-makers.

TEXT BOX 21.3

Anti-Terrorist Exercises for "Top Officials"

Connecticut: Simulated chemical attack on the New London waterfront and a simulated mustard gas attack.

New Jersey: Simulated biological attack involving "terrorists" spreading plague from an SUV in Union County, eventually "killing" 8,694 and "sickening" some 40,000.[22]

The New Jersey Domestic Security Preparedness Task Force will dissect how every state department performed during exercise. And the Homeland Security Department will analyze the performance of the more than 200 agencies that participated in TopOff 3 and issue an "after action" report.

"This is not over until we fully capture all of the lessons learned," said Robert Stephan, director of the agency's Incident Management Group. "This phase is … showing us where we did well and where we need to make improvement."[23]

Canada: "Triple Play" Nova Scotia and New Brunswick. Coordinated by Canada's Department of Public Safety and Emergency Preparedness and the RCMP, eighteen Canadian federal departments, as well as the provinces of New Brunswick and Nova Scotia, took part in the mock terror attack.

"Officials circulate word the ocean-going ship Castlemaine, en route to Halifax, carries a container holding chemicals for creating a weapon of mass destruction—possibly like the deadly substance already released in the United States and Britain. A meeting is hastily called to devise a plan."[24]

United Kingdom: "Atlantic Blue". Operation Atlantic Blue consisted of mock terrorist attacks by Al Qaeda using dirty bombs and plane hijacks. Britain's Home Office officials collaborating with the Metropolitan Police are said to have studied Al Qaeda's strategies before developing a series of ideas for mock attacks.[25]

According to official statements, an "actual terrorist attack" of the type envisaged under TOPOFF 3 would inevitably lead to a Code Red Alert. The latter in turn, would create conditions for the ("temporary") suspension of the normal functions of civilian government

The Role of the Military

What would be the involvement of the Military in an emergency situation?

In theory, the Posse Comitatus Act of 1878 adopted in the wake of the US civil war, prevents the military from intervening in civilian police and judicial functions. This law has been central to the functioning of constitutional government.

While the Posse Comitatus Act is still on the books, in practice the legislation is no longer effective in preventing the militarization of civilian institutions.[26]

Both the legislation inherited from the Clinton administration and the post 9/11 PATRIOT Acts I and II have "blur[red] the line between military and civilian roles". They allow the military to intervene in judicial and law enforcement activities even in the absence of an emergency situation.

In 1996, legislation was passed which allows the Military to intervene in the case of a national emergency (e.g., a terrorist attack). In 1999, Clinton's Defense Authorization Act (DAA) extended those powers under the 1996 legislation, by creating an "exception" to the Posse Comitatus Act, which henceforth permits the military to be involved in civilian affairs "regardless of whether there is an emergency".[27] This exception to the Posse Comitatus Act further expands the controversial measure already adopted by Congress in 1996.

> Under that new [1999] measure, which was proposed by the Defense Department, the military would be authorized to deal with crimes involving any chemical or biological weapons—or any other weapon of mass destruction—regardless of whether there is an "emergency." In addition, the new proposal would lift requirements that the mil-

itary be reimbursed for the cost of its intervention, thus likely increas-
ing the number of requests for military assistance.

Under this new provision ... Nojeim said, "the mere threat of an
act of terrorism would justify calling in military units. That represents
a loophole large enough to drive a battalion of army tanks through."

The defense authorization bill would also require the Pentagon to
develop a plan to assign military personnel to assist Customs and
the Immigration and Naturalization Service to "respond to threats
to national security posed by entry into the US of terrorists or drug
traffickers."

"The mere threat of an act of terrorism would justify calling in
military units. That represents a loophole large enough to drive a
battalion of army tanks through."[28]

The legal and ideological foundations of the "war on terrorism", therefore, were already laid under the Clinton Adminstration.

Despite this 1999 "exception" to the Posse Comitatus Act", which
effectively invalidates it, this has not prevented both the Pentagon
and Homeland Security, from actively lobbying Congress for the
outright repeal of the 1878 legislation:

New rules are needed to clearly set forth the boundaries for the use
of federal military forces for homeland security. The Posse Comitatus
Act is inappropriate for modern times and needs to be replaced by
a completely new law. ...

It is time to rescind the existing Posse Comitatus Act and replace
it with a new law. ... The Posse Comitatus Act is an artifact of a different conflict—between freedom and slavery or between North and
South, if you prefer. Today's conflict is also in a sense between freedom and slavery, but this time it is between civilization and terrorism. New problems often need new solutions, and a new set of rules
is needed for this issue.

President Bush and Congress should initiate action to enact a
new law that would set forth in clear terms a statement of the rules
for using military forces for homeland security and for enforcing
the laws of the United States.[29]

The Posse Comitatus Act is viewed by Homeland Security analysts as a "Legal Impediment to Transformation":

[The Posse Comitatus Act constitutes] a formidable obstacle to our nation's flexibility and adaptability at a time when we face an unpredictable enemy with the proven capability of causing unforeseen catastrophic events. The difficulty in correctly interpreting and applying the Act causes widespread confusion at the tactical, operational, and strategic levels of our military. Given that future events may call for the use of the military to assist civil authorities, a review of the efficacy of the PCA is in order.[30]

The ongoing militarization of civilian justice and law enforcement is a bi-partisan project. Democrat Senator Joseph Biden, a former Chairman of the powerful Senate Foreign Relations Committee, has been waging in consultation with his Republican counterparts, a battle for the outright repeal of the Posse Comitatus Act since the mid-1990s.

The PATRIOT Legislation
In turn, the Bush administration's PATRIOT Acts have set the groundwork of the evolving Homeland Security State. In minute detail, they go much further in setting the stage for the militarization of civilian institutions.

The USA PATRIOT Act of 2001 entitled "Providing Appropriate Tools Required to Intercept and Obstruct Terrorism Act of 2001" as well as the "Domestic Security Enhancement Act of 2003," ("PATRIOT Act II"), create the conditions for the militarization of justice and police functions. Frank Morales describes the PATRIOT legislation as a "Declaration of War on America":

> The "PATRIOT Act" is a repressive "coordination" of the entities of force and deception, the police, intelligence and the military. It broadens, centralizes and combines the surveillance, arrest and harassment capabilities of the police and intelligence apparatus. Homeland defense is, in essence, a form of state terrorism directed against the American people and democracy itself. It is the Pentagon Inc. declaring war on America.
>
> The "domestic war on terrorism" hinges upon the Pentagon's doctrine of homeland defense. Mountains of repressive legislation are being enacted in the name of internal security. So called "homeland

security", originally set within the Pentagon's "operations other than war", is actually a case in which the Pentagon has declared war on America. Shaping up as the new battleground, this proliferating military "doctrine" seeks to justify new roles and missions for the Pentagon within America. Vast "legal" authority and funds to spy on the dissenting public, reconfigured as terrorist threats, is being lavished upon the defense, intelligence and law enforcement "community."

All this is taking place amidst an increasingly perfected "fusion" of the police and military functions both within the US and abroad, where the phenomena is referred to as "peacekeeping", or the "policization of the military". Here in America, all distinction between the military and police functions is about to be forever expunged with the looming repeal of the Posse Comitatus Act.

In other words, the "New World Law and Order" based on the repeal of the Posse Comitatus Act, requires a system of domestic and global counterinsurgency led by the Pentagon.[31]

Even under a functioning civilian government, the PATRIOT Acts have already instated several features of martial law. The extent to which they are applied is at the discretion of the military authorities.

The 2003 PATRIOT Act II goes very far in extending and enlarging the "Big Brother functions" of control and surveillance of people. It vastly expands the surveillance and counterinsurgency powers, providing government access to personal bank accounts, information on home computers, telephone wire tapping, credit card accounts, etc.[32]

US Northern Command (NorthCom)

Northern Command (NorthCom) based at Peterson Air Force Base, Colorado, was set up in April 2002 in the context of "the preemptive war on terrorism".

The creation of NorthCom is consistent with the de facto repeal of the Posse Comitatus Act. In fact, the position of Homeland Defense Command "in the event of a terrorist attack on US soil", had already been envisaged in early 1999 by Clinton's Defense Secretary William Cohen.[33]

Following the Bush Administration's decision to create NorthCom, the White House instructed Justice Department lawyers "to review the Posse Comitatus law in light of new security requirements in the war on terrorism." The 1878 Act was said to "greatly restrict the military's ability to participate in domestic law enforcement".[34]

The role of Northern Command defined in the Pentagon's "Joint Doctrine for Homeland Security" (JP-26), constitutes a blueprint on how to defend the Homeland.

According to Frank Morales, "the scenario of a military takeover of America is unfolding". And Northern Command is the core military entity in this takeover and militarization of civilian institutions.

A coup d'État could be triggered even in the case of a bogus terror alert based on fabricated intelligence. Even in the case where it is known and documented to senior military officials that the "outside enemy" is fabricated, the military coup d'Etat characterized by detailed command military/security provisions, would become operational almost immediately.

NorthCom's "Command Mission" encompasses a number of "non-military functions" including "crisis management" and "domestic civil support". Under NorthCom jurisdiction, the latter would imply a process of "military support to federal, state and local authorities in the event of a terror attack". The latter would include:

> the preparation for, prevention of, deterrence of, preemption of, defense against, and response to threats and aggression directed towards US territory, sovereignty, domestic population, and infrastructure; as well as crisis management, consequence management, and other domestic civil support.[35]

NorthCom is said to have a "Creeping Civilian Mission".[36] Since its inception, it has been building capabilities in domestic intelligence and law enforcement. It is in permanent liaison with the DHS and the Justice Department. It has several hundred FBI and CIA officers stationed at its headquarters in Colorado.[37] It is in permanent liaison, through an advanced communications system, with municipalities and domestic civilian law enforcement agencies around the country.[38] Moreover, the CIA, which has a unit operating out of NorthCom, has extended its mandate to issues of "domestic intelligence".

In the case of a national emergency, Northern Command would deploy its forces in the air, land and sea. Several functions of civilian government would be transferred to NorthCom headquarters, which already has structures which enable it to oversee and supervise civilian institutions.

NorthCom's "command structure" would be activated in the case of a Code Red terror alert. In accordance with the provisions of the 1999 Defense Authorization Act (DAA), however, NorthCom does not require a terror alert, an attack or a war-like situation to intervene in the country's civilian affairs.

The Center for Law and Military Operations, based in Charlottesville, Virginia has published a "useful" Handbook entitled "Domestic Operational Law for Judge Advocates," which prepares for new "law enforcement" missions for the Military. According to Frank Morales, the Handbook:

> attempts to solidify, from a legal standpoint, Pentagon penetration of America and it's 'operations other than war,' essentially providing the US corporate elite with lawful justification for its class war against the American people, specifically those that resist the "new world law and order" agenda.[39]

In other words, "the 'war on terrorism' is the cover for the war on dissent".[40]

North-American Integration
The jurisdiction of the Northern Command now extends from Mexico to Alaska. Under bi-national agreements signed with Canada and Mexico, Northern Command can intervene and deploy its forces and military arsenal on land, air and sea in Canada (extending into its Northern territories), throughout Mexico and in parts of the Caribbean.[41]

Taken together, the existing legislation grants the military extensive rights to intervene in any "emergency situation", and, in practice, without the prior approval of the Commander in Chief.

Upon the creation of Northern Command in April 2002, Defense Secretary Donald Rumsfeld announced unilaterally that NorthCom would have jurisdiction over the entire North American region.

Canada and Mexico were presented with a *fait accompli*. The "War on Terrorism" was the main justification of this restructuring of the North-American defense structures.

US Northern Command's jurisdiction as outlined by the US Department of Defense includes, in addition to the continental US, all of Canada, Mexico, as well as portions of the Caribbean, contiguous waters in the Atlantic and Pacific oceans up to 500 miles off the Mexican, US and Canadian coastlines as well as the Canadian Arctic.

NorthCom's stated mandate is to "provide a necessary focus for [continental] aerospace, land and sea defenses, and critical support for [the] nation's civil authorities in times of national need."[42]

Defense Secretary Donald Rumsfeld is said to have boasted that:

> NorthCom—with all of North America as its geographic command—"is part of the greatest transformation of the Unified Command Plan [UCP] since its inception in 1947."[43]

Following Canada's refusal to join NorthCom, a high-level so-called "consultative" Bi-National Planning Group (BPG), operating out of the Peterson Airforce base in Colorado, was set up in late 2002, with a mandate to "prepare contingency plans to respond to [land and sea] threats and attacks, and other major emergencies in Canada or the United States".[44]

Following consultations between Washington and Ottawa, bi-national "military contingency plans" were established, which could be activated in the case of a terror attack or "threat".

Under the so-called Civil Assistance Plan (CAP), NorthCom is to assist civilian governmental bodies such as municipalities in both the US and Canada. Military commanders would "provide bi-national military assistance to civil authorities". In other words, it would respond "to national requests for military in the event of a threat, attack, or civil emergency in the US or Canada".[45]

In the case of a Code Red Alert, these "requests" (e.g., from a Canadian municipality) could result in the deployment of US troops or Special Forces inside Canadian territory. In fact, with an integrated command structure, Canadian and US servicemen would be integrated into the same bi-national military operations.

What these initiatives suggest is that the Bush administration is using the "War on Terrorism" as a pretext to exert military as well as political control over Canada and Mexico.

In this regard, Canada's National Security Policy is a copy and paste version of US National Security doctrine, which commits Canada to "regular national and international exercises involving civilian and military resources to assess the adequacy of the national system against various emergency scenarios." Moreover, under the 1999 Canada-US Chemical, Biological, Radiological and Nuclear (CBRN) Guidelines and Smart Border Accord, Canada has committed itself to "engage with the US in joint counter-terrorism training activities, including exercises."[46]

Consolidating the Big Brother Data Banks

In the wake of September 11, the Bush Administration established its proposed Big Brother data bank: the Total Information Awareness Program (TIAP).

TIAP was operated by the Information Awareness Office (IAO), which had a mandate "to gather as much information as possible about everyone, in a centralized location, for easy perusal by the United States government."[47] This would include medical records, credit card and banking information, educational and employment data, records concerning travel and the use of the Internet, email, telephone and fax. TIAP was operated in the offices of the Defense Advanced Research Projects Agency (DARPA), a division of the Pentagon in Northern Virginia.[48]

Ironically, when it was first set up, TIAP was headed by a man with a criminal record, former National Security Adviser Admiral John Pointdexter.

Pointdexter, who was indicted on criminal charges for his role in the Iran-Contra scandal during the Reagan Administration, subsequently resigned as TIAP Director and the program was "officially" discontinued.[49]

While the Information Awareness Office (IAO) no longer exists in name, the initiative of creating a single giant "Big Brother data bank" encompassing information from a number of State agencies, has by no means been abandoned. Several US Government bodies including Homeland Security, the CIA and the FBI, respectively oversee their own data banks, which are fully operational. They also collaborate in the controversial Multistate Anti-Terrorism Information Exchange (MATRIX). The latter is defined as "a crimefighting database" used by law enforcement agencies, the US Justice Department and Homeland Security.[50]

The National Intelligence Reform Act of 2004, sets the framework for establishing a centralized "Information Sharing Network" which will coordinate data from "all available sources". The proposed network would bring together the data banks of various government agencies under a single governmental umbrella.[51] This integration of Big Brother data banks also includes tax records, immigration data as well as confidential information on travelers.

Similar procedures have been implemented in Canada. In December 2001, in response to the 9/11 attacks, the Canadian government reached an agreement with the Head of Homeland Security Tom Ridge, entitled the "Canada-US Smart Border Declaration." Shrouded in secrecy, this agreement essentially hands over to the Homeland Security Department, confidential information on Canadian citizens and residents.

It also provides US authorities with access to the tax records of Canadians. Under the ongoing US-Canada integration in military command structures, "Homeland Security" and intelligence, Canadian data banks would eventually be integrated into those of the US. Canada Customs and Revenue has already assembled confidential information on travelers, which it shares with its US counterparts. In early 2004, Ottawa announced under the pretext of combating terrorism that "US border agents will soon have access to the immigration and tax records of Canadian residents".

Moreover, under Canada's controversial Bill C-7, the Public Safety Act of 2004, Canadian police, intelligence and immigration authorities are not only authorized to collect personal data, they also have the authority to share it with their US counterparts.[52]

What these developments suggest is that the process of binational integration is not only occurring in the military command structures but also in the areas of immigration, police and intelligence. The question is what will be left over within Canada's jurisdiction as a sovereign nation, once this ongoing process of binational integration—including the sharing and/or merger of data banks—is completed.

America at a Critical Crossroads

As outlined in Chapter XX, the coded terror alerts and "terror events" are part of a disinformation campaign carried out by the CIA, the Pentagon, the State Department and Homeland Security.

US intelligence is not only involved in creating phony terror warnings, it is also behind the terror groups, providing them with covert support.

Meanwhile, the militarization of civilian institutions is not only contemplated, it has become a talking point on network television; it is openly debated as a "solution" to "protecting American democracy" which is said to be threatened by "Islamic terrorists".

The implications of a Code Red Alert are rarely the object of serious debate. Through media disinformation, citizens are being prepared and gradually conditioned for the unthinkable.

Bipartisan Consensus

A large section of US public opinion thought that a change in direction might occur if the Democrats had won the 2004 presidential elections.

Yet the Democrats are not opposed to the illegal occupation of Iraq and Afghanistan. Nor are they opposed to the militarization of civilian institutions, as evidenced by their 1996 initiative to repeal the Posse Comitatus Act. Moreover, their perspective and understanding of 9/11 and the "war on terrorism" is broadly similar to that of the Republicans.

This ongoing militarization of America is not a Republican project. The "war on terrorism" is part of a bipartisan agenda. Furthermore, successive US Administrations since Jimmy Carter have supported the Islamic brigades and have used them in covert intelligence operations.

While there are substantive differences between Republicans and Democrats, Bush's National Security doctrine is a continuation of that formulated under the Clinton Administration in the mid-1990s, which was based on a "strategy of containment of Rogue States".

In 2003, the Democrats released their own militarization blueprint, entitled "Progressive Internationalism: A Democratic National Security Strategy". The latter called for "the bold exercise of American power, not to dominate but to shape alliances and international institutions that share a common commitment to liberal values."[53]

The militarization of America is a project of the US corporate elites, with significant divisions within the corporate establishment on how it is to be achieved.

The corporate establishment and its associated think tanks and semi-secret societies (The Bildeberg, Council on Foreign Relations, Trilateral Commission, etc.), however, is by no means monolithic. Influential voices within the elites would prefer a "softer" police state apparatus, a "democratic dictatorship" which retains the external appearances of a functioning democracy.

The Democrats' "Progressive Internationalism" is viewed by these sectors as a more effective way of imposing the US economic and military agenda worldwide. For instance, the Kerry-Edwards ticket in the 2004 presidential elections was supported by billionaire George Soros, who had waged a scathing denunciation of George W. Bush and the Neocons.

While the US Congress and the bipartisan consensus constitutes the façade, the Military (and its Intelligence counterparts) are, from the point of view of the corporate elites, mere foreign policy "pawns", to use Henry Kissinger's expression, acting on behalf of dominant business interests.

The Wall Street financial establishment, the military-industrial complex, led by Lockheed Martin, the big five weapons and aerospace defense contractors, the Texas oil giants and energy conglomerates, the construction and engineering and public utility companies not to mention the biotechnology conglomerates, are indelibly behind this militarization of America.

The "war on terrorism" is a war of conquest, which supports American and British)economic and strategic interests. Its underpinnings are supported by both Democrats and Republicans.

Under the legislation put into place by both parties since the 1990s, a Coup d'État could be triggered in the wake of a Code Red Alert.

If emergency measures are maintained, the militarization of civilian institutions will become entrenched, leading to the suspension of civil liberties and the outright repression of the anti-war movement. It would make any form of reversal back to civilian forms of government much more difficult to achieve.

Yet it should be understood that a step-by-step militarization of civilian institutions, as distinct from an outright Military Coup d'État, would essentially lead America in the same direction, while maintaining all the appearances of a "functioning democracy".

In this regard, the contours of a functioning Police State under the façade of Constitutional government have already been defined:
— the Big Brother surveillance apparatus, through the establishment of consolidated data banks on citizens;
— the militarization of justice and law enforcement;
— the disinformation and propaganda network;
— the covert support to terrorist organizations;

- political assassinations, torture manuals and concentration camps;
- extensive war crimes and the blatant violation of international law.

Notes

1. Transcript of the complete March 2005 speech of Homeland Secretary Michael Chertoff at http://www.dhs.gov/dhspublic/display?theme=42&content=4392.

2. *Ibid.*

3. Homeland Security Council (HSC), *Planning Scenarios*, July 2004, http://www.globalsecurity.org/security/library/report/2004/hsc-planning-scenarios-jul04_exec-sum.pdf.

4. *Ibid.*

5. *Ibid.*

6. *Ibid.*

7. Reuven Pedatzur, "The US removes the Nuclear Brakes", *Haaretz*, 26 May 2005.

8. Federal Emergency Management Agency (FEMA), http://www.fema.gov/pdf/areyouready/security.pdf.

9. *Washington Post*, 28 February 2002.

10. See the Continuity in Government website at http://www.continuityofgovernment.org/home.html.

11. National Security Council, *op cit.*

12. See www.USAonWatch.org.

13. Citizen Corps, Guide for Local Officials, President Bush's introductory remarks, http://www.citizencorps.gov/pdf/council.pdf.

14. For full text, see Department of Homeland Security, "Summary Conclusions From National Exercise", Office of the Press Secretary, December 19, 2003, http://www.dhs.gov/dhspublic/display?content=2693. The first TOPOFF 1 exercise was conducted on a small scale in May 2000 under the Clinton Administration. It consisted in a simulated aerosol plague attack in a Denver, Colorado, concert hall. *Wall Street Journal*, 2 May 2003.

15. See Department of Homeland Security, TOPOFF 2 Summary Report, Washington, December 19, 2003 at http://www.dhs.gov/interweb/assetlibrary/T2_Report_Final_Public.doc.

16. *Ibid.*

17. Department of Homeland Security spokesperson at Press Conference, April, 2005, complete transcript at http://www.allamericanpatriots.com/m-news+ article+storyid-9058.html.

18. *Ibid.*

19. *New York Times,* 26 February 2005.

20. Voice of America, 8 April 2005.

21. Department of Homeland Security, http://www.dhs.gov/dhspublic/inter-app/editorial/editorial_0588.xml.

22. Asbury Park Press, New Jersey, 9 April 2005 http://www.app.com/apps/pbcs.dll/article?AID=/20050409/NEWS03/504090432/1007.

23. *New Jersey Ledger,* 9 April 2005.

24. Jim Bronskill, "Plague, explosions and mystery cargo: Terror drill looks ahead to next 9/11, Cnews (Canoe Network), 8 April 2005.

25. US Federal News, 28 March 2005.

26. Frank Morales, "Homeland Defense" and the Militarization of America, Centre for Research on Globalization, 15 September 2003, http://globalresearch.ca/articles/MOR309A.html.

27. See American Civil Liberties Union (ACLU), "Congress Moves to Expand Military Involvement in Law Enforcement", 14 September 1999, http://www.aclu.org/NationalSecurity/NationalSecurity.cfm?ID=8683&c=24.

28. *Ibid.*

29. John R. Brinkerhoff, "The Posse Comitatus Act and Homeland Security", *Homeland Security Journal,* February 2002, http://www.homelandsecurity.org/journal/Articles/brinkerhoffpossecomitatus.htm John R. Brinkerhoff is former associate director for national preparedness of the Federal Emergency Management Agency (FEMA).

30. Donald J. Currier, "The Posse Comitatus Act: A Harmless Relic from the Post-Reconstruction Era or a Legal Impediment to Transformation?" Army War College Strategic Studies Institute, Carlisle Barracks, Pa., September 2003.

31. Frank Morales, "Homeland Defense: The Pentagon Declares War on America", Centre for Research on Globalization, December 2003, http://globalresearch.ca/articles/MOR312A.html.

32. For further details, see bibliography and analysis of www.Ratical.org at http://www.ratical.org/ratville/CAH/USAPA2.html#DSEAanalysis.

33. Lynne Wilson, "The Law of Posse Comitatus: Police and military powers once statutorily divided are swiftly merging", *Covert Action Quarterly,* Fall 2002.

34. *National Journal,* Government Record, 22 July 2002.

35. Global Security website: "Northern Command", http://www.globalsecurity.org/military/agency/dod/northcom.htm.

36. David Isenberg, *Asian Times*, 5 December 2003.

37. *National Journal*, 1 May 2004.

38. David Isenberg, *op cit.*

39. Frank Morales, "Homeland Defense and the Militarization of America", *op cit.*

40. *Ibid.*

41. See The Global Security Website: "Northern Command", http://www.globalsecurity.org/military/agency/dod/northcom.htm.

42. "Canada-US Relations-Defense Partnership", Canadian American Strategic Review (CASR), July 2003, http://www.sfu.ca/casr/ft-lagasse1.htm.

43. *Ibid.*

44. Text of the Canada US Security Cooperation Agreement, Canadian Embassy, Washington, http://www.canadianembassy.org/defence/text-en.asp.

45.See Canada, National Defense, The Bi-National Planning Group http://www.forces.gc.ca/site/Newsroom/view_news_e.asp?id=1528.

46. Department of Homeland Security, "Fact Sheet: TOPOFF 3 Exercising International Preparedness", Washington, 28 March 2005.

47. See Source Watch, Center for Media Democracy, at http://www.source-watch.org/index.php?title=Total_Information_Awareness.

48. See *Washington Post*, 11 Nov 2002.

49. See Admiral John Pointdexter's PowerPoint presentation at http://www.darpa.mil/darpatech2002/presentations/iao_pdf/slides/poindexteriao.pdf.

50 See The Multistate Anti-Terroism In formation eXchange (MATRIX) website at http://www.matrix-at.org/.

51. *Deseret Morning News*, 29, 2004.

52. House of Commons, Text of the C-7 Public Safety Act, Ottawa, 2002, http://www.parl.gc.ca/37/3/parlbus/chambus/house/bills/government/C-7/C-7_3/C-7TOCE.html, see also Transcripts of the House of Commons, http://www.parl.gc.ca/common/bills_ls.asp?Parl=37&Ses=3&ls=c7.

53. Mark Hand, "'It's Time to Get Over It' John Kerry Tells Antiwar Movement to Move On", *Press Action*, 9 Feb 2004.

CHAPTER XXII
The London 7/7 Bomb Attacks *

On the 7th of July 2005 at 8.50 am, three bombs exploded simultaneously on underground trains in central London. The fourth explosion occurred approximately one hour later on a double-decker bus in Tavistock Square, close to King's Cross. Tragically, 56 people were killed and more than seven hundred people were injured. The alleged suicide bombers were reported to have died in the blast.

The explosions coincided with the opening sessions of the Group of Eight (G-8) meetings at Gleneagles, Scotland, hosted by Britain's Prime Minister Tony Blair.

Without supporting evidence, the attacks were presented as an assault on the "civilized world" by "Islamic terrorists". Immediately following the explosions, Prime Minister Tony Blair, stated that:

> Those engaged in terrorism [should] realize that our determination to defend our values and our way of life is greater than their deter-

---

* At the time of the London 7/7 attacks, this book was going to press. What we are presenting here are observations pertaining to the police investigation as well as a preliminary asssessment of the broader political implications of 7/7 in the context of the "war on terrorism".

mination to cause death and destruction to innocent people in a
desire to impose extremism on the world.

Whatever they do, it is our determination that they will never
succeed in destroying what we hold dear in this country and in other
civilized nations throughout the world.[1]

7/7 versus 9/11

There are marked similarities between 7/7 and 9/11. Prime Minister
Blair's words on 7/7 echo the statement of President Bush in the
immediate wake of 9/11. At 11 o'clock on 9/11, Al Qaeda was held
responsible for the attacks on the World Trade Center (WTC) and
the Pentagon. (Chapter I.) Similarly, within hours of the 7/7 London
bomb attacks, and prior to the conduct of a police investigation, the
British authorities had already identified "Enemy Number One"
as the mastermind behind the 7/7 attacks.

A mysterious Islamist website had posted a statement from an
alleged "Al-Qaeda-linked group" claiming responsibility for the
London attacks. On that same day, July 7, another website linked
to "Al-Qaeda's Iraq frontman Abu Musab al-Zarqawi" confirmed
it had executed the Egyptian ambassador to Iraq, who had been
abducted a few days earlier.[2]

Two weeks later, there was a second bomb attack in London, in
which the detonators failed to go off. And two days later, on July 23,
a triple attack in Egyptian Red Sea resort of Sharm al-Sheikh left
64 people killed.

Following the 21 July attacks a massive police hunt was launched.

The Post 7/7 Disinformation Campaign

The 7/7 bomb attacks occurred at a critical moment. Widely
acknowledged, President Bush and his British ally Prime Minister
Tony Blair were guilty of innumerable war crimes and atrocities.

The political standing of Prime Minister Tony Blair in the country as well as within his Party was in jeopardy, following the release
of the Secret Downing Street memorandum. The latter confirmed
that the war on Iraq had been waged on a fabricated pretext: "The
intelligence and facts were being fixed around the policy."

The 7/7 attacks served to distract public attention from the broader issue of the war, which had resulted in more than 100,000 civilian deaths in Iraq since the outset of the occupation.[3]

The London 7/7 attacks provided a new legitimacy to those who had ordered the illegal invasion of Iraq. They contributed to signifcantly weakening the antiwar and civil rights movements, while triggering an atmosphere of fear and racial hatred across Britain and the European Union.

Tony Blair stated authoritatively that extremism is "based on a perversion of the true faith of Islam but nonetheless is real within parts of our community here in this country".[4]

Meanwhile, the British media had launched its own hate campaign directed against Muslims and Arabs. The nature of the Iraqi resistance movement was distorted. The London bombings were being linked to the activities of "terrorists" and "armed gangs" in Iraq and Palestine.

Several "progressive" voices added to the confusion, by describing the London 7/7 attacks as retribution for the US-UK invasion of Iraq: "If we hadn't gone to Iraq, they might not have bombed us."

Secret State Police

On both sides of the Atlantic, the London 7/7 attacks were used to usher in far-reaching police state measures.

The US House of Representatives renewed the USA PATRIOT Act "to make permanent the government's unprecedented powers to investigate suspected terrorists". Republicans claimed that the London attacks had "shown how urgent and important it was to renew the law".[5]

Barely a week prior to the London attacks, Washington announced the formation of a "domestic spy service" under the auspices of the FBI. The new department—meaning essentially a Big Brother "Secret State Police"—was given a mandate to "spy on people in America suspected of terrorism or having critical intelligence information, even if they are not suspected of committing a crime".[6] Of significance, this new FBI service, would not be accountable to the Department of Justice. It is controlled by the

Directorate of National Intelligence headed by John Negroponte, who has the authority to order the arrest of "terror suspects". According to Timothy Edgar, of the American Civil Liberties Union (ACLU):

> The FBI is effectively being taken over by a spymaster who reports directly to the White House. ... It's alarming that the same person who oversees foreign spying will now oversee domestic spying too.[7]

Meanwhile in the UK, the Home Office was calling for a system of ID cards as an "answer to terrorism". Each and every British citizen and resident will be obliged to register personal information, which will go into a giant national database, along with their personal biometrics: "iris pattern of the eye, fingerprints and "digitally recognizable facial features". Similar procedures were being carried out in the European Union. Sweeping controls on the movement of people, both within and across international borders were introduced. Tony Blair called for "extended powers to deport or bar from the UK foreigners who encourage terrorism".[8] Particular categories of people will be targeted and prevented from travelling.

The Police Investigation

Within a few days of the 7/7 attacks, the police investigation had already identified the names and identities of the alleged "London bombers". Reminiscent of 9/11, credit cards and drivers licenses were apparently found among the debris in the London underground.

Based on scanty evidence, the police concluded that the suicide attacks were carried out by four British-born men, three of whom were of Pakistani descent.

Three of the men were reported dead "after belongings were found at the scenes". The alleged bombers are Shehzad Tanweer, 22, of Beeston, Leeds, Hasib Mir Hussain, 18, also of Leeds and Mohammed Sidique Khan, 30, of Beeston, The fourth bomber's identity was later revealed to be Jamaican-born Lindsey Germaine.

A few days after the bombings, police announced that they were hunting for a fifth man who was said to have left the UK prior to the attacks.

"All Roads Lead to Pakistan"

Three of the four suicide bombers had allegedly visited Pakistan in the year prior to the attacks, where they had established contacts with several Islamic organizations, including the two main Kashmir rebel groups Jaish-e-Mohammed and Lashkar-e-Toiba, both of which have ties to Al Qaeda.[9]

Pakistan immediately became the focus of the investigation. London police detectives were rushed off to Islamabad.

According to police statements, both Mohammed Sidique Khan and Shehzad Tanweer, had established close ties to Jaish-e-Mohammed. Tanweer had apparently been trained at a Jaish camp for "young jihadists" situated north of Islamabad. There were also reports that he had visited a madrassa run by Jamaat-ud Dawa, a Kashmiri group previously associated with Lashkar-e-Toiba.[10]

> In Pakistan, [British] police are painstakingly analyzing the mobile phone records of the two 7/7 suspects who visited the country. While officials stress that it is a tedious process, it has already yielded the name of at least one significant suspect: Masoud Azhar, leader of the Jaish -e-Mohammed (Army of Mohammed).[11]

The Role of Pakistan's Military Intelligence (ISI)

The British investigation was being conducted in collaboration with Pakistan's Military Intelligence (ISI), which is known to have supported both Lashkar-e-Taiba, (Army of the Pure) and Jaish-e-Muhammad (Army of Mohammed), which claimed responsibility for the attacks on the Indian parliament in December 2001. (See Chapter II.)

Instead of being the object of the police investigation, the ISI's collaboration was sought by the British authorities. The ISI was providing "documentation" to the British on Islamic organizations, which they had supported and financed:

> A list of telephone numbers believed to be shared by British intelligenceofficials with their Pakistani counterparts has been the focus of attentionafter suggestions that the two men may have phoned fellow militants during their visit [to their parents in 2004].[12]

This was not the first time that the ISI's assistance had been sought in "going after the terrorists". In the immediate wake of 9/11, a far-reaching agreement was signed at the US State Department with the head of Pakistan's Military Intelligence, which defined the terms of Pakistan's "cooperation" in the "war on terrorism". (See Chapter III.)

Amply documented, Pakistan's ISI has supported the terror network. It has acted in close liaison with its US counterpart, the CIA.

"Al Qaeda's Webmaster"

British investigators had also uncovered that the "Yorkshire bombers" were in contact with a mysterious Pakistani engineer named Mohammed Naeem Noor Khan, also known as Abu Talha, who was allegedly behind the August 2004 planned terror attack on Wall Street, the World Bank and the IMF. (See Chapter XX.)

In the July 2005 news coverage of the London attacks, Naeem Noor Khan was described as Al Qaeda's webmaster: "he was sending messages for Osama bin Laden."

The British and US media immediately concluded that the attacks on the London subway were part of a broader coordinated plan, which also included financial buildings in the United States:

> All roads seem to lead to Pakistan and an apparent al Qaeda summit meetings in April of last year, where it appears both the London subways and US financial buildings were approved as targets.[13]

Naeem Noor Khan had, according to the news reports, played a central role in the preparations of the London 7/7 attacks:

> The laptop computer of Naeem Noor Khan, a captured al Qaeda leader [arrested in July 2004], contained plans for a coordinated series of attacks on the London subway system, as well as on financial buildings in both New York and Washington.[14]

Mohammed Naeem Noor Khan had allegedly stored the maps of the London underground on his computer hard disk. He was said to be in close contact with two of the London suicide bombers, Shehzad Tanweer and Hasib Hussain, during their visits to Pakistan.

For Scotland Yard, Noor Khan's laptop computer was central to their investigation:

> There's absolutely no doubt he [Noor Khan] was part of an al Qaeda operation aimed at not only the United States but Great Britain," explained Alexis Debat, a former official in the French Defense Ministry who is now a senior terrorism consultant for ABC News.[15]

Faulty Intelligence

The assertions regarding Naem Noor Khan contradict the findings of American and Pakistani investigators, following his arrest in July of 2004 by Pakistan's ISI.

According to (former) US Homeland Security Secretary Tom Ridge in an August 2004 statement, Noor Khan had "top secret information" on his laptop computer pointing to an imminent terror attack—involving multiple targets—on US-based financial institutions.

This information on Noor Khan`s computer was used as a pretext to trigger a Code Orange Alert at the height of the presidential election campaign.

The FBI, however, subsequently confirmed that the material on his computer included outdated pre-9/11 photos and diagrams, which were publicly available. This material did not point to an impending terror threat. Quite the opposite. Following the August 2004 investigation, the "top secret information" extracted from Noor Khan`s laptop was dismissed as being largely irrelevant. (See Chapter XX.)

Secret Maps of the London Subway

In none of these August 2004 reports, however, was there reference to the existence of maps of the London underground or "plans for a coordinated series of attacks on the London subway system" as suggested by ABC News in its July 2005 reports. While the latter referred to the participation of Noor Khan in an "Al Qaeda Summit", where the London bombings were being planned, the same news source, namely ABC News, confirmed back in August

2004 that the information on Noor Khan's computer was "outdated" and was not indicative of a terror threat.[16]

Following Noor Khan's July 2004 arrest, there was indeed mention of the existence of outdated maps of Heathrow Airport, but there was no mention of the London underground:

> Photographs and maps of the airport, along with underpasses running beneath key buildings in London, were found on the laptop computer of Mohammad Naeem Noor Khan when he was arrested in Pakistan last month [July 2004], although the computer file was four years old and created before 9/11.[17]

Moreover, according to a spokesman of Pakistan's military-intelligence:

> The computer and the other information obtained from Mohammad Naeem Noor Khan revealed that there were certain maps [of Heathrow airport] and some other plans. But let me clarify that none of these were new; they were the old maps and old plans.[18]

In other words, it was only a year later, in the wake of the July 2005 attacks, that the maps of the London underground allegedly on Noor Khan's laptop surfaced in the British and American press. They had never been reported on previously.

Terror Suspect Recruited by the ISI

Moreover, when Naem Noor Khan was arrested in July 2004, he was not charged or accused of masterminding a terror attack on Wall Street and the IMF as suggested in the July 2005 reports. In fact quite the opposite: he was immediately recruited by Pakistan's military intelligence (ISI):

> Khan had been arrested in Lahore on July 13 [2004], and subsequently "turned" by Pakistan's Inter Services Intelligence Agency. When his name appeared in print [in early August 2004], he was working for a combined ISI/CIA task force sending encrypted e-mails to key al Qaeda figures in the hope of pinpointing their locations and intentions.[19]

At the time the "Yorkshire bombers" visited Pakistan (November 2004-February 2005) and allegedly had "secret meetings" with Noor Khan, with a view to planning the attacks on London's underground, Noor Khan had already been hired by the ISI as an informer on a CIA sponsored program.

If there had been an "Al Qaeda Summit" or a plan masterminded in Pakistan, in which Naem Noor Khan had participitated, as suggested by the London police investigation, both the ISI and the CIA would have known about it.

Al-Muhajiroun

Meanwhile, another "prime terror suspect" had emerged. Barely three weeks after the 7/7 bombings, Scotland Yard reported that they had identified a British citizen named Haroon Rashid Aswat, who was living in Lusaka, Zambia.

Aswat had apparently been in touch with the "Yorkshire bombers" and had also traveled to Pakistan, where the planning of the attacks was said to have occurred. Aswat was a member of Al-Muhajiroun, a British based Islamist organization led by radical cleric Sheikh Omar Bakri Mohammed.

Al-Muhajiroun ("The Emigrants") is described as "an arm of Al Qaeda". It was involved in the recruitment of Mujahideen to fight "the holy war" in Afghanistan, Bosnia, Chechnya and Kosovo. It became active in the UK in the mid-1980s, recruiting British volunteers to join the ranks of the Mujahideen in the Soviet-Afghan war. The foreign fighters in America's proxy war against the Soviet Union were trained in Pakistan in CIA sponsored camps. (See Chapter II.)

In the late 1990s, terror suspect Haroon Rashid Aswat joined Al Muhajiroun where he was said to have participated in the recruitment of volunteers in Britain's Muslim community, who were sent to fight in the ranks of the Kosovo Liberation Army (KLA), largely supporting NATO's war effort:

> Back in the late 1990s, the leaders [of Al Muhajiroun] all worked for British intelligence in Kosovo. Believe it or not, British intelligence

actually hired some Al-Qaeda guys to help defend the Muslim rights in Albania and in Kosovo. That's when Al-Muhajiroun got started. … The CIA was funding the operation to defend the Muslims, British intelligence was doing the hiring and recruiting.[20]

In Kosovo, US, British and German intelligence (BND) were involved in training the Kosovo Liberation Army (KLA), which was also being supported by Al Qaeda.

According to a report published in 1999, the US Defense Intelligence Agency (DIA) had approached The British Secret Service (MI6) to arrange a training program for the KLA. While British SAS Special Forces in bases in Northern Albania were training the KLA, military instructors from Turkey and Afghanistan, financed by the "Islamic jihad", were familiarizing the KLA with guerrilla and diversion tactics (See Chapter III.)

Aswat was said to have recruited the "Yorkshire bombers". He was also from West Yorkshire, where the alleged bombers were living. He is suspected of having visited the bombers in the weeks leading up to the attacks.[21]

He is said to have played a central role in planning the 7/7 attacks. Press reports initially referred to him as a possible "mastermind" of 7/7:

> Cell phone records show around 20 calls between him and the 7/7 gang, leading right up to those attacks, which were exactly three weeks ago."[22]

At the time of his arrest in Zambia, however, much to the embarrassment of the British authorities, Scotland Yard's "prime suspect" was reported as being protected by the British Secret Service (MI6):

> This is the guy [Aswat], and what's really embarrassing is that *the entire British police are out chasing him, and one wing of the British government, MI6 or the British Secret Service,* has been hiding him. And this has been a real source of contention between the CIA, the Justice Department, and Britain.[23]

According to intelligence analyst John Loftus, Al-Muharijoun was an "intelligence asset" of MI6. Londoin Met's terror suspect was being used either as an informer or a "double agent":

JOHN LOFTUS: Yeah, *all these guys should be going back to an organization called Al-Muhajiroun, which means The Emigrants. It was the recruiting arm of Al-Qaeda in London;* they specialized in recruiting kids whose families had emigrated to Britain but who had British passports. And they would use them for terrorist work.

JERRICK: So a couple of them now have Somali connections?

LOFTUS: Yeah, it was not unusual. Somalia, Eritrea, *the first group of course were primarily Pakistani. But what they had in common was they were all emigrant groups in Britain, recruited by this Al-Muhajiroun group.* They were headed by the, Captain Hook, the imam in London the Finsbury Mosque, without the arm. He was the head of that organization. Now his assistant was a guy named Aswat, Haroon Rashid Aswat.

JERRICK: Aswat, who they picked up.

LOFTUS: *Right, Aswat is believed to be the mastermind of all the bombings in London.*

JERRICK: On 7/7 and 7/21, this is the guy we think.

LOFTUS: This is the guy, and *what's really embarrassing is that the entire British police are out chasing him, and one wing of the British government, MI6 or the British Secret Service, has been hiding him.* And this has been a real source of contention between the CIA, the [US] Justice Department, and Britain.

JERRICK: *MI6 has been hiding him. Are you saying that he has been working for them?*

LOFTUS: Oh I'm not saying it. This is what the Muslim sheik said in an interview in a British newspaper back in 2001.

JERRICK: So he's a double agent, or was?

LOFTUS: *He's a double agent.*

JERRICK: *So he's working for the Brits to try to give them information about Al-Qaeda, but in reality he's still an Al-Qaeda operative.*

LOFTUS: *Yeah. The CIA and the Israelis all accused MI6 of letting all these terrorists live in London* not because they're getting Al Qaeda information, but for appeasement. It was one of those you leave us alone, we leave you alone kind of things.

JERRICK: Well we left him alone too long then.

LOFTUS: Absolutely. *Now we knew about this guy Aswat. Back in 1999 he came to America. The Justice Department wanted to indict him in Seattle because him and his buddy were trying to set up a terrorist training school in Oregon.*

JERRICK: So they indicted his buddy, right? But why didn't they indict him?

LOFTUS: Well it comes out, we've just learned that *the headquarters of the US Justice Department ordered the Seattle prosecutors not to touch Aswat.*

JERRICK: Hello? Now hold on, why?

LOFTUS: *Well, apparently Aswat was working for British intelligence.* Now Aswat's boss, the one-armed Captain Hook, he gets indicted two years later. So the guy above him and below him get indicted, but not Aswat. Now there's a split of opinion within US intelligence. Some people say that the *British intelligence fibbed to us.* They told us that Aswat was dead, and that's why the New York group dropped the case. *That's not what most of the Justice Department thinks. They think that it was just again covering up for this very publicly affiliated guy with Al-Muhajiroun. He was a British intelligence plant.* So all of a sudden he disappears. He's in South Africa. We think he's dead; we don't know he's down there. Last month the South African Secret Service come across the guy. He's alive.

JERRICK: *Yeah, now the CIA says, oh he's alive. Our CIA says OK let's arrest him. But the Brits say no again?*

LOTFUS: *The Brits say no. Now at this point, two weeks ago, the Brits know that the CIA wants to get a hold of Haroon. So what happens? He takes off again, goes right to London. He isn't arrested when he lands, he isn't arrested when he leaves.*

JERRICK: Even though he's on a watch list.

LOFTUS: He's on the watch list. *The only reason he could get away with that was if he was working for British intelligence.* He was a wanted man.

JERRICK: And then takes off the day before the bombings, I understand it—

LOFTUS: And goes to Pakistan.

JERRICK: And Pakistan, they jail him.

LOFTUS: The Pakistanis arrest him. They jail him. *He's released within 24 hours.* Back to Southern Africa, goes to Zimbabwe and is arrested in Zambia. Now the US—

JERRICK: Trying to get across the—
LOFTUS: —we're trying to get our hands on this guy.[24]

The interview conveys the impression that there were "disagreements" between American, British and Israeli intelligence officials on how to handle the matter. It also suggests that "the Brits" might have misled their US intelligence counterparts.

This interview, however, reveals something which news coverage on the London 7/7 attacks has carefully ignored, namely the longstanding relationship of Western intelligence agencies to a number of Islamic organizations including Al-Muhajiroun.

Haroon Rachid Aswat was reportedly in London for two weeks before the July 7 attacks, "fleeing just before the explosions". If he had been working for MI6, his movements and whereabouts, including his contacts with the "Yorkshire bombers", might have been known to British intelligence.

The broader role of Al-Muhajiroun since its creation in the 1990s, as well as its alleged links to MI-6 requires careful review.

Mock Terror Drill on the Morning of 7/7

A fictional "scenario" of multiple bomb attacks on London's underground took place at exactly the same time as the bomb attack on July 7, 2005.

Peter Power, Managing Director of Visor Consultants, a private firm on contract to the London Metropolitan Police, described in a BBC interview how he had organized and conducted the antiterror drill, on behalf of an unnamed business client.

The fictional scenario was based on simultaneous bombs going off at exactly the same time at the underground stations where the real attacks were occurring:

> POWER: At half past nine this morning [July 7, 2005] we were actually running an exercise for a company of over a thousand people in London based on simultaneous bombs going off precisely at the railway stations where it happened this morning, so I still have the hairs on the back of my neck standing up right now.

HOST: To get this quite straight, you were running an exercise to see how you would cope with this and it happened while you were running the exercise?

POWER: Precisely, and it was about half past nine this morning, we planned this for a company and for obvious reasons I don't want to reveal their name but they're listening and they'll know it. And we had a room full of crisis managers for the first time they'd met and so within five minutes we made a pretty rapid decision that this is the real one and so we went through the correct drills of activating crisis management procedures to jump from slow time to quick time thinking and so on.[25]

Following his interviews with the BBC, in response to the flood of incoming email messages, Peter Power—who is a former senior Scotland Yard official specializing in counterterrorism—answered in the form of the following "automatic reply":

"Thank you for your message. Given the volume of emails about events on 7 July and a commonly expressed misguided belief that our exercise revealed prescient behavior, or was somehow a conspiracy (noting that several websites interpreted our work that day in an inaccurate/naive/ignorant/hostile manner) it has been decided to issue a single email response as follows:

It is confirmed that a short number of 'walk through' scenarios planned well in advance had commenced that morning for a private company in London (as part of a wider project that remains confidential) and that two scenarios related directly to terrorist bombs at the same time as the ones that actually detonated with such tragic results. One scenario in particular, was very similar to real time events.

However, anyone with knowledge about such ongoing threats to our capital city will be aware that (a) the emergency services have already practiced several of their own exercises based on bombs in the underground system (also reported by the main news channels) and (b) a few months ago the BBC broadcast a similar documentary on the same theme, although with much worse consequences. It is hardly surprising therefore, that we chose a feasible scenario - but the timing and script was nonetheless, a little disconcerting.

In short, our exercise (which involved just a few people as crisis managers actually responding to a simulated series of activities involving, on paper, 1000 staff) quickly became the real thing and the players that morning responded very well indeed to the sudden reality of events.

Beyond this no further comment will be made and based on the extraordinary number of messages from ill informed people, no replies will henceforth be given to anyone unable to demonstrate a bona fide reason for asking (e.g., accredited journalist / academic).

[signed] Peter Power.[26]

Power's email response suggests that mock drills are undertaken very frequently, as a matter of routine, and that there was nothing particularly out of the ordinary in the exercise conducted on July 7th, which just so happened to coincide with the real terror attacks.

There was nothing "routine" in the so-called "walk through" scenarios. Visor's mock terror drills (held on the very same day as the real attack) was by no means an isolated "coincidence".

There have been several mock drills and anti-terror exercises conducted by the US and British authorities since 9/11. A scenario of a mock terror attack of a plane slaming into a building organized by the CIA, took place on the morning of September 11, 2001, exactly at the same time as the real attacks on the World Trade Center. (See Chapter XVII.). Another high profile mock terror drill was held in late October 2000 (more than ten months prior to 9/11) which consisted in the scenario of a simulated passenger plane crashing into the Pentagon. (See Chapter XVII.)

"Atlantic Blue"

A mock terror drill on London's transportation system entitled "Atlantic Blue" was held in April 2005, barely three months prior to the real attacks. (See Chapter XXI.) "Atlantic Blue" was part of a much larger US sponsored emergency preparedness exercise labelled TOPOFF 3, which included the participation of Britain and Canada. It had been ordered by the UK Secretary of State for the Home Department, Mr. Charles Clarke, in close coordination with his US counterpart Michael Chertoff. (See Chapter XXI.)

The assumptions of the Visor Consultants mock drill conducted on the morning of July 7th were similar to those conducted under

"Atlantic Blue". This should come as no surprise since Visor Consultants was involved, on contract to the British government, in the organization and conduct of "Atlantic Blue", in coordination with the US Department of Homeland Security.

As in the case of the 9/11 simulation organized by the CIA, the July 7, 2005 Visor mock terror drill, was casually dismissed by the media, without further investigation, as a "bizarre coincidence" with no relationship to the real event.

Foreknowledge of the 7/7 Attack?

According to a report of the Associated Press correspondent in Jerusalem, the Israeli embassy had been advised in advance by Scotland Yard of an impending bomb attack:

> Just before the blasts, Scotland Yard called the security officer at the Israeli Embassy to say they had received warnings of possible attacks, the official said. He did not say whether British police made any link to the economic conference.[27]

Israeli Finance Minister Benjamin Netanyahu was warned by his embassy not to attend an economic conference organized by the Tel Aviv Stock Exchange (TASE) in collaboration with the Israeli embassy and Deutsche Bank.

Netanyahu was staying at the Aldridge Hotel in Mayfair. The conference venue was a few miles away at the Great Eastern Hotel close to the Liverpool subway station, where one of the bomb blasts occurred.

Rudolph Giuliani's London Visit

Rudolph Giuliani, who was mayor of New York City at the time of the 9/11 attacks, was staying at the Great Eastern hotel on the 7th of July, where TASE was hosting its economic conference, with Israel's Finance Minister Benjamin Netanyahu as keynote speaker.

Giuliani was having a business breakfast meeting in his room at the Great Eastern Hotel, close to Liverpool Street station when the bombs went off:

"I didn't hear the Liverpool Street bomb go off," he explains. "One of my security people came into the room and informed me that there had been an explosion. We went outside and they pointed in the direction of where they thought the incident had happened. There was no panic. I went back in to my breakfast. At that stage, the information coming in to us was very ambiguous."[28]

Israeli Finance Minister Benjamin Netanyahu and Rudolph Giuliani knew each other. Giuliani had officially welcomed Netanyahu when he visited New York City as Prime Minister of Israel in 1996. There was no indication, however, from news reports that the two men met in London at the Great Eastern. On the day prior to the London attacks, July 6th, Giuliani was in North Yorkshire at a meeting.

After completing his term as mayor of New York City, Rudi Giuliani established a security outfit: Giuliani Security and Safety. The latter is a subsidary of Giuliani Partners LLC. headed by former New York head of the FBI, Pasquale D'Amuro.

After 9/11, D'Amuro was appointed Inspector in Charge of the FBI's investigation of 9/11. He later served as Assistant Director of the Counterterrorism Division at FBI Headquarters and Executive Assistant Director for Counterterrorism and Counterintelligence. D'Amuro had close links to the Neocons in the Bush adminstration.

It is worth noting that Visor Consultants and Giuliani Security and Safety LLC specialize in similar "mock terror drills" and "emergency preparedness" procedures. Both Giuliani and Power were in London at the same time within a short distance of one of the bombing sites. While there is no evidence that Giuliani and Power met in London, the two companies have had prior business contacts in the area of emergency preparedness. [29]

Concluding Remarks

The British police investigation although formally under the jurisdiction of a "civilian police force", involves the participation of British intelligence and the Ministry of Defense. In fact, several key organizations of the military-intelligence apparatus including MI6, MI5, British Special Forces (SAS), Israel's Mossad, the CIA and

Pakistan's Military Intelligence (ISI) are directly or indirectly involved in the investigation.

The evidence presented in this book suggests that these same Western intelligence agencies, which are collaborating with Scotland Yard, are known to have supported the "Islamic jihad". This applies not only to Pakistan's Military Intelligence, which supports the two of main Kashmir rebel groups, it also pertains to MI6, which has alleged links to Al-Mahajiroun, going back to the 1990s.

Notes

1. Statement by Prime Minister Tony Blair, 7 July 2005.

2. AFX News, Cairo, 7 July 2005.

3. Riyadh Lafta, Richard Garfield, Jamal Khudhairi and Gilbert Burnham, "Mortality before and after the 2003 invasion of Iraq: cluster sample survey", *Lancet*, October 2004.

4. Statement of Tony Blair at a Press Conference together with visiting Afghan President Hamid Karzai, following his meeting with 25 Muslim leaders, AFP, 9 July 2005.

5. Reuters, 21 July 2005.

6. NBC Tonight, 29 June 2005.

7. Quoted in Mike Whitney, "Genesis of an American Gestapo", *Dissident Voice*, 16 July 2005.

8. BBC, 5 August 2005.

9. *Washington Post,* 5 August 2005.

10. *The Guardian,* 1 August 2005.

11. *Christian Science Monitor,* 1 August 2005

12. *Financial Times,* 2 August 2005.

13. ABC News, 18 July 2005.

14. Quoted by ABC News, 14 July 2005.

15. ABC News, 14 July 2005.

16. ABC Good Morning America, 3 August 2004.

17. *Sunday Herald,* 8 August 2004.

18. Statement by Pakistan's Inter-Service Public Relations (ISPR) Director-General Maj-Gen Shaukat Sultan, PTV World, Islamabad, 16 August 2004.

19. *The Herald,* 9 August 2005.

20. Statement of intelligence expert John Loftus in an interview on Fox News, 29 July 2005.

21. *New Republic*, 8 August 2005.

22. Fox News, 28 July 2005.

23. John Loftus, *op. cit.*, emphasis added.

24. *Ibid.*, emphasis added.

25. BBC Radio Interview, 7 July 2005.

26. Quoted in London Underground Exercises: Peter Power Responds, Jon Rappoport, July 13, 2005. http://www.infowars.com/articles/London_attack/power_responds_terror_drills.htm).

27. AP, 7 July 2005.

28. Quoted in the *Evening Standard*, 11 July 2005.

29. Peter Power served on the Advisory Board to the Canadian Centre for Emergency Preparedness (CCEP), together with Richard Sheirer, Senior Vice President of Giuliani and partners. (http://wcdm.org/wcdm_advs.html) Sheirer was previously Commissioner at the NYC Office of Emergency Management, and Director of New York City Homeland Security, responsible for emergency preparedness. Peter Power of Visor, who coordinated Atlantic Blue, held in April 2005, had a close relationship with the US Department of Homeland Security.

Appendix A
Intelligence based on Plagiarism: The British "Intelligence" Iraq Dossier
by Glen Rangwala

A close textual analysis of the British Intelligence report quoted by Colin Powell in his UN Address suggests that its UK authors had little access to first-hand intelligence sources and instead based their work on academic papers, which they selectively distorted.

US Secretary of State Colin Powell, in his presentation to the Security Council on February 5, sought to reinforce his argument by referring to a British intelligence report.

> What we are giving you are facts and conclusions based on solid intelligence. ... I would call my colleagues' attention to the fine paper that the United Kingdom distributed ... which describes in exquisite detail Iraqi deception activities. (Sec. Colin Powell, United Nations Security Council, 5 February 2003)

Powell was referring to "Iraq Its Infrastructure Of Concealment, Deception And Intimidation", released barely a few days prior to his historical February 5 address to the UN body.

On 2 February 2003, British Prime Minister Tony Blair released a report allegedly prepared by the Secret Intelligence Service (MI6) entitled "Iraq: Its Infrastructure of Concealment, Deception and

Intimidation". The following day, the Prime Minister told the House of Commons on how grateful we should be to receive this information. "It is obviously difficult when we publish intelligence reports, but I hope that people have some sense of the integrity of our security services."

Yet to me, the document seemed oddly familiar. Checking it against three journal articles published over the past six years, I discovered that most of the Downing Street report—including the entire section detailing the structures of the Iraqi security services—had been lifted straight from the on-line versions of those articles. The writings of three academics, including that of a California-based postgraduate student and primarily using information from 1991, had become caught up in the justification for war.

The authors of the dossier are members of Tony Blair's Press Relations Office at Whitehall. Britain's Secret Service (MI6), either was not consulted, or more likely, provided an assessment that did not fit in with the politicians' argument. In essence, spin was being sold off as intelligence.

The bulk of the 19-page document (pp. 6-16) had been directly copied without acknowledgement from an article in the September 2002 *Middle East Review of International Affairs* entitled "Iraq's Security and Intelligence Network: A Guide and Analysis". The author of the piece is Ibrahim al-Marashi, a postgraduate student at the Monterey Institute of International Studies. He has confirmed to me that his permission was not sought by MI6; in fact, he didn't even know about the British document until I mentioned it to him.

Two articles from the specialist security magazine, *Jane Intelligence Review*, were indirectly copied. On-line summaries of articles by Sean Boyne in 1997 and Ken Gause in 2002 were on the GlobalSecurity.org website, and these texts were also amalgamated into the dossier prepared for Prime Minister Tony Blair.

Even the typographical errors and anomalous uses of grammar were incorporated into the Downing Street document. For example, Marashi's had written:

> "Saddam appointed, Sabir 'Abd al-'Aziz al-Duri as head" …

Note the misplaced comma. Thus, on p.13, the British dossier incorporates the same misplaced comma:

"Saddam appointed, Sabir 'Abd al-' Aziz al-Duri as head" ...

The fact that the texts of these three authors are copied directly results in a proliferation of different transliterations (e.g., different spellings of the Ba'th party, depending on which author is being copied).

The only exceptions to these acts of plagiarizing were the tweaking of specific phrases. The reference to how the Iraqi Mukhabarat was "aiding opposition groups" in neighboring states and "monitoring foreign embassies in Iraq" in Marashi's article turned into a statement in the MI6 Document of how it was "supporting terrorist groups" and "spying on foreign embassies in Iraq". A mention in Boyne's article on how the "Fedayeen Saddam" (Saddam's Self-Sacrificers) was made up of "bullies and country bumpkins" was shorn of its last three words in the dossier: Iraqi country bumpkins, clearly, are not about to launch an attack on the UK, and so have no role in the document's rhetorical strategy.

Numbers are also increased or are rounded up. So, for example, the section on "Fedayeen Saddam" (pp.15-16) is directly copied from Boyne, almost word for word. The only substantive difference is that Boyne estimates the personnel of the organization to be 18,000-40,000 (Gause similarly estimates 10-40,000). The British dossier instead writes "30,000 to 40,000". A similar bumping up of figures occurs with the description of the Directorate of Military Intelligence.

Finally, there is one serious substantive mistake in the British text, in that it muddles up Boyne's description of General Security (al-Amn al-Amm), and places it in its section on p.14 of Military Security (al-Amn al-Askari). The result is complete confusion: it starts on p.14 by relating how Military Security was created in 1992 (in a piece copied from Marashi), then goes onto talk about the movement of its headquarters—in 1990 (in a piece copied from Boyne on the activities of General Security). The result is that it gets the description of the Military Security Service wholly wrong, claiming that its head is Taha al-Ahbabi, whilst really he was head of General Security in 1997 and that Military Security was headed by Thabet Khalil.

Apart from the obvious criticism that the British government has plagiarized texts without acknowledgement, passing them off as the work of its intelligence services, there are two other serious considerations:

1) It indicates that the UK at least really does not have any independent sources of information on Iraq's internal politics—they just draw upon publicly available data. Thus any further claims to information based on "intelligence data" must be treated with even more scepticism.

The authors state that they drew "upon a number of sources, including intelligence material." In fact, they copied material from at least three different authors. They plagiarized, directly cutting and pasting or near quoting.

2) The information presented as being an accurate statement of the current state of Iraq's security organizations is not anything of the sort. Marashi—the real and unwitting author of much of the document has as his primary source the documents captured in 1991 for the Iraq Research and Documentation Project. His focus is the subject of his PhD thesis is on the activities of Iraq's intelligence agencies in Kuwait from August 1990 to January 1991 prior to the onslaught of the Gulf War. As a result, the information presented as relevant to how Iraqi agencies are currently engaged with Unmovic is 12 years old.

When the document was first released as a Word document, I checked the properties of the text in the File menu. It revealed the authors of the text as P. Hamill, J. Pratt, A. Blackshaw, and M. Khan. Those names were removed within hours from the downloadable file. However, journalists have since checked who these individuals are, and revealed them all to be responsible for the UK government's press relations. In essence, then, spin was being sold off as intelligence.

The dossier is ordered as follows:
– p.1 is the summary.

- pp. 2-5 are, firstly, a repetition of Blix's comments to the Security Council in January on the difficulties they were encountering. Further claims about the activities of al-Mukhabarat follow. These claims are not backed up, for example the allegation that car crashes are organized to prevent the speedy arrival of inspectors. Some of these claims have since been denied by UNMOVIC head Hans Blix.
- p. 6 is a simplified version of Marashi's diagram at: http://cns.miis.edu/research/iraq/pdfs/iraqint.pdf.
- p. 7 is copied (top) from Gause (on the Presidential Secretariat), and (middle and bottom) from Boyne (on the National Security Council).
- p. 8 is entirely copied from Boyne (on the National Security Council).
- p. 9 is copied from Marashi (on al-Mukhabarat), except for the final section, which is insubstantial.
- p. 10 is entirely copied from Marashi (on General Security), except for the final section, which is insubstantial.
- p. 11 is entirely copied from Marashi (on Special Security), except for the top section (on General Security), which is insubstantial.
- p. 12 is entirely copied from Marashi (on Special Security).
- p. 13 is copied from Gause (on Special Protection) and Marashi (Military Intelligence).
- p. 14 is wrongly copied from Boyne (on Military Security) and from Marashi (on the Special Republican Guard).
- p. 15 is copied from Gause and Boyne (on al-Hadi project/project 858).
- pp. 15-16 is copied from Boyne (on Fedayeen Saddam). A final section, on the Tribal Chiefs' Bureau, seems to be copied from Anthony H. Cordesman, "Key Targets in Iraq", February 1998, http://www.csis.org/stratassessment/reports/iraq_targets.pdf.

Why did the UK government put out such a shoddy piece of work? The first dossier dated September 2002 addressed what is purportedly the rationale for military action against Iraq: Saddam Hussein's alleged production of nuclear, chemical and biological weapons. The problem was that these claims could be checked: Iraq invited UN inspectors to visit the sites of concern, and they have found nothing to raise suspicions.

With the argument about the large-scale development of prohibited weapons looking increasingly implausible, the US shifted tack. Now the problem was not the immediate threat of Iraq, but Saddam Hussein's "unique evil". Ever eager to support the changing US line, the British government responded with a second dossier. This was on human rights in Iraq, and largely about the crimes committed by the Iraqi regime in the 1980s. As human rights organizations said at the time, this was a crass and opportunistic attempt to justify a war on the basis of events that had been committed largely with the compliance of the UK and US at the time. Defense Secretary Rumsfeld was hobbled when the story of his 1983 meeting with Saddam Hussein—possibly giving the green light to Iraq's use of chemical weapons—reappeared on the front pages of US newspapers.

And so the US focus changed again. Now the problem was primarily phrased in terms of the ineffectiveness of weapons inspections in the absence of Iraq's full cooperation. On the face of it, this is an implausible argument: a key role of inspections is to deter through its monitoring activities any attempt by Iraq to reconstruct its industries to produce these weapons. In present circumstances, Iraq may be able to hide a few vials and canisters of agents that have largely decomposed, but it cannot develop the means to threaten the outside world.

However, as Secretary of State Powell made clear that his statement to the Security Council of 5 February would concentrate on this theme, Mr Blair may have sensed that his government needed to produce something quickly to substantiate the US position.

The case for war on Iraq has largely been made on the back of information that politicians claim to be presenting from the intelligence services. In this case, the intelligence services either were not consulted even though the information was sourced to them; or, possibly more likely, they provided an assessment that did not fit in with the politicians' argument. Downing Street, in trying to pander to the US stance without the argumentative means to do so, resorted to petty plagiarism.

Appendix B
The Financial Interests behind the World Trade Center Lease

On October 17, 2000, eleven months before 9/11, Blackstone Real Estate Advisors, of The Blackstone Group, L.P, purchased, from Teachers Insurance and Annuity Association, the participating mortgage secured by World Trade Center, Building 7.[1]

On April 26, 2001 the Port Authority leased the WTC for 99 years to Silverstein Properties and Westfield America Inc,

The transaction was authorized by Port Authority Chairman Lewis M. Eisenberg.

This transfer from the New York and New Jersey Port Authority was tantamount to the privatization of the WTC Complex. The official press release described it as "the richest real estate prize in New York City history". The retail space underneath the complex was leased to Westfield America Inc.[2]

On 24 July 2001, 6 weeks prior to 9/11, Silverstein took control of the lease of the WTC following the Port Authority decision of April 26, 2001.

Silverstein and Frank Lowy, CEO of Westefield Inc. took control of the 10.6 million-square-foot WTC complex. "Lowy leased the shopping concourse called the Mall at the WTC, which comprised about 427,000 square feet of retail space."[3]

Explicitly included in the agreement was that Silverstein and Westfield "were given the right to rebuild the structures if they were destroyed".[4]

In this transaction, Silverstein signed a rental contract for the WTC over 99 years amounting to 3,2 billion dollars in installments to be made to the Port Authority: 800 million covered fees including a down payment of the order of 100 million dollars. Of this amount, Silverstein put in 14 million dollars of his own money. The annual payment on the lease was of the order of 115 million dollars.[5]

In the wake of the WTC attacks, Silverstein sued for some $7.1 billion in insurance money, double the amount of the value of the 99 year lease.[6]

WTC Financial Interests

Silverstein Properties Inc. is a Manhattan-based real estate development and investment firm that owns, manages, and has developed more than 20 million square feet of office, residential and retail space.

Westfield America, Inc. is controlled by the Australian based Lowy family with major interests in shopping centres. The CEO of Westfield is Australian businessman Frank Lowy.

The Blackstone Group, a private investment bank with offices in New York and London, was founded in 1985 by its Chairman, Peter G. Peterson, and its President and CEO, Stephen A. Schwarzman. In addition to its Real Estate activities, the Blackstone Group's core businesses include Mergers and Acquisitions Advisory, Restructuring and Reorganization Advisory, Private Equity Investing, Private Mezzanine Investing, and Liquid Alternative Asset Investing.[7]

Blackstone chairman Peter G. Peterson is also Chairman of the Federal Reserve Bank of New York and Chairman of the board of the Council on Foreign Relations (CFR). His partner Stephen A. Schwarzman is a member of the Council on Foreign Relations

(CFR). Peter G. Peterson is also named in widow Ellen Mariani's civil RICO suit filed against George W. Bush, et al.

Kissinger McLarty Associates—Henry Kissinger's consulting firm—has a "strategic alliance" with the Blackstone Group "which is designed to help provide financial advisory services to corporations seeking high-level strategic advice." [8]

Notes

1. Business Wire, 17 October 2000.

2. See Paul Goldberger in *The New Yorker*, 20 May 2002.

3. C. Bollyn, "Did Rupert Murdoch Have Prior Knowledge of 9/11?" Centre for Research on Globalization, www.globalresearch.ca, 20 October 2003.

4. Goldberger, *op. cit.*

5. Associated Press, 22 November 2003. See also Die Welt, Berlin, Oct 11, 2001.

6. Alison Frankel, *The American Lawyer*, Sept 3 2002.

7. Business Wire, *op. cit.*

8. The Blackstone Group website at http://www.blackstone.com.

INDEX

MEMBER OF SCABRINI GROUP

Québec, Canada
2005